Socrates

A Life Examined

Luis E. Navia

Socrates
A Life Examined

Prometheus Books
59 John Glenn Drive
Amherst, New York 14228-2197

Published 2007 by Prometheus Books

Inquiries should be addressed to
Prometheus Books
59 John Glenn Drive
Amherst, New York 14228–2197
VOICE: 716–691–0133, ext. 207
FAX: 716–564–2711
WWW.PROMETHEUSBOOKS.COM

11 10 09 08 07   5 4 3 2 1

Library of Congress Cataloging-in-Publication Data

Navia, Luis E.
    Socrates, a life examined / Luis E. Navia.
        p. cm.
    Includes bibliographical references and index.
    ISBN 978–1–59102–501–6 (alk. paper)
    1. Socrates. I. Title.

B317.N37 2007
183'.2—dc22

2006102731

Printed in the United States on acid-free paper

Contents

$\mathscr{P}$reface

$\mathscr{I}$n the preparation of this book, it has been my goal to re-create the essence of what I interpret to be Socrates' legacy, that is, the fundamental lesson he sought to communicate and what appears to be his most lasting and important contribution. During his long life in ancient Athens, he seems to have been consumed by the need to find some hidden treasure that he sought with unbounded energy and indefatigable persistence. He spoke of it often and in many ways, but was generally not particularly clear as to what he thought it was. Perhaps, he wanted those with whom he spoke to search for it by themselves and discover its essence on their own. Perhaps, too, he himself may not have been altogether certain about its nature. Yet, its elusive and mysterious presence kept him in constant motion and agitation, pursuing it, as he once remarked, as a hunting hound pursues its prey or as a donkey runs after a carrot or a bit of green placed in front of it. At the end of his life, when he was sentenced to death, he was still unsure of having found the hidden treasure, for which reason he expressed the pious hope that if death was, as many believe, the beginning of another life,

7

he could spend eternity searching for what, while in this world, had eluded him.

The treasure of Socrates' quest is, I submit, the enthronement of reason as the one and only means to render human life meaningful and happy. This enthronement is possible only by turning the eye of the soul in the right direction, that is, inward into the recesses of consciousness, and becoming blind to all the kaleidoscopic illusion that most people mistake for reality. An unexamined life, according to him, is not worth living because—and this is Socrates' faith—only through the constant process of self-examination can we attain the clarity of mind that is the necessary and sufficient condition for a good and happy life. This is his legacy.

Socrates died twenty-four centuries ago. No writings have ever been attributed to him, and we can be reasonably sure that he wrote nothing. With him, therefore, the word was always spoken or heard, not written or seen. Accordingly, whatever we know or claim to know about him is what we can extract from authors who wrote about him, a few among them his contemporaries, and who left for us testimonies not always in agreement with one another, giving us the impression that either they wrote about different people or that Socrates was indeed several people in one body.

Since Socrates' death in 399 BCE, innumerable books, articles, works of art, and even musical compositions have been created in an effort to reconstruct his paradoxical ideas and enigmatic presence. In what has been said and written about him, what we find is an enormous mosaic of opinions and interpretations, so that it is possible to say that everyone who has endeavored to make sense of him and his philosophy has expressed his own idiosyncratic reaction to his presence. Even those who were close to him and were engaged in daily conversations with him carried away very different interpretations of the lesson he endeavored to teach. Antisthenes, Plato, Euclides, and Aristippus, for instance, men who lived for years under his shadow, each discovered in different ways what others had failed to discern in him and ignored aspects of his presence that others found to be its very essence.

In the *Euthyphro*, an early dialogue of Plato, Socrates tells us that his lineage is traceable to Daedalus, the legendary sculptor who made marvelous statues that had the strangest quality. Once completed, they would at once begin to move aimlessly in all directions, making it impossible to seize them. As soon as anyone would approach them, they would run away like tantalizing ghosts.

Somehow, Socrates' reference to the magical Daedalus makes perfect sense, for his ideas and convictions and, indeed, his personality are not unlike the sculptor's moving statues. The moment we think we can attribute anything to him and are under the impression that we have succeeded in grasping him, he either assumes another form or simply vanishes into thin air, leaving us as perplexed as before. In the end, Socrates seems to elude us and goes away, as if playing some game with us and laughing at the whole world at our expense, as he is described in Plato's *Symposium*, for which reason Alcibiades reminds everybody that *no one* really knows who Socrates is.

I have devoted many years to the study of Socrates and have read countless accounts and interpretations of him, hoping to discover a unifying idea, some firmly upheld conviction that can sum up his philosophical message, his legacy. Almost intuitively, I have always suspected that he had something important and urgent to say about the human condition and that he had accurately diagnosed the sickness that has afflicted us since time immemorial. Like a clever physician of the soul, as he once called himself, and as the Cynics, who followed in his footsteps, called themselves, he also prescribed the only effective medication.

That humanity has always been afflicted by some dreadful

disease, I have never doubted, for I also suffer from it. Indeed, it only takes a small dosage of lucidity to recognize it and conclude, as Schopenhauer did, that human life gives every indication of being some kind of a mistake. Still, at least from Socrates' perspective, although the disease is real and pandemic, it is curable, and remedy is, so to speak, there, ready for the taking. If human life is a mistake, it is we, not God or nature or even society, that are responsible for the mistake, and if so, it is we, in our own individuality, who have to attempt to correct it.

This is ultimately the optimistic sentiment that animated Socrates, and this is perhaps the reason why he was willing to offer himself as a sacrificial victim in the presence of the jury that sentenced him to death. He needed to emphasize what he appears to have conceived of as a self-evident truth, namely, that an examined life leads inexorably to righteousness, and righteousness to happiness, along the path delineated by the right use of reason.

In chapter 1, I endeavor to draw a biographical portrait of Socrates, extracting from the very few facts known about him some semblance of the actual man. The sources, both primary and secondary, provide plentiful information that, although never altogether certain, allows us to re-create his life, albeit in a sketchy way. Socrates is not a legend.

Chapters 2, 3, and 4 undertake a review of the testimonies of the three major witnesses: Aristophanes, Xenophon, and Plato. In chapter 5, I appeal to the testimony of Aristotle, who, while not directly acquainted with Socrates, must have been privy to much reliable information about him. Not having, as they say, an ax to grind about him, either attacking him or defending him, Aristotle is a valuable and informative witness.

Chapters 6 and 7 attempt to reconstruct Socrates' philosophy. It may at first appear futile to look for *his* philosophy because what we know about it is mostly couched in Plato's language, and it is difficult to distinguish what Socrates could have said from what Plato made him say throughout his dialogues. Still, a fair and balanced review of the sources, especially Plato's early dialogues, Xenophon's *Memorabilia*, Aristotle's references to him, and what one finds in Cynic and other traditions, can yield some modicum of information about what Socrates was, said, and thought. From this, it is possible to formulate the principles of his philosophy and, ultimately, his fundamental message, that is, his legacy. This legacy, as will be made clear in chapter 7, is embodied in Socrates' conviction that reason, and reason alone, furnishes human beings with the means to render their lives meaningful and good and as happy as the limitations imposed by nature allow.

In order to shed light on the meaning of Socrates' legacy, I have appealed to Kant, who, as has been noted by many scholars, shared much in common with him. Like Socrates, he, too, early in his life directed his attention to the physical world that surrounds us—the universe in which we are confined to live. Yet, also like Socrates, he eventually came to recognize the illusory and inconsequential character of that knowledge, and its uselessness when sought for its own sake. In the footsteps of the Greek philosopher, Kant came to the conclusion that the principal role of reason is to lead us to an unwavering commitment to self-knowledge, which paves the way to the attainment of *Heiligkeit*—holiness, as he wrote not long before his death in 1804. To know and understand for the sake of knowing and understanding is a misguided and futile activity, a pastime, a *ludus puerum*—a childish game—that amounts to nothing and leads nowhere. If, for Socrates, an unexamined life is *not* worth living, for Kant a life whose goal is not holiness is also *not* worth living. Yet, in this respect Socrates and Kant stand on the same ground because for Socrates the only purpose of subjecting one's life to examination is also holiness understood in the sense of approaching in this life *to agathon*, that is, the absolute Good. If philosophy and science are not conducive to the restructuring of human life along rationally understood moral principles that help us find this treasure, they are altogether useless. This is the Socratic legacy, of which Kant's conviction is a distant echo.

The bibliography includes all the works quoted or mentioned in the text, as well as a representative selection of works on Socrates published in English. For a comprehensive bibliography, it may be useful to consult my *Socrates: An Annotated Bibliography* (New York: Garland Publishing, 1988), in which almost two thousand works are extensively annotated.

There are two aspects of this book that may trouble its reviewers and readers as much as they have troubled me. First, there is the hesitation with which I venture to affirm anything I have written about Socrates. This, I think, is the result of attempting to be as honest as I can possibly be. About Socrates, it is always unwise to claim to know more than can be known. Regardless of all scholarly efforts to resurrect him, he remains an elusive ghost that refuses to be pinned down to a simple set of formulas. To speak dogmatically about him displays either intellectual dishonesty or a great deal of wishful thinking. Secondly, in my attempt to reconstruct the portrait of Socrates as a man and a philosopher, it has proven impossible to avoid repetitions, if nothing else, because the representations of Socrates found in the principal sources—Aristophanes, Xenophon, Plato, and Aristotle—deal with one and the same person and, thus, include common elements that are bound to reappear in various chapters throughout this book.

As with my previous books, I am grateful to my wife, Alicia, and to my daughters, Monica, Olga, Melissa, and Soraya, for their encouragement in my work and for having commented on every page of the manuscript. Without their presence, I do not think that I would have made any progress in the quest for Socrates' legacy. They are a living testimony that Schopenhauer's terrible comment about human life being a mistake is plainly wrong. If I may be allowed to borrow the language of

John Stuart Mill in dedicating his *On Liberty* to his wife, I, too, wish to dedicate this unassuming work on Socrates to my wife, who has been "the inspirer, and in part the author, of all that is best in my writings—the friend and wife whose exalted sense of truth and right has been my strongest incitement, and whose approbation has been my chief reward."

I owe a great debt to Eduardo Santa—renowned philosopher, historian, sociologist, poet, and exquisite writer. I acknowledge his persistent and supportive presence in my life, a presence that is faithfully reflected in the pages of this book.

Special words of appreciation are due to Mariela Angel de Cadena for her continuous and generous moral support.

I wish to thank Gerri Brown for her meticulous and patient reading of the manuscript. I am also thankful to Hector F. Cadena, Ian Cutler, Angela Morgan Cutler, Charles L. Defanti, and Jonathan Zenir for their assistance. In those occasional moments of despair, when I have been tempted to set aside the search for Socrates, they, as much as my wife and my daughters, have forced me to remain faithful to my mission.

CHAPTER 1
The Socratic Enigma

*T*here are not many things that are known about Socrates with certainty. We know that he was born in Athens in 469 BCE and that he died in Athens in 399 BCE. It is certain that he was executed, probably by hemlock poisoning, after being found guilty of irreligiosity by an Athenian jury. Beyond these and a few other facts, we enter into a field of conjectures and controversies from which it is difficult, if not impossible, to escape.

Indeed, much has been written about Socrates. The bibliography that has grown around him since his death and even before his death is exceedingly extensive.[1] Literally thousands of books, articles, works of art, plays, and musical compositions have been devoted to him, as if his life were a magnet that attracts the imagination of those who endeavor to re-create his presence. Yet, as one reviews the Socratic bibliography, one cannot but conclude that there must have been more than one philosopher by that name, for little agreement is found among the many things said and written about him. From Aristophanes, who wrote a comedy about him in 423 BCE when Socrates was a middle-aged man, to authors of the twenty-first century, works about him continue to be written and in them one seldom finds a solid portrayal of consistency and agreement. Who and what, then, can we say that Socrates was? What ideas and ideals can be truthfully associated with him? What sort of legacy are we entitled to associate with him? What is the basis for the extraordinary influence he has managed to exert during the twenty-four centuries that have elapsed since his death? What sense can we make of the man whom Nietzsche once called "that ironic and amorous monster and Pied Piper of Athens"?

The reasons for Socrates' historical elusiveness are many; chief among them is the fact that he, like Confucius, Buddha, and Jesus, left no writings. He is reported to have had an aversion to written language and a passion for the spoken word, as we learn from Plato. Conversing, not writing, was the medium he chose to communicate his message. Written words, he said, are dead things, like paintings, and are unable to answer whomever wishes to question them: "I cannot help feeling, Phaedrus, that writing is unfortunately like painting; for the creations of the painter have the appearance of life, and yet if you ask them a question they preserve a solemn silence" (*Phaedrus* 275d).

Another reason for his elusiveness is undoubtedly his own personality, to which there are numerous references in the sources. In Plato's *Euthyphro* (11c), for instance, Socrates speaks of Daedalus as the founder of his lineage. Why? Well, because this legendary character would make statues that, as soon as they were made, would not stay still but would move aimlessly. Like those statues, too, Socrates' personality and statements gave the impression of moving in all sorts of directions as if avoiding being pinned down to something definite. Again, in Plato's *Symposium* (216c) we have a revealing comment from Alcibiades, who says to those around him: "Let me tell you that none of you knows Socrates; but I shall reveal him to you." The others thought they knew Socrates, but they were mistaken and could have reversed Alcibiades' comment back to him because in reality no one knew or knows anything about him.

In Aristophanes' *Clouds* (446–52) we encounter a clear description of Socrates that unveils the complexity of his personality: "A bold rascal, a fine speaker, impudent, shameless, a braggart, and adept at stringing lies, and an old stager at quibbles, a complete table of laws, a thorough rattle, a fox to slip through any hole, supple as a leathern strap, slippery as an eel, an artful fellow, a blusterer, a villain, a knave with one hundred faces, cunning, intolerable, a gluttonous dog." Whatever its biographical correctness may be, this is quite a description of Socrates as Aristophanes must have seen him. Others, indeed, must have seen him precisely as he did, and still others did not fail to experience a sort of vertigo in his presence as if stung by a stingray, as we read in Plato's *Meno* (80a).

Socrates' refusal to write about himself and his ideas and the sort of person he seems to have been explain still another reason for his historical elusiveness. Anything we can possibly think, say, or write about him is bound to be based on the writings of others, that is, on what we call the sources. These are generally classified either as primary or as secondary, the former being the writings of Socrates' contemporaries and the latter the enormous collection of writings of others who did not share his time on earth. Obviously, these latter sources depend on the primary sources.

A review of the sources yields at first a discouraging result: there is hardly any consistent and cohesive account of who Socrates was and what his philosophical message could have been. It is as if those who wrote about him were bent on projecting themselves into what they saw or learned about Socrates. From Aristophanes, our earliest source, to the writers of late classical times that is precisely what we find. To a great extent, moreover, that is also what we discover as we review modern writings about Socrates. We confront in the end a problem, the Socratic problem as this is known, one that can be stated in simple terms: despite all our knowledge about Socrates, little of substance can be affirmed without hesitation. Any trait associated with him, any idea attributed to him, can be contradicted by adducing passages from various sources.

It is, therefore, not surprising that some scholars and historians have concluded that the actual Socrates, the man made of flesh and bone, is bound to remain a perfect X, that is, an insoluble problem. Neither is it surprising that others have opted for a solution that entails the acceptance of *one* source alone as the true testimony about who Socrates was and what his ideas were. This one source is often Plato's writings, although a review of those writings reveals at once that there are in them various characters named "Socrates" who are often at odds with one another. For some, too, Aristophanes, not Plato or Xenophon, is seen as the writer who captured best the essence of the Socratic presence, and then Socrates turns out to be a disruptive and dangerous man who lived his meaningless life confusing and misguiding those who were unfortunate enough to cross his path.

There is also the persistent idea that when dealing with Socrates' philosophy we must turn to Antisthenes. It is true that hardly any of Antisthenes' writings are extant. Yet, the philosophical movement that seems to have ensued from him, Cynicism, may have been the most genuine offshoot of Socrates' ideas. Diogenes of Sinope, the archetype of the Cynic philosopher, who lived one century after Socrates, may be, after all, despite the radicalism and exaggerated character of his style of life and ideas, the man who understood most clearly the essence of the Socratic message. The designation of Diogenes, attributed to Plato, as a "Socrates gone mad" (DL 6.54) is revealing, as is the statement ascribed to Diogenes that it was Plato who was mad in betraying the spirit of philosophy by using Socrates' name to expound his senseless political and metaphysical ideas.[2]

The Socratic problem is, therefore, quite complex. First, there is the absence of writings on the part of Socrates himself. Then, there is the apparently protean nature of his personality, allegedly accompanied by significant changes during the course of his life. And then, as the result of these two circumstances, there is the multiplicity of portrayals created by the sources. The main primary sources, namely, Aristophanes, Xenophon, and Plato, do not create one consistent portrayal but various representations, and the secondary sources, beginning with Aristotle, furnish us with a mosaic of features and attributes that form a kaleidoscopic photograph of Socrates.

Are we, however, forced to despair? Can the Socratic presence be resurrected, not simply as the comic character of Aristophanes' *Clouds*, nor as the judicious citizen of Xenophon's *Memorabilia*, nor as the imposing Platonic philosopher created by Plato, nor as the raving rebel of Cynic traditions, nor still as the crafty and dangerous man of those who spoke and wrote against him, but as the man, as he refers to himself in Plato's *Apology* (34d), "sprung from human parents," that is, the actual man?

There may be, however, a way out of the Socratic labyrinth. Although as noted above, there is much discrepancy among the sources, it is still possible to sift through them in order to find certain common elements and construct out of them a tentative sketch of Socrates as a man and as a philosopher. In so doing, it is important to recognize the fact, found in the writings of all major historical figures, that the writers themselves saw their subjects from their own perspectives. Through them, they recognized those features and details that they found worthy of mention and always from their own points of view. In writing about Socrates, accordingly, they left a firsthand account or an account of what they had learned. The word *person* is derived from the Latin *persona*, a word that literally means *mask*. An actual person is, however, inevitably a collection of masks that the true self presents to the world. Both self and masks undergo variations in time, sometimes profound variation, and, thus, there should not be anything strange in encountering a variety of masks in the reports and writings about Socrates.

This is, we suspect, most likely the case with Socrates. The primary sources saw in him what their inclinations, abilities, and goals allowed them to see in him. They incorporated their experiences into themselves and created out of the masks they encountered in him the images they eventually portrayed. Likewise in the instance of the secondary sources: they learned about Socrates what they were able and inclined to learn and dismissed as inconsequential or false other reports.

The solution could then be to recognize these undeniable circumstances and ask, what common features are present in at least many of the sources? Whatever the result may be, it will have to be tentative and sketchy, and we may be compelled to repeat with Alcibiades that no one really knew who or what Socrates was. We may have to add that in the end we must be satisfied with having identified certain reasonably assured facts and ideas about him. These can grant us some justification in attempting to speak intelligently about his legacy.

We can begin by recounting some pieces of information about Socrates that are seldom, if at all, contradicted by any of the sources. The dates of his birth and death can be ascertained. He was born in 469 BCE (fourth year of the 77th Olympiad) and died in 399 BCE (first year of the 95th Olympiad) at the age of seventy. The report (DL 2.44) that he died at the age of sixty does not appear to hold much ground. The coincidence of his birth and death with the Athenian festival of Apollo and Artemis (DL 2.44; Porphyry, *De vita Platonis* 2.96) may be a legend created in Hellenistic times, although the testimony of Plato lends support to the belief that Socrates was executed at the conclusion of the Delian festival of Apollo, as we learn from the *Crito* and in the *Phaedo*. Both his birth and death took place in Athens. His father was a statuary or sculptor named Sophroniscus, and his mother was a midwife named Phaenarete.[3] Both were Athenian, and their son was, therefore, an Athenian citizen.

Socrates appears to have come from a working class background; he was neither an aristocrat like Alcibiades or Plato nor a member of the poor class. This is supported by testimonies that tell us that he served as an infantry soldier in the Athenian army.[4] Wealthy citizens would normally serve in the cavalry, as in the case of Xenophon, whereas the poor would serve as auxiliaries. In later years, it seems that Socrates' financial resources became diminished because of his choice of philosophy as his vocation. He devoted himself to intellectual pursuits, refusing to receive payment for his teaching. Aristoxenus's statement that Socrates made money by teaching (DL 2.20) is not supported by Plato or Xenophon. In Aristophanes' *Clouds* (98), there is a reference to Socrates' practice of collecting fees. In Xenophon's *Oeconomicus* (2.1–4), Socrates states that his possessions did not exceed more than 100 minae (about 1,000 dollars), which would have placed him in the fourth and lowest of social classes among the citizens according to the constitution of Solon. Moreover, there are several references to his poverty in Plato's testimony as in the *Apology* (19d, 31c).

There is a report in Diogenes Laertius (2.20) that in his youth, Socrates worked as a statuary and that he was rescued from this occupation by Crito, a wealthy man himself. Neither Plato nor Xenophon, however, mentions anything about having ever worked for a living. In the *Crito* (45a), we learn that he was the beneficiary of his friends' generosity and in Diogenes Laertius (2.25), we hear about their willingness to provide for his needs. It is clear that he enjoyed a great deal of leisure, which was nothing exceptional among the free Athenians of his time, who looked upon the need to work for a living as something embarrassing.

He was married to a woman named Xanthippe, who is mentioned by Plato and Xenophon (*Phaedo* 60a, 116a; Xenophon's

Symposium 2.10). The report attributed (DL 2.26) to Aristotle
that Socrates was also married to a certain Myrto, a daughter of
Aristides the statesman, is not found in the existing Aristotelian
works and is not confirmed by the primary sources. According
to Diogenes Laertius, Myrto was Socrates' second wife and the
mother of his two youngest children, Sophroniscus and Menexenus. In the *Phaedo* (60a), however, it is clear that it was Xanthippe who was Socrates' wife at the time of his death and also
the mother of his youngest child. The reference in the *Memorabilia* (2.2.1–14) to the mother of Lamprocles, his oldest son, is
inconclusive because her name is not given.[5] In Aristophanes,
on the other hand, there are no allusions to Socrates' family, but
this is not surprising. The Athenians paid little attention to the
details and circumstances of a man's married life, and Aristophanes' silence about Xanthippe, therefore, has no special significance.

In the secondary sources, Xanthippe is often portrayed as an
impatient and difficult wife, one who would not stop nagging
and complaining, as Diogenes Laertius reports (2.34–37). This
characterization is also found in Xenophon in whose *Symposium*
(2.26) Socrates says that he chose her as his wife in order to
learn to cope even with the most irritating and difficult people.
From Plato, however, nothing definite can be deduced about
her character or background. One suspects that her uncompli-
mentary reputation is partly the result of exaggeration and distortion born out of the low esteem in which women were often
held among the Greeks.

Little is known about Socrates' children, except for their
names and approximate ages at the time of their father's death.
Plato does not mention them by name, but states that the oldest
(Lamprocles) was a boy already reaching manhood (*Apology*
34d), while the youngest was small enough to be held in his
mother's arms (*Phaedo* 60a) at the time of Socrates' execution.
Xenophon gives us only the name of the oldest son but says

nothing about the other two, whose names appear in Diogenes Laertius (2.26). Some information about them can be gathered from the secondary sources. For instance, in Aristotle (*Rhetoric* 1390b) and in Plutarch (*Cato* 20), they are said to have been stupid and vulgar and to have amounted to little in life.

Knowledge about Socrates' education is difficult to sort out. We hear that he was a student of Anaxagoras, Damon, and Archelaus the natural philosopher (DL 2.19). In Ameipsias's comedy the *Connus*, a certain Connus is introduced as Socrates' music teacher (cf. *Euthydemus* 272c, 295d). Also, in the *Phaedo* (97c ff.), we learn of his having studied a work by Anaxagoras. Yet, both Plato and Xenophon are emphatic in asserting that Socrates had no formal teachers and that he regarded himself as a student of no one.

It is, however, possible to distinguish two stages in Socrates' intellectual development—a first stage during which he studied under one or more teachers and was interested in issues concerning natural science, and a second stage during which he declared his independence from the ideas of others and turned his attention exclusively inward, that is, toward his own self. The mature Socrates, accordingly, was someone who could have regarded himself as having no intellectual or philosophical mentors and as a thinker wholly indifferent toward the problems of natural philosophy or science. The point in time that separates these two stages constitutes an enigmatic aspect of his life. There is some justification in identifying that point with the famous Delphic pronouncement about him and perhaps with the performance of Aristophanes' *Clouds* in 423 BCE. One thing, however, is certain. The Socrates who speaks in the writings of Plato and Xenophon, and who inspired the numerous reports of the secondary sources, is a man thoroughly knowledgeable about the philosophical developments of his time and a person of refined culture in a variety of fields, indeed, someone who could have easily warranted the Pythia's statement about him, namely, that of all living men he was truly the wisest.

Of Socrates' social relations we can construct a reasonably accurate picture from the testimonies of Plato and Xenophon. In them, he is described as a gregarious man who was willing and able to enter into discourse with all sorts of people. We find him conversing with statesmen and generals, philosophers and sophists, poets and musicians, wealthy foreigners, people of humble background, and slaves—in sum, he approached almost everyone he encountered with an irresistible passion to communicate his message. He is portrayed far removed in this respect from the portrait created by Aristophanes, according to whom Socrates was an antisocial recluse living indoors and surrounded by a close entourage of stupefied disciples.

In Xenophon's and Plato's testimonies, Socrates is an outgoing person whose ideas, as we read in Plato's *Apology* (33b), are never revealed in secret or by esoteric means. He converses always in public and in a language accessible even to uneducated people and couched in metaphors related to the activities of shoemakers, horse trainers, and other working folk. He is well at ease among the aristocrats, as well as among simple citizens, and is invariably an example of politeness and civility. He is loved and admired by a small group of devoted friends, who, as in the case of Xenophon, regard him as a philosophical master whose words and memory deserve to be revered (*Memorabilia* 1.2.61), or who, as with Plato, regard him as the best, wisest, and most righteous man (*Phaedo* 118a). Others, like Meno (*Meno* 80a–b), stand befuddled and perplexed in his presence and, as if stung by a stingray, are unable to speak or move. Still others, like the passionate Alcibiades, as we are told in Plato's *Symposium* (215 ff.), are literally in love with him and are unable to dispel the spell he has cast upon their souls.

For his part, Socrates responds to his friends by returning their love with an even greater love. For love, he says (*Theages*

128b),[6] is the only subject in the world in which he regards himself an unsurpassed master. In Xenophon's *Symposium* (8.2), he makes the remarkable statement that he cannot remember a time in his life when he was not in love with someone. Love is the decisive force that animates and sustains all his endeavors.

Yet the circle of Socrates' friends must have been small. In this respect, the testimony of Aristophanes agrees with those of Plato and Xenophon. In the *Clouds*, the group of his disciples is very small. Furthermore, in none of the primary or secondary sources does he appear as a charismatic leader addressing the masses. His message is not heard amid large gatherings of people but is one that touches quietly only those few who have the right ears for his words. His style is not what is heard in courts or political assemblies (*Apology* 17d).

We can assume that for most Athenians, Socrates was merely an eccentric and colorful figure in the marketplace and the public buildings, perhaps a clever sophist and a restless philosopher, but in reality nothing else. Athenians were probably unconcerned about his activities and indifferent toward his philosophical preoccupations, although, as the testimony of the comedians show, they must not have missed the opportunity of laughing at his expense in the performances at the theater of Dionysus. In Diogenes Laertius (2.21), we read that often, as a result of his vehement questioning, people would set upon him with their fists and tear out his hair. He succeeded in antagonizing his interlocutors with his frank comments and persistent interrogations.

This does not entail, however, that he earned for himself so dreadful a reputation as to be considered a public enemy. Certainly, his trial does not appear to have had the trappings of a popular lynching. The comment attributed by Plutarch to Aristoxenus (*On the Malice of Herodotus* 856d), that even though Socrates was an uneducated and impudent fellow, there was no real harm in him—this comment probably echoed the general sentiment of the Athenians toward him. For them, he must have been a mild but tolerable public nuisance. If we assume this attitude on their part, we understand the otherwise surprising impunity with which he lived in a city that, despite its democratic traditions and openness, was sometimes far from liberal and tolerant. In his seventh letter (*Epist.* 7.325b), Plato explains Socrates' ability to remain unpunished for so long to an element of chance, and, indeed, this must have been the case. Still, the climate of public indifference that surrounded the philosopher must also be taken into account. We have enough information to conclude, moreover, that the trial did not really have to take place and that what the prosecutors wanted was for him to leave the city.

Nevertheless, there is another aspect of Socrates' life that should be kept in mind. Side by side with his devoted friends and against the background of the indifference of most people, there was the genuine hatred and dislike of a few who saw in him an enemy of Athenian society, more formidable and dangerous than the Spartan infantry that during the Peloponnesian War would devastate the Attic countryside. Socrates' enemies were few but sufficiently influential to create for him an atmosphere of danger, of which he was obviously well aware (e.g., *Memo* 94e). They looked upon him as a dangerous man who would question and challenge the beliefs and practices of the state religion, who would pour contempt on long-established political practices and customs, such as the selection of public officials by lot, and who would persuade the youth to break away from parental authority. By means of linguistic trickery he would baffle and corrupt the best among the citizens, and through public interrogations he would embarrass prominent political figures.

Foremost in their minds, there must have been the curious yet historically ascertainable circumstance that many of Socrates' associates were men who at one time or another had gained notoriety for their unpatriotic leanings and immoral behavior—men like Alcibiades, Critias, Charmides, Meno, and others. The enemies of Socrates would argue that such people had been misguided and corrupted by him and had become, under his influence, the seeds of the destruction of the Athenian empire. This destruction eventually took place in the year 404 BCE, when the Spartans compelled the city to surrender. From this point on, the history of Athens was colored by decadence and confusion, and the last five years of Socrates' life witnessed the most unhappy period of its history.

In 403 BCE the Spartans left and the democracy was reinstated. Feelings of revenge for the defeat soon surfaced, and this, more than anything else, was responsible for the execution of Socrates. The democrats who assumed power—Anytus, one of Socrates' prosecutors, among them—must have sought to punish those who had either sympathized with the Spartans or had at least created a climate of uncertainty in the city. Socrates had already been accused of laconism, that is, sympathizing with the Spartans, in Aristophanes' *Birds*, a comedy performed several years earlier. Moreover, Socrates' occasional expressions of admiration for the Spartans, which appear in the testimonies of Plato and Xenophon, as well as his unabashed dislike for democracy, set in motion those who would accuse him in 399 BCE.

It was then that he was indicted before an Athenian jury on a charge of irreligiosity, known in Athenian law as *asebeia*, which literally means irreverence, fearlessness, or lack of respect for the gods accepted by the state and, consequently, for the laws. Forty years earlier and at the urging of Pericles, the assembly had passed a law that made *asebeia* a crime. A certain Diopeithes had proposed that law. The trial took place in the spring. Socrates was found guilty and sentenced to death. One month later he was executed.

These are the bare facts about Socrates' life. More extensive biographical information is not available. Surely, all sorts of reports began to circulate after his death, but many of them cannot be confirmed by reference to the primary sources. Some of them, as can be expected, are the result of the imagination of later writers. The secondary sources provide innumerable anecdotal details and comments about Socrates' ideas, but, in general, it is difficult to assess their historical and philosophical value.

NOTES

1. For a review of about two thousand works related to Socrates, see L. E. Navia and E. Katz, *Socrates: An Annotated Bibliography* (New York: Garland Publishing, 1988).

2. The relationship between Socrates and the Cynic movement is explored in detail in L. E. Navia, *Diogenes the Cynic: The War against the World* (Amherst, NY: Humanity Books, 2005).

3. The name of Socrates' father is given by Plato in *Euthydemus* 297e, *Hippias Major* 298b, and *Laches* 180d. His mother is mentioned by Plato in *Theaetetus* 149a. They are also mentioned by Diogenes Laertius (2.18).

4. Socrates' military service is mentioned in Plato's *Apology* 28e, *Laches* 181b, and *Symposium* 221a.

5. There are reports that in the late fifth century BCE, at the height of the Peloponnesian War, the Athenian assembly made it possible for citizens to take on a second wife. The war had left many women widowed and many more unmarried. Socrates then could have taken on Myrto as a wife while remaining married to Xanthippe.

6. The authenticity of the *Theages* is generally rejected. Still, it is possible to find in it useful information about Socrates.

CHAPTER 2

Socrates on the Comic Stage

*T*he sources of information about Socrates can be divided into two categories, primary and secondary. The primary sources include the writings of Socrates' contemporaries. Among them, we encounter the comedies of the playwrights who ridiculed him on the stage, the writings of Socrates' associates, a reconstruction of the indictment attributed to Polycrates, several books by Xenophon, and statements of other writers such as Isocrates. If all these sources were extant, an enormous collection of documents would be available. Unfortunately, however, this is not the case. The circumstances and accidents of bibliographical history have brought about the irreparable loss of the bulk of the Socratic and related literature of Socrates' time.

Of the fifty-four comedies attributed to Aristophanes, only eleven have survived, and of the many comedies written by other comic playwrights none is extant except in the form of fragments. Thus, the references probably made to Socrates in those works cannot be retrieved. The numerous writings of the sophists have also disappeared, again, except for fragments.

Whatever light they might have shed on the Socratic presence can no longer be rekindled.

More important still is the loss of the works of the minor Socratics, to whom Diogenes Laertius attributes a great number of writings. Aristippus, for example, is said to have been the author of thirty-five volumes. Dozens of works are attributed to other Socratics, but, without exception, only fragments found in quotations of later writers are available. It is difficult not to assume that in most of these writings, many of them written in the style of Xenophon's and Plato's dialogues, the influence of Socrates must have been present in practically every line, for it was he who led such authors into the pursuit of philosophy.

Of Antisthenes' writings, also hardly anything has survived of his sixty-two works. The loss of these works is especially regrettable because from what we know about Antisthenes, he seems to have been Socrates' closest associate and the man who, according to some, was the most genuine heir of the Socratic presence.[1] Through his own direct influence on Diogenes of Sinope, he was responsible for the rise of classical Cynicism, the philosophical movement that planted the seeds for the rise of Stoicism and that ultimately rose on the basis of his interpretation of Socrates.[2]

Concerning the circumstances and accidents responsible for the preservation of some primary sources and the destruction of others, several comments can be made. We could mention the repeated burnings of the ancient libraries where, whether at Alexandria, Pergamum, or other centers of learning, thousands of irreplaceable manuscripts perished at the hands of conquering armies or thoughtless religious zealots. Then there was the process of natural decay undergone by the original documents. Thus, either through design or accident, the majority of documents of antiquity no longer exist.

Important, too, is the process of bibliographical selectiveness that must be imputed to the scholars and librarians in whose hands the ancient documents were placed. They were the ultimate judges of what deserved to be preserved. What they saw fit to preserve and copy survived and what they deemed less important or ideologically offensive simply rotted away in the underground chambers of the libraries or was consigned to fire. Ancient scholars, it seems, were not interested in preserving for posterity all the writings of their ancestors but only what in their estimation was valuable and edifying.

As noted earlier, in the instance of Aristophanes' comedies, we have only a small number of them. In some of these, we come upon Socrates in several passages and in one of them, the *Clouds*, we find him as the protagonist. In all of them, the portrayal of him is consistent, as if the playwright had never changed his mind about him.

The *Clouds* was performed in Athens in 423 BCE and is the earliest notice of Socrates known to us. On that occasion, three comedies were performed at the Great Dionysia festival: Cratinus's *Bottle*, Ameipsias's *Connus*, and Aristophanes' *Clouds*. The theatrical prizes were awarded in that order, the first going to the aged Cratinus. Neither his comedy nor that of Ameipsias has survived except for fragments from which it is nearly impossible to reconstruct the entire pieces. What we can affirm, however, is that in them a character named "Socrates" plays an important part.

It may have been a coincidence that Socrates was the subject of the three competing comedies. It is possible that for unknown reasons he may have attracted public attention at that time either for something he did or for something he said. He could have then become a perfect subject for the comic stage. In Ameipsias's comedy, the protagonist is a harpist and music teacher named Connus, with whom we are acquainted through Plato's references (*Euthydemus* 272c, 295d). Socrates is introduced to the audience by Connus, his music teacher, and is accompanied by a chorus of thinkers. He is depicted as a ridiculous man who, despite his intellectual pretensions, is described as totally empty and worthy of ridicule. Much more cannot be said about the Socrates of Ameipsias.

A great deal, however, can be said about the Socrates of Aristophanes because the *Clouds* has survived in its entirety. Its extant form seems to reflect not its original version of 423 BCE but a revision made by the playwright. Significant parts of the original version are believed to have been different from those of the text available to us. Parts in the latter, such as the contest between the Just Discourse and the Unjust Discourse, as well as the last scene in which Socrates' school is burned, were probably not in the original version. Possibly, Aristophanes' failure to secure the first prize made him revise his comedy in order to gain greater acceptance from the audience. It is probable, however, that the comedy was performed only once.

It may be unsettling that the earliest appearance of Socrates is as the protagonist of a comedy in which he is portrayed as a ridiculous man and as the fittest subject for public laughter. Somehow, we face a paradoxical situation: Socrates, who is described by Plato as a virtuous and almost saintly man and by Xenophon as a model of rectitude, enters into history as a ridiculous buffoon. The former compels us to think and reflect, but the latter moves us to laughter. Yet, with Socrates all sorts of things are possible including amusement and reflection, ridicule and canonization, accusation and vindication, condemnation and apotheosis. Moreover, there may be an element of justice in Aristophanes' choice of him as a subject for ridicule. The playwright makes the crowd laugh at a man who, as Alcibiades remarks in the *Symposium* (216e), "spends his whole life playing his little game of irony and laughing up his sleeve at all the world."

In classical comedy no less than in classical tragedy, we assume that at the basis of the playwright's effort there is a desire to imitate some actual person or situation. Surely, the subject of imitation varies from comedy to tragedy. In the latter, the playwright aims at imitating a person of great character and praiseworthy achievements, as Aristotle says in his *Poetics*. In comedy, things are very different. Comedy, according to Aristotle (*Poetics* 1449a), is the art of imitating bad and vicious characters in order to render them ridiculous. Thus, in selecting Socrates as the protagonist of his comedy, Aristophanes chose a bad character and brought to the surface those among his traits that made him especially ridiculous. Socrates must have been for him a bad and ridiculous man, which is confirmed by passages from his *Frogs* (1491) and *Birds* (1555).

It is unreasonable to assume that Aristophanes' Socrates is altogether unrelated to the historical man, that is, just a creation of his imagination. Plato's own testimony makes this untenable. In the *Apology* (18d), Socrates mentions a "writer of comedies," whom he names later on as one of his accusers and as the source of the false charges circulating against him. There is also the anecdotal report that at the performance of the *Clouds*, as strangers and foreigners would ask, "Who is this man Socrates?" the philosopher, who was in the audience, would silently stand up as if to reply, "Here is the man himself."[3] Thus, everyone could see at least how well the mask makers had succeeded in reproducing his actual physical features. Considering the protagonists of Aristophanes' other comedies, one realizes that most of them are imitations of actual people. The requirements of Athenian comedy would not have permitted otherwise, because the audiences would not have appreciated altogether fictional characters.

If the *Clouds* involves the imitation of Socrates, several questions arise. Was it accurate and justified even within the liberal parameters of Athenian comedy that allowed for distortion and exaggeration? Is the playwright's character a travesty of the real person? What could have been the playwright's motivation for choosing Socrates? Was it only for the purpose of amusing the crowd? Is it possible that beneath the jokes and preposterous scenes there was a political, moralistic, or personal agenda for which Socrates was used as the most appropriate medium?

Questions also arise about the consequences of the comedy for Socrates himself. Did the comic jokes succeed in transforming themselves twenty-four years later into the accusations brought against him at the trial, as Plato suggests in the *Apology*? What impact did the comedy have on Socrates? Could it have been a sort of catalyst that forced him to undergo some form of conversion?

Little is known with certainty about the origin of comedy. Aristotle himself confessed his limited knowledge in this respect (*Poetics* 1449). Still, general statements can be made with some assurance. As much as with tragedy, the origin of comedy is related to emotional needs and religious longings that became crystallized and structured in ritualistic celebrations and festivals. Comedy was probably a transformation of the ancient rites in which Dionysus was worshiped as the god of fertility at the conclusion of the vintage. Also known as Bacchus, Dionysus was revered as the god of intoxication and ecstatic revelries. Bacchanalian processions of revelers would travel from place to place, carrying huge phallic symbols, singing and dancing wildly, all in a spirit of total licentiousness, often preceded and followed by comic performances. It must have been in the countryside and small villages where such celebrations took place. The etymological connection between the word *comedy* and the word *comos* (which means in Attic Greek *merrymaking* and in Doric Greek *village*) suggests that the origin of comedy was rural. In time, however, the Dionysian *comos* found its way into the cities, transformed into comic plays in which actors entertained the crowd.

The first recorded comic competition took place in Athens in 487 BCE. From this time onward, comedy became an important part of Athenian life—at least for Athenian men, since women, although often represented on the stage by male actors, were not allowed in the theater. To enter the competitions, the playwrights would present their comedies to an Athenian magistrate, who would grant or deny a license for the performance. The production was paid for by wealthy citizens. Three comedies were chosen for the yearly festivals, and their performance took place at the theater of Dionysus below the Acropolis. After the performances, a panel of jurors would rank the pieces and award the prizes. It seems that the only basis for the jurors' decision was the reaction of the audience: the louder and longer the laughter, the greater was the chance of winning the first prize.

A great deal has been written about the significance of comedy among the Athenians. Much discussion has taken place about the fact that in a society as sophisticated as that of Athens, so vulgar a form of entertainment could have flourished. Athenian comedy, as a scholar has noted, "reflected the eternal spectacle of human nature and its weaknesses, [and was] the most complete reflection of its age, far surpassing any other type of literature or art in fullness and accuracy."[4]

Its distinguishing feature was the permissiveness in which it functioned. What people were not allowed to do or say in public and what was forbidden by social norms were acceptable if done or said on the stage. The scenes were vulgar, the costumes offensive, and the dances obscene. The language, despite its poetical form, was unrestricted.

During the performances, the audience, moved by the libidinous license seen on the stage, behaved in ways that imitated those of the actors. Practically nothing was sacred on the comic stage. Even the gods, with the exception of Athena, were not spared from ridicule. The government, political parties, and military alliances, the Homeric heroes and respected statesmen, aristocratic leaders and democratic demagogues, citizens and foreigners—all were chosen at one time or another as the subjects of ridicule. Indeed, as Aristophanes notes in his *Peace*, the more important the victim, the greater was the opportunity for ridicule. Among all ancient cultures, it has been said, "Athens definitely reached the highest level of toleration of any other society known to us."[5]

Occasionally, the authorities imposed restrictions on the comedians, as was the case shortly after the Samian revolt of 440 BCE, when Pericles persuaded the Assembly to ban comedies in which the Athenian policies were ridiculed. After this, playwrights and their producers had to obtain a license for their comedies. The playwrights could be indicted by those whom they had ridiculed or maligned on the stage, as happened in the case of Cleon, an important politician, who prosecuted the man responsible for the production of Aristophanes' *Babylonians*. Aristophanes himself was indicted by Cleon for the production of *Acharnians* in 425 BCE. Such accusations, however, were seldom successful.

Often, as in Aristophanes' works, the choice of the characters was motivated by political position or popularity. Unimportant people were not worth the comedian's effort, and the chances for success were greater when the subject was well known. It would be surprising not to find philosophers among the subjects of comedies because they often were and still are viewed as eccentric, disruptive, and ridiculous. In the eyes of ordinary people, they give the impression of having lost touch with reality and of posing a constant danger to the normalcy and sanity in which most people live. It was precisely for such people that the playwrights wrote.

Comedy originated in the country villages and retained its peasant character for a long time. Its origins had left on it a mark that was discernible long after it had made its entrance in cities. Its language was peasant language. The vulgarity of its idioms, the roughness of its mannerisms, and its phallic songs and dances were reminders of its origin. The main character is often a peasant uprooted from his country village who lives in the city where he feels lost. He is cheated and abused by the decadence of urban life. The city, with its political machinery, its courts and juries, its system of education, and its emphasis on affluence and comfort, has brought upon him distress and mischief and has corrupted his children. He longs for the simple life he once enjoyed.

This theme must have been appreciated by the spectators who during the Peloponnesian War were forced to leave their country homes and farms. Pericles had urged the peasants to take refuge in the city in order to avoid the danger posed by the Spartan army in the western districts of Attica. Thus, the city became filled with displaced peasants who must have found it hard to adjust to urban conditions. Conservative and traditionalistic, they must have resented those aspects of urban life that were imposed on them.

The character of Strepsiades in the *Clouds* is a typical peasant who blames city life for his unhappiness. "My life in the country," he insists, "was the most pleasant life, untidy, easygoing, unrestrained." On his arrival in Athens, he marries a sophisticated lady, a woman used to perfumes and luxuries, who teaches him the art of tongue-kissing. Many among the audience would have had no difficulty in empathizing with the wretched man because his fate was not uncommon. How much, indeed, they would also have preferred to live in the farmlands away from the politicians, philosophers, and foreigners with whom Athens was teeming.

Socrates, for his part, appears as the antithesis of Strepsiades. Born in the city and bred in its customs, he feels at home only in the marketplace and crowded streets of the city. The countryside has no appeal for him. Phaedrus, a young friend of his, once remarked to him, "You strike me as the oddest of men. Anyone would take you for a stranger being shown the countryside by a guide instead of a native—never leaving the city, nor even, I believe, so much as setting foot outside the walls. [To which Socrates replies] You must forgive me, dear Phaedrus, for I am a lover of learning, and trees and the world of nature cannot teach me anything. The people in the city, however, do" (*Phaedrus* 230d).

The comedy's cast calls for nine characters and a chorus of twenty-four voices. The chorus is a group of personified clouds, which explains the comedy's title. Of the nine characters, two represent types of ideas, namely, the Just Discourse and the Unjust Discourse. Of the other characters, four are marginal, while three are constantly in the foreground. The latter are Strepsiades, his son Phidippides, and Socrates.

The plot unfolds along simple lines. After being forced to leave his country house because of his marriage with a city lady, Strepsiades finds himself in the midst of a bad financial situation brought about by the habits of his horse-loving son. The lazy and irresponsible boy, completely corrupted by city life, thinks of nothing other than horses. He dreams of them. Distressed and confused by his debts and by the behavior of his son, Strepsiades spends restless nights thinking about ways to extricate himself from his plight. How, he asks himself, could he avoid paying his debts? At last he comes upon the idea of taking Phidippides to a school run by Socrates. Here, the boy would learn to avoid paying his creditors. The father himself would then learn from his son. The Thinking Establishment, as the school is called, is then his only hope. He remembers that Socrates teaches that

> Heaven is one vast fire-extinguisher
> Placed round about us, and that we are the cinders.
> Yes, and they'll teach (only they'll want some money),
> How one may speak and conquer, right or wrong. . . .
> They teach to talk unjustly and prevail.
> Think then, you only learn that Unjust Discourse,
> And all the debts, which I have incurred through you,
> I'll never pay, no, not one cent of them.

> (*Clouds* 95–98, 115–19)

The son is not, however, willing to enter the school, and this is why the father himself decides to become a disciple of Socrates.

From the start, his experiences are bizarre. He is greeted with the news that he is responsible for the miscarriage caused by his knocking on the door, perhaps an allusion to Socrates' reference to himself as a midwife (*Theaetetus* 149 ff.). Inside, he meets Socrates' disciples, among whom Chaerephon holds an important place. This Chaerephon is surely the same person mentioned in Plato's dialogues (*Apology* 21a, *Gorgias* 447a) and in Xenophon's *Memorabilia* (1.2.48).

Strepsiades soon realizes that Socrates' disciples are strange people. Pale and emaciated, they resemble imprisoned wild beasts. Their eyes are fixed on the ground. They explain to him that they are searching for things under the earth. They also study the stars. Science is an important subject for them because their master is especially interested in it. As Strepsiades learns, an embarrassing accident had just happened to Socrates:

> Why, as He Himself, with eyes and mouth wide open,
> Mused on the Moon, her paths and revolutions,
> A lizard from the roof squirted full on him.

> (*Clouds* 171–73)

The idea of a lizard spattering on the philosopher amuses and delights Strepsiades. He then hears about the miscarriage he caused by knocking on the door. Socrates, he is told, had been trying to measure the length of the jump of a flea that had bitten Chaerephon's forehead and had bounced off to Socrates' head. To accomplish this scientific feat, which is referred to as one of their "high mysteries," Socrates

> warmed some wax, and then caught the flea,
> And dipped its feet into the wax he had melted.
> Then he let it cool, and there were Persian slippers!
> These he took off, and so he found the distance.

> (*Clouds* 149–53)

Yet, despite these and other absurdities, Strepsiades insists on meeting Socrates, the head of so strange a school. He finds him suspended in a floating basket. In it, Socrates says, he can contemplate the sun at short range and can live close to his beloved Clouds, the only gods he worships. Strepsiades discloses the purpose of his visit, saying that he has come "to learn to speak" in order to avoid paying his debts. Will Socrates, he inquires, be willing to take him on as a disciple? The plot continues amid nonsensical language games, jokes and puns of all types, and embarrassing scenes that deserve to be read attentively because they all add to the portrayal of Socrates. Especially revealing, for instance, are the statements uttered by the chorus of Clouds and the dialogue between the Just Discourse and the Unjust Discourse.

Finally, Strepsiades is unable to learn the lessons. Reluctantly, he decides once more to ask his son to enter the school. Perhaps, he hopes, the young man might find it easier to understand the lessons. Phidippides agrees and profits well from Socrates' guidance. At last, he emerges from the school as a transformed person who no longer dreams of horses but whose mind is wrecked. He has become as mad as the Socratic disciples. He no longer obeys or respects his father and does not hesitate to abuse him. He even threatens to beat his mother.

Dismayed by so dreadful a transformation, Strepsiades decides to avenge himself by setting fire to the school. His concluding words, in which we discern an anger not quite in line with what we would expect in a comedy, reveal the real message of the *Clouds*:

> For with what aim did you insult the Gods,
> And pry around the dwellings of the Moon?
> Strike, smite them, spare them not, for many reasons,
> But most because they have blasphemed the Gods!

> (*Clouds* 1504–1508)

It is impossible to know how the original version of the *Clouds* ended. Perhaps what led Aristophanes to rewrite the play was his initial failure. He had not been harsh enough, and because of this he had to introduce the burning scene. Socrates' unpopularity at that time must have been great, as is suggested by Diogenes Laertius (2.21): "Frequently, owing to his vehemence in argument, men set upon him with their fists and tore his hair out; and for the most part he was despised and laughed at, yet bore all this ill-usage patiently."

What did people in general and the audience in particular see in him? What did he do to earn the dislike and hatred of many? What did Aristophanes find so reprehensible in him to justify so drastic an end for the *Clouds*?

The *Wasps*, a comedy performed one year later, gives us a clue. In it, the playwright complains bitterly about his failure to secure the first prize with his *Clouds*, and then explains his purpose in ridiculing Socrates:

> But he [Aristophanes], when the monstrous form he saw,
> No bribe he took and no fear he felt,
> For you [the people] he fought, and for you he fights.
> And then last year with adventurous hand
> He grappled besides with the Spectral Shadows,
> The maladies and fevers that plagued our land,
> That loved in the darksome hours of the night
> To throttle fathers, and grandfathers choke,
> That laid them down on their restless beds,
> And against your quiet and peaceful folk
> Kept welding together proofs and legal documents
> And oath against oath, till many a man
> Sprang up, distracted with wild affright,
> And ran off in haste to the magistrate.

> (*Wasps* 1035–42)

These harsh lines clearly disclose his purpose. He speaks unambiguously of his fight on behalf of the "quiet and peaceful folk" against "the Spectral Shapes" that plague Athens and disturb family relationships by means of "proofs and legal documents" and "oath against oath." He presents himself as the protector of the common people against the threat posed by Socrates and philosophers like him. His frustration is great because in the *Clouds* he attempted to tackle the greatest enemy of the Athenians by means of the "cleverest comedy a man, since the world began, has witnessed."

Aristophanes' words should incline us to abandon the idea that the *Clouds* was only an amusing and clever farce of no significance. If there is anything that distinguishes him from other comic playwrights, it is his sense of mission and his desire to set aright the city's cultural and political climate. Beneath the jokes and ludicrous scenes, there is an earnestness that lurks behind every comic line. His comedies were not always the best in the eyes of the audiences. Of his eleven extant comedies, only three are known to have received the first prize: *Acharnians*, *Knights*, and *Frogs*. In the case of the *Clouds*, he received, as we saw earlier, only the third prize. A review of his comedies reveals that he is at war with what he saw as a great evil afflicting the city—the unscrupulous demagogues and politicians, the irrationality and excesses of the Athenian jury system, the imperialism of the government, the senselessness of the democratic warmongers, the lawlessness of oligarchs, the philosophers, in a word, the sources of social and cultural unhealthiness—the Spectral Shadows that haunted the streets of Athens. For him, Socrates was one of those shadows.

The reconstruction of the image of Socrates in the *Clouds* yields several clear points. Socrates is the head of a school, the Thinking Establishment, where the disciples live in submission to their Master, to whom they refer as "He Himself." They appear distraught, open-mouthed, pale and emaciated, stupefied, as if their minds had been taken away from them. The Master and his thoughtless disciples pass their time thinking about astronomy and geography, about things in the sky and below the earth, and about things such as the length of the jump of a flea.

The school's curriculum is also career-oriented because the disciples learn the art of speaking, something that would prepare them to succeed in the world. They could then take advantage of others, avoid paying taxes and debts, and escape from indictments and accusations. Questions about ethical values, the nature of virtue and vice, and the difference between truth and falsity are not part of their studies because such matters are useless. If they learn to succeed, the goal of the school will have been achieved. The school is not entirely closed to outsiders. It welcomes new recruits if they are willing to pay. Neither Socrates nor his disciples live like the rest of the Athenians. The former live indoors and have no external interests since they are detached from political and social affairs, whereas the latter enjoy living in the open and are constantly engaged in public life.

Other points emerge with clarity. Socrates worships and follows his own gods, the Clouds, who are not part of Athenian religion. He does not believe in the accepted gods of the city. When the pious Strepsiades reminds him that Zeus is unquestionably a god, Socrates bluntly replies that there is no such thing as Zeus. This lesson is at last learned by Strepsiades, who eventually convinces his son that the gods do not exist.

The teachings of Socrates are obviously detrimental to the boy, for he is also taught to disregard the morality of language and actions and to disobey and abuse his parents. His behavior at the end of the comedy shows this with clarity: he insults and strikes his aged father while displaying obedience to his new master. Strepsiades might have cured his son from the obsession with horses, but he has ultimately lost him. The boy now belongs to Socrates.

Indeed, Socrates emerges as a man who has lost touch with reality, as is shown by his living in a hanging basket. He is truly a madman who stares stupidly at the sun. Unable and unwilling even to bathe himself, he stands for all that is undesirable in the eyes of the Athenians. He represents the decadence afflicting the city, a decadence for which he is responsible. In Aristophanes' words, already quoted in the previous chapter, Socrates is "a bold rascal, a fine speaker, impudent, shameless; a braggart, and adept at stringing lies, an old stager at quibbles, a complete table of laws, a thorough rattle, a fox to slip through a hole; supple as a leather strap, slippery as an eel, an artful fellow, a blusterer, a villain; a knave with one hundred faces, cunning, intolerable, a gluttonous dog" (*Clouds* 446–52).

If *this* is what Socrates was and if such was his influence over the Athenians, the burning of his school and the disbanding of his disciples would have been only a mild punishment for him. Athens was tolerant and forgiving, but it was also watchful for its own welfare. It seldom hesitated to impose severe punishments, whether death or exile, on those whom it judged dangerous or disruptive. Why then was Socrates allowed to live for so many years, unmolested and with impunity, while exhibiting such traits as we find in Aristophanes' comic character? In the *Apology*, the Platonic Socrates expresses surprise as to why the indictment against him was not drawn many years before. Why was he left in peace for so many years and brought to trial only in his old age?

According to Plato, this was the result of mere chance (*Epist.* 7.325b). He mentions certain political changes that may have been responsible for the timing of the indictment: "To be sure, in those days too, full of disturbance as they were, there were many things occurring to cause offense, nor is it surprising that in time of revolution men in some cases took undue revenge on their enemies. Yet for all that, the restored exiles displayed great moderation. As luck would have it, however, some of those in control brought against this associate of mine, Socrates, a most sacrilegious charge, which he least of all men deserved" (*Epist.* 7.325b).

This element of chance increases in proportion to the accuracy of Aristophanes' portrait of Socrates. Yet, such a portrait may not be accurate, otherwise why would Plato have spoken of him as someone who deserved less than any other man the punishment he suffered? The Socrates of Aristophanes is an atheist, an ungodly man who not only does not believe in the gods but who teaches others not to believe in them. Atheism, according to Plato himself (*Laws* 10.910d), is the worst of all crimes and must be punished by death. Thus, we must raise the issue of the accuracy of Aristophanes' portrayal. Is his Socrates a faithful representation of the historical man? Is it not possible that when the *Clouds* was written, Socrates, then a forty-six-year-old man, could have resembled at least in some ways the comic character that bore his name, only to undergo a *metanoia*, that is, a conversion or change of mind from which he might have emerged precisely as he is described by Plato?

The essence of Greek comedy was the exploitation of well-known people and situations as sources of entertainment. Surely, if the comedian remained restricted to the bare imitation of his subjects, the desired effect would not be attained. There are few actual persons, if any, that are so ridiculous to keep large audiences in a prolonged state of laughter. Hence, the imitation of which Aristotle speaks is only a point of departure. The rest, the greater part, is the result of exaggeration, distortion, and invention, intertwined in a series of surprising and unexpected sequences.

Laughter is generally aroused by the awareness of the gap between what is actual and what is encountered, but only if two conditions are present. First, what is actual must be something that does not give rise to grief or sadness, and second, the gap between the actual and the invented does not result in disbelief.

This, as Schopenhauer observed, is the process that explains the phenomenon of jokes. This explains why the characters of Aristophanes' comedies are real people well known to the audiences, but who, once on the stage, are transformed into caricatures that involve distortion and exaggeration.

Aspasia, Pericles' common-law wife, for instance, was a sophisticated lady, attractive and intelligent, sufficiently liberated to mingle freely with men, and influential enough to attract other women who shared her aspirations. This is a reasonable historical portrait. On the comic stage, however, she became another person, as Aristophanes portrays her in *Acharnians*, in which she is a libertine who uses her wits and appearance to manipulate the social world around her and maintain a brothel to satisfy the needs of prominent Athenians. Cleon was a democratic leader whose behavior was not always an example of rectitude. Yet, in the hands of Aristophanes, he appears as a political monster and a man worthy of contempt (*Acharnians* 516). Cleon may have taken bribes, as was customary among politicians, but on the stage he literally eats his bribe money only to vomit it in the presence of the audience. The Athenian jury system was inadequate and inefficient in some regards, and the jurors were often ignorant and vulgar. On the stage, however, they were all corrupted wasps characterized by greed, vengefulness, and stupidity, which is how Aristophanes depicts them in the *Wasps*. In general, then, the historical person and the comic character stand related to each other as a photograph to a caricature. The question is whether this could also be the case with the historical Socrates and the Socrates of the *Clouds*.

Unfortunately, the question is complex. There are no historical accounts of Socrates' character and habits at the time of the performance of the *Clouds* other than what we hear from Aristophanes. He appears in history many years later and is then generally presented in a very different light. Yet, even then, the portrayals of him are not quite in agreement with one another. Still, even in the absence of direct historical information of the time of the *Clouds*, it seems reasonable to assume that the comic Socrates is a distorted and exaggerated imitation of a historical person. In this respect, he does not differ from Aspasia, Cleon, and other Aristophanic characters, for they, too, are types of individuals who, in the eyes of the comedian, stand for a whole assortment of habits, traits, and ideas fit for ridicule. Thus, the comic Socrates is a focal point where an array of characteristics and issues converge and where, magnified and blown out of proportion, they can be exposed before an audience. Socrates himself may have in fact possessed some of those characteristics.

As a focal point for the comic denunciation, the character of Socrates has much in common with other philosophers of his time and earlier times. We find in him traces of Thales of Miletus, who was ridiculed for staring fixedly at the sky and making strange statements about the universe. Anaxagoras, too, and other natural philosophers can be found in Socrates, as well as the many sophists who were his contemporaries. The sophists' relativism, moral nihilism, and indifference toward social concerns are also found in him. In a word, in him we are in the presence of everything Aristophanes judged to be a source of political and moral decadence. What better way could there have been for him than to combine in one character all those social ills?

We could also consider the little we know about the relationship between Socrates and the playwright. Even in the absence of specific information in this regard, we can assume that they were well acquainted with each other. It must have been relatively easy in ancient Athens for many people to be in contact with many people at one time or another. The geographical parameters were small, and the number of citizens was not large. Besides, the outgoing and gregarious personality of Socrates, as depicted by Plato and Xenophon, conveys the impression of a man always willing to engage people in conversation (*Euthyphro* 3c, *Memorabilia* 1.1.10).

It is conceivable that in his reported effort to make sense of the Delphic statement about him, Socrates could have approached the young Aristophanes in order to question him about the meaning and purpose of his comedies.[6] Plato makes Socrates utter these words: "After I had questioned the politicians, I approached the dramatic and lyric poets and all the rest, in the expectation that I could demonstrate in front of them my lack of knowledge. I chose their best poetical compositions, and I asked them to explain to me their meaning, hoping that in that way I might also be somehow enlightened by them" (*Apology* 22b). Not surprisingly, the result was disappointing. They, too, knew nothing: "What they composed they composed not by wisdom."

The poets, including the playwrights, must have reacted to Socrates' inquiries with anger and resentment, for they held a position of prominence and were seen as sources of public instruction. Socrates' embarrassing questions proved to ordinary people that the poets were, after all, far from wise. Meletus, a "fanatical champion of religion," as he has been called,[7] was the accuser at Socrates' trial who spoke on behalf of the poets victimized by the Socratic inquisitiveness (*Apology* 23e), thus acting as some sort of mouthpiece for Aristophanes.

If we return to the issue of the relationship between Aristophanes and Socrates, several similarities between passages from the *Clouds* and statements found in other sources can be mentioned. There is, for instance, a parallelism between the reference to the miscarriage of a thought (*Clouds* 137) and Socrates' role as an intellectual midwife as outlined in the *Theaetetus* (149 ff.). Then there is the method of teaching employed by the Socrates of the *Clouds* (e.g., 478 ff.), in which we detect elements of Socrates' *elenchus*, that is, his method of questioning, as described by Plato. In the *Clouds* and in Plato's dialogues, he often begins by examining the character of his prospective student or interlocutor, and then, through interrelated questions, leads him to the solution of the initial question. In some cases, as is evident in the *Euthyphro* and the *Protagoras*, the final result is mostly negative. In the end, neither Socrates nor those he questioned can reach a conclusion. These and other similarities render Aristophanes' direct acquaintance with Socrates at least probable.

Although there are no references to Aristophanes in the writings of Xenophon, we do find them in two of Plato's dialogues. He is mentioned twice in the *Apology*, where, as we have seen, he is referred to in passing as one of Socrates' original accusers. In the *Symposium*, however, he plays an important role. This dialogue, no less than others, may include much that is fictional, although also much that is biographically and historically genuine. We can imagine that a conversation such as is described in the *Symposium* did take place twenty years before Socrates' death. The principal participants are all historical persons, and the setting itself is historically probable, from which we may conclude that the content of the conversation may also be more than a literary invention of Plato.

The conversation is narrated by Apollodorus, one of Socrates' closest friends, who in the *Phaedo* (117d) is said to have been present at Socrates' execution. It takes place in Agathon's house, where several people have gathered to spend an evening of relaxation. Aristophanes, we are told (*Symposium* 176b), is just recovering from the heavy drinking of the previous night and has developed a severe case of hiccup as a result of overeating (185c). He is described as a man who has devoted his life to Dionysus and Aphrodite, that is, indulging and gratifying his physical urges. During the conversation, he makes a colorful speech about love, in which he recounts an ancient mythological tale that describes how the gods punished human beings for their arrogance by cutting them into halves, male and female, and how each person is condemned to be forever in search of his or her other half (189–93). Socrates finds this speech "a magnificent display" (194a). At the end of the lengthy conversation, when most of the participants have either left or fallen asleep, Agathon, Aristophanes, and Socrates remain engaged in a conversation about the nature of tragedy and comedy and the relationship between them.

There are several cross-references between Aristophanes' statements about Socrates in the *Symposium* and those from the *Clouds*. There is Socrates' habit of swaggering and glancing sideways (*Symposium* 221b, *Clouds* 362) and his going barefoot and thinly clad (*Symposium* 220b; *Clouds* 103, 362). Whether Plato introduced such statements through his knowledge of the *Clouds* or whether Plato and Aristophanes discovered those traits in Socrates is difficult to establish, but the latter possibility appears more reasonable. The presence of Aristophanes in the *Symposium*, if taken together with the other factors mentioned earlier in this chapter, appears to support the idea that he must have been personally acquainted with Socrates and that some of the characteristics attributed to Socrates in the *Clouds* must have been the result of the comedian's direct knowledge.

Several comments can be made concerning the motives that may have led Aristophanes to choose Socrates as the main character for the *Clouds*. In this respect, however, there is much uncertainty. We do not know, for instance, whether there was animosity on the part of the comedian. In Plato's *Symposium*, there is no trace of animosity or enmity, but what transpires in the midst of a social gathering is not always a reflection of people's true feelings and attitudes. Civility goes a long way in covering up human feelings. What is certain, however, is that if personal animosity was a factor in Aristophanes' choice of Socrates for the *Clouds*, this feeling must have been in him for many subsequent years. This can be gathered from various references to Socrates in later comedies (e.g., *Birds* 1554, *Frogs* 1491).

Whatever Aristophanes' motives could have been, the effect was the same. Socrates was ridiculed and exposed before the audience as a dangerous fool, and the persistence and magnitude of this effect can be appreciated by considering once more what the Platonic Socrates says about Aristophanes in the *Apology*, namely, that the *Clouds* lies at the basis of the accusations against him: "Over the years, there have been many such people who have been accusing me. They made a powerful impression on you when you were most vulnerable to their slander, that is, when some of you were quite young [twenty-four years before the trial], and they actually won their case by default, because then no one defended me from them. What is extraordinary is that I cannot even remember their names, except for the name of one of them who happens to be a certain comic playwright" (*Apology* 18c).

A few lines later, the comic playwright is mentioned by name:

> Well then, what did my accusers say about me? Allow me to read directly from the official accusation of the prosecuting citizens: Socrates is guilty of criminal activities insofar as he spends his time investigating things below the earth and in the sky [cf. *Clouds* 172, 187]; furthermore, he teaches how to make a weak argument appear strong [cf. *Clouds* 110 ff.], and others imitate his example. Such is then the gist of the accusation, as you may have seen it in the comedy of Aristophanes, where Socrates is depicted as going around and saying that he can walk on air, and making all sorts of nonsensical statements about subjects of which I myself am perfectly ignorant. (*Apology* 19b–c)

The portrayal of Socrates in the comedy was indeed so effective that it succeeded in gaining a firm hold of public opinion. Obviously, as in the case of social prejudices, a brief legal defense could have never undermined its force. As an ingrained attitude, it lived in the minds and hearts of countless Athenians who, after seeing the comedy, were unable to distinguish the real Socrates from the character on the stage. The two had become one. Thus, if the latter had been punished with severity, why should the former remain unpunished?

Still, something can be said on behalf of Aristophanes. The political climate when his comedy was performed was different from that of the trial. In 423 BCE, Athens was the optimistic and vigorous center of an enormous empire, able to withstand calamities such as the plague of 429 BCE and willing to allow for a great deal of *parrhesia*—freedom of speech or, more precisely, the right to say it all. But as the Peloponnesian War progressed, Athens' fortune changed, and by 404 BCE, good fortune had turned into misfortune. The city had been defeated and its empire dismembered. As Plato remarks in his seventh letter, that was a time when people longed to vent their anger and frustration on anyone even remotely responsible for the political collapse.

Why, then, was apparently nothing mentioned in Socrates' trial about such matters? According to Plato, Socrates was accused of atheism, corrupting the youth, and meddling with natural science, in a word, irreligiosity. Yet, nothing specific was said about his possible role in undermining the strength of the city. Why should this be so?

When the democracy was reinstated several months after Athens' defeat, the entire citizenry became bound by a solemn oath never even to mention in public anything related to their misfortune. Several political trials took place shortly before that of Socrates' trial, but those involved remained faithful to the oath of silence. Irreligiosity or fearlessness (*asebeia*) was the common charge, which is precisely what we find in the case of Socrates' trial. His embarrassing questions, his intellectual restlessness, his insistence on abiding only by his convictions—the voice of God he claimed he heard—and other traits of his must have convinced many that he, too, had contributed to Athens' defeat, but they were unwilling to say it.

As we consider the value of Aristophanes' Socratic testimony, we face several possibilities. The most obvious one, often favored in modern scholarship, is that given the information about Socrates that comes from Plato, Xenophon, and other sources, Aristophanes' *Clouds* must be viewed only as an insulting travesty of no solid biographical value. Nothing of significance can be learned about Socrates from the comedy. Whether moved by his conservative political considerations the playwright intended to inflict harm on Socrates or simply sought to amuse the crowd, the effect of the comedy was the same. The damage had been done. As times change, jokes often have the ability of transforming themselves into accusations and indictments. In the case of Socrates, the jokes belong to Aristophanes, but the indictment belongs to the prosecutors, even though the two are identical.[8]

Another possibility would lead us to the seldom entertained conclusion that in the comic Socrates we come upon the real man both at the time of the *Clouds* and at the time of his execution. A sort of clownish and ironic man then emerges before our eyes, a sophist and manipulator, a self-serving individual who devoted himself to the art of duping others to the detriment of the social fabric, an atheistic and rebellious person distant from moral and social values—in sum, the Socrates of Aristophanes. His trial and execution, therefore, were well deserved. Even the most liberal among societies cannot afford to tolerate someone like him.

What, then, about the portrayals created by Plato, Xenophon, and others that stand in sharp opposition to that of the protagonist of the *Clouds*? If Aristophanes' testimony is the most faithful one, those portrayals must be the result of the active imagination of their creators who used the name of Socrates to voice their own philosophical and political agendas. We hear that once when Socrates heard someone reading a passage from Plato's *Lysis*, he exclaimed, "By Hercules, what a number of lies this young man is telling about me." "Plato," adds the biographer, "has included in his dialogues much that Socrates never said" (DL 3.35). The same might apply to others who wrote about him, of course, on the assumption that the

Clouds offers the solution to Socrates' enigma. Yet, is this so? Is it not possible that, as suggested earlier, it may not be anything but a deformation of him?

It is difficult to make substantive progress in this matter. It is reasonable to affirm, however, that in his comedy, Aristophanes was addressing himself to a cultural phenomenon that he saw as detrimental to the Athenian polity. Somehow, then, Socrates suddenly emerged for him as a focal point on which various manifestations and ramifications of that phenomenon converged. As a comic playwright, Aristophanes saw himself as a great critic of Athenian culture, and comedy as the most important medium of censorship.

More generally speaking, we can affirm that the comic playwrights acted as if they were the conscience of the city, not only of this or that political party, this or that constituency, but of the ordinary Athenian people for whom the comedies were written. In order to appreciate their literary creations, one must understand the audiences, those noisy crowds who, as Plato remarked, would hiss and whistle during the performances (*Laws* 3.700c, *Republic* 6.492b). It was for *them* that the playwrights wrote and for *them* alone that the comedies were performed.

We must ask, however, who or what could be more detestable and worthy of ridicule for the Athenian masses and their descendants than the philosophers, whom they were and are condemned never to understand and appreciate, and whom they were and are compelled to regard as somehow superior to them? In philosophers, the ordinary specimens of humanity are bound to see something different, foreign, and peculiar that unsettles their comfortable status quo and their vulgar state of normalcy. For them, as Nietzsche put it, the philosopher is "a portentous man, around whom there is always rumbling and mumbling and gaping and something uncanny going on."[9]

In the Athens of Aristophanes, who was a philosopher in the eyes of the masses? He was anyone whose ideas differed from what was accepted as traditional and ordinary, whether his thoughts were directed toward the phenomena of nature under the earth or in the sky, or toward ethical and political issues, or toward any other subject that demanded a rational explanation. He was someone who had dismissed accepted explanations that appealed to superstition, fantasy, emotion, or the opinions of the many. He exemplified a hybrid genus that embraced all sorts of species like the astronomer, the physicist, the sophist, and the tragic playwright. He belonged to a generic breed under which various types could be subsumed. What, however, could have been more appropriate than to give this breed of humanity a single familiar name and what better name than that of Socrates?

The Socrates of the *Clouds* appears from this perspective as the stereotype of an intellectual class, the Athenian intelligentsia. He stands for its two most important tendencies, namely, the natural philosophers who in the tradition of Thales had been endeavoring to find a rational explanation for the universe, and with whom the Athenians had become acquainted through Anaxagoras, and the sophists who had turned their attention toward the problem of human existence.

It is certain, moreover, that in the conservative and religious atmosphere of the Athens of the second half of the fifth century BCE, neither group was viewed as beneficial or productive in the eyes of ordinary people. The sophists, however, had at least one redeeming quality. They served as tutors and teachers of rhetoric and politics for the sons of affluent families, and were able to create the semblance of being somehow useful.

The natural philosophers (whom we might call scientists), however, had nothing redeeming. Their reputation for wisdom notwithstanding, they were often considered indifferent about religion, unconcerned about human affairs, and intent on explaining the world by appealing to reason, something seldom understood by ordinary people. Their behavior was often seen as eccentric and ridiculous, as can be learned from anecdotes about Thales, Heraclitus, Anaxagoras, and others. Thales, for instance, is said to have fallen in a ditch while looking at the stars, for which someone commented to him, "How can you expect to know about the heavens, when you cannot even see what is just before your feet?" (DL 1.34).

Heraclitus had the reputation of being a misanthrope who felt contempt for all human affairs. His death—an appropriate one for such a man, was said to have been strange: "He asked his doctors whether anyone could by emptying the intestines draw off the moisture, and when they said it was impossible, he put himself in the sun and asked his servants to plaster him over with cow dung. Being thus stretched, he died the following day and was buried in the marketplace" (DL 9.4). In another version, he is said to have been unable to tear off the dung from his body and to have been eaten by a pack of dogs (DL 9.4). The message is clear. The man who hated human company and whose language was always dark was buried in the marketplace of Ephesus, where he would be stepped on by everybody or devoured by dogs.

There are similar stories about other philosophers. In them, we come upon the same idea: they were demented and antisocial and a danger to society. Their failure to agree among themselves about the nature of the universe must have baffled the minds of ordinary people. Could it be, the latter must have asked, that what the natural philosophers said was mostly nonsense? What benefit could such people accrue to society when all they did was to ridicule Homer and Hesiod, speak irreverently of the gods, claim to have knowledge about the origin of things, and despise ordinary people?

In the Socrates of the *Clouds*, this is precisely what we find. He is eccentric and absentminded and spends his time contemplating the sky (*Clouds* 225). Like Anaxagoras, his older contemporary, he, too, conceives of himself as belonging not to any community or city, but to the universe at large. He could have said what Anaxagoras replied when asked why he was not concerned about his country. Pointing to the sky, he ironically said, "I am greatly concerned about my country" (DL 2.7). It was his conviction that the highest purpose of human life was the study of the sun, the moon, and the stars, anything else being unimportant (DL 2.10). No wonder, then, people found him and those like him peculiar and ridiculous.

Around 450 BCE, the Athenian assembly issued a decree that included the prohibition of delving into matters related to the study of the universe. The decree of Diopeithes, as it became known, was designed to curtail the activities and teachings of philosophers like Anaxagoras who was indicted and exiled (Plutarch, *Pericles* 32). Several philosophers were subsequently indicted on the basis of the decree. Even long after Socrates' trial, natural philosophers were tried and found guilty as was the case with Aristarchus of Samos, the astronomer who advanced for the first time a heliocentric hypothesis (Plutarch, *De facie in orbe lunæ* 922–23).

In a subsequent chapter, we will examine the relationship between Socrates and another group of philosophers, the sophists. In the *Clouds*, Socrates is also portrayed as one of them. The similarities between the sophists and Socrates, as described perhaps unfairly by Aristophanes, are many. Like the sophists, Socrates teaches the art of speaking as an instrument for success and instructs people in the techniques of persuasion. His rhetorical skills are the means by which people avoid having to pay debts and taxes, and his semantical games confuse his interlocutors. Like a linguistic juggler, he can make the best argument appear to be the worst and the worst to be the best. For him, truth is relative, which ultimately means that nothing is true or false because everything is both true and false. He is skeptical and agnostic, and is willing to give his assent to an idea only when it is to his own advantage. In all these traits and ideas of the comic Socrates, it is not difficult to detect an echo of the habits and thoughts customarily associated with the sophists. Even the reference to his demanding pay for his instruction points unmistakably to the sophists.

The Aristophanic Socrates appears, therefore, as a composite portrait of various styles of life and ideas, all of which in the opinion of the playwright deserved to be exposed to the light of ridicule. This Socrates is, accordingly, a generic Socrates and not quite the representation of one single historical person. Of course, even the generic Socrates resembles in some ways the actual man.

Yet, it is difficult to avoid the temptation of arguing that despite all the exaggerations and distortions created by Aristophanes, his comic character may after all resemble Socrates— not the mature Socrates of sources like Plato and Xenophon, but a younger Socrates. As suggested earlier in this chapter, we could envision a moment of conversion on his part from which he would emerge as the antithesis of what he had been on the stage. Perhaps a review of the testimonies of Xenophon, Plato, and Aristotle that we are about to undertake may shed some light on this and other related issues.

NOTES

1. For a documented and critical examination of Antisthenes as a witness of the Socratic presence, see L. E. Navia, *Antisthenes of Athens: Setting the World Aright* (Westport, CT: Greenwood Press, 2001).

2. For a detailed discussion of the influence of Socrates on Antisthenes and Diogenes, see L. E. Navia, *Diogenes the Cynic: The War against the World* (Amherst, NY: Humanity Books, 2005).

3. In Diogenes Laertius (2.36), Socrates is reported to have said on the occasion of his being used as a comic character: "We ought not to object to be subject for the comic poets, for if they satirize our

faults they will do us good, and if not, they do not touch us." In Plutarch's *De liberis educandis* (10c), we read that when Socrates was asked if he was angry at the way Aristophanes had abused him in the *Clouds*, he replied, "Good heavens, no! He made his joke against me in the theater as if it were a party of friends."

4. W. Jaeger, *Paideia: The Ideals of Greek Culture*, vol. 1, trans. G. Highet (New York: Oxford University Press, 1965), p. 358.

5. G. Murray, *Aristophanes: A Study* (Oxford: Clarendon Press, 1965), p. 31.

6. At the time of the performance of the *Clouds*, Aristophanes was about twenty years old.

7. J. B. Bury, "The Age of Illumination," *The Cambridge Ancient History*, vol. 5 (Cambridge: Cambridge University Press, 1927), p. 391.

8. Writing in the eighteenth century, Moses Mendelssohn saw in Aristophanes an instrument used by Socrates' enemies. His words deserve to be quoted:

> [The enemies of Socrates] hired, there is reason to believe, the comic playwright Aristophanes to compose a ludicrous piece, which, at that time, was called Comedy, in order to expose Socrates to public ridicule and hatred, that they might test the sentiments of the common people concerning him, and give such impressions as, if their artifice succeeded, might lead to some more decisive stroke against him. The farce bore the name of *The Clouds*. Socrates was the principal character; and the person by whom he was represented endeavored to exhibit him according to life: his dress, walk, gestures, and voice, were all studiously copied and imitated. The piece itself, to the honor of the persecuted philosopher, is still extant. But a composition more wild and extravagant can hardly be imagined.
>
> Socrates was accustomed to visit the theater only when the plays of Euripides, which some think he helped to compose, were performed. The day, however, on which this farce was performed, he was in the audience. Hearing some strangers enquire for the original of this Socrates who was so

much abused on the stage, he stepped forward in the midst of the performance, and remained until the piece ended standing in one place, where every person could see and compare him with the copy. This was a mortal wound to the playwright and his comedy. The most ridiculous incidents in it could no longer make any impression on the audience, as the appearance of Socrates commanded respect, and raised a kind of astonishment at his undauntedness of mind. The piece, of course, met with no success. The playwright altered it and brought it the following year upon the stage, but with no better fortune. The enemies of the philosopher found the necessity of dropping their intended persecution until a more favorable opportunity.

9. Friedrich Nietzsche, *Beyond Good and Evil* (New York: Modern Library, 1954), p. 292.

CHAPTER 3
Xenophon's Recollections

We can now leave behind the Socrates of the *Clouds* in order to examine a second portrayal of him. The nonsensical utterances, the vulgar gibes, the riotous jokes, the man in the basket, and the shadowy and batlike disciples must now be set aside. We are now in the presence of a clear-minded citizen, a man concerned with the affairs of the city, a judicious gentleman always able and willing to render himself useful to others, who respects religious traditions and does not neglect to honor the gods. He is a family man, whose fate at the hands of the state is an embarrassing travesty of justice. This is the Socrates of Xenophon.

As a younger contemporary of Socrates, Xenophon must have experienced his captivating charisma and, as an affectionate disciple, he must have felt the need to vindicate the memory of the man who had been so maligned by the state. At the conclusion of his *Apology* (34), Xenophon sums up his sentiments in these words: "And so, in contemplating the man's wisdom and nobility of character, I find it beyond my power to forget him or, in remembering him, to refrain from praising him. If among those who make virtue their aim any one has ever been brought into contact with a person more helpful than Socrates, I count that man worthy to be called blessed."

The word *helpful* appears repeatedly in Xenophon's testimony, for helpfulness was indeed the main attribute of the philosopher in his estimation. In Aristophanes, the opposite is the case. His Socrates is a destructive influence on those who, like Strepsiades, come to seek his assistance. The comic Socrates renders useless those who approach him, but the Socrates of Xenophon is a source of support for friends and strangers.

In the context of the Socratic problem, Xenophon presents a formidable challenge that requires a balanced approach. With him, we face many questions. Are we justified in giving credence to his recollections of Socrates? Is there a solid ground for accepting his alleged close intimacy with Socrates, to which he occasionally makes reference? Is his perception of the philosopher more faithful to the reality of the historical man than the comic jests of Aristophanes or the idealized descriptions of Plato? Was Xenophon endowed with the intellectual insightfulness to grasp adequately the Socratic presence?

There have been few scholars willing to accept Hegel's contention that "in regard to the content of Socrates' teaching and the point reached by him in the development of thought, we have in the main to look to Xenophon."[1] Most scholars see in his testimony something edifying and interesting, but not something of great consequence. As one reviews the pertinent literature, the list of unfavorable epithets given to him is long, so long that one is tempted to conclude that his only merit as an author was his ability to write in simple and clear Greek.

We read that Xenophon was "a military man, not very liberally endowed with brains" and that his relationship with Socrates is comparable to that between a stupid man and a clever man.[2] We hear that his Socrates is a simple-minded self-portrayal of no value. Plato's philosophical gifts, we are told, were altogether lacking in him to such an extent that "in spite of all the veneration for the master he defended, [Xenophon] shows in his Socratic writings such a lack of understanding for all that was essential in his [Socrates'] personality and work that he has contributed most to the distortion of the true picture of Socrates."[3] According to some, Xenophon and Plato stand in absolute contradiction with respect to their accounts of Socrates. Since that of Plato must be the correct one, that of Xenophon must be wrong. A Socrates without irony and without paradox, that is, as Xenophon portrays him, cannot be the real Socrates.[4]

Modern unfavorable comments often question Xenophon's motives in writing about Socrates and other subjects. Self-glorification and the promotion of a certain political agenda, among others, have been suggested. Inaccuracy and distortion have been mentioned in the context of his two historical works, the *Anabasis* and the *Hellenica*. His role in the retreat of the Greek army from Persia, described in the *Anabasis*, is occasionally viewed as an invention on his part. Surely, these criticisms cannot be ignored because, if justified, they would force us to doubt his reliability as a Socratic witness.

Yet, as in the case of Aristophanes' testimony, a final determination cannot be reached. The sources of information are defective and often at odds with one another. A reading of the *Anabasis*, for instance, may lead us to conclude that its author was bent on presenting himself as the heroic commander responsible for the successful retreat of the Greeks. The problem is that there are no other extant contemporary accounts of the circumstances. Later accounts, moreover, do not challenge the significant details provided by Xenophon.

Xenophon's works can be divided into three groups: (1) the historical writings, which include the *Anabasis*, also known as *The March of the Ten Thousand*, and the *Hellenica*; (2) the Socratic writings, which comprise the *Apology*, the *Memorabilia*, and the *Symposium*; and (3) various works such as the *Cyropaedia*, the *Oeconomicus*, the *Hiero*, the *Ways and Means*, *The Constitution of Sparta*, the *Cavalry Commander*, and short pieces on hunting, horsemanship, and dog breeding. His *Constitution of the Athenians* is generally viewed as inauthentic.

We encounter the presence of Socrates in most of these works. In the historical works we find him in the *Anabasis*, in which we are told that Xenophon, after being invited by Proxenus, a disciple of Gorgias, who was at that time (401 BCE) recruiting mercenaries for the expedition, spoke to Socrates about the matter. The philosopher advised Xenophon to ask the Delphic oracle whether he should accept the invitation. He went to Delphi and found the answer *he* wanted, but Socrates was not pleased with the way he approached the oracle: "Socrates found fault with him [Xenophon] because he did not first put the question whether it was better for him to go or to stay, but decided for himself that he was to go and then asked the god as to the best way of going. However, he added, 'since you did put the question that way, you must do as the god directed'" (*Anabasis* 3.1.5–7).

Xenophon then joined the ten thousand Greek mercenaries whose mission was to invade what is known today as Iraq and to overthrow the Persian king. Two years later, the defeated Greeks were on their way back to Greece under the command of Xenophon. In the spring of 399 BCE, they reached Greek territory on the southern coast of the Black Sea at precisely the time when Socrates was executed in Athens. Obviously, Xenophon could not have been with him during his last days.

In the *Hellenica* (I, vii, 15), a lengthy historical account of Greece after 415 BCE, Socrates is mentioned in the context of the trial of the generals of Arginusae accused in 406 BCE. Here, the stubborn philosopher refuses to alter his stand despite the threatening will of the Assembly: "When some of the prytanes [the magistrates in charge of the government] refused to put the question to the vote [to proceed with the trial] in violation of the law, Callixeinus again mounting the platform urged the same charge against them. The crowd cried out to summon to court those who refused. The prytanes, stricken with fear, agreed to put the question—all of them except Socrates the son of Sophroniscus. He said that he would never act except in accordance with the law" (*Hellenica* 1.7.15).

This incident, also reported by Plato (*Apology* 32b), is significant, for it gives us a glimpse of Socrates' attitude toward the relationship between legality and morality. Its historical authenticity can be taken for granted, and we can even assume that both Xenophon and Plato were present on that occasion. Despite the objections of Socrates, who was one of the prytanes, the assembly proceeded with the trial of the eight generals, six of whom were executed.

With respect to the third group of Xenophon's writings, some comments may suffice. These works reveal the versatility of their author and speak clearly of his convictions and style of life. In them, we hear about his boundless admiration for the laws and customs of the Spartans, of his predilection for a monarchical form of government, and of his conviction that political power and intellectual enlightenment must be united. These works disclose a practical and efficient man of the world, perhaps not philosophically sophisticated, but an impressively knowledgeable and perceptive Athenian.

Among them, the *Oeconomicus* occupies a special place. Its influence among classical writers was considerable. As with some of his other works, it was written between the years 380 and 370 BCE in the form of a dialogue, while living away from Athens in an estate given to him by the Spartans. It deals with a variety of subjects such as the management of a household,[5] public and private finances, the duties and virtues of conjugal life, and others. Socrates is generally the main speaker.

The Socrates of the *Oeconomicus* can be described as a character created by Xenophon in order to introduce the subjects under discussion, guide the conversation, and advance ideas and opinions, most of which, according to many, are those of the author himself. Yet, not every aspect of this Socrates is fiction. Certain elements remind us of the Socrates who speaks in Xenophon's *Apology* and *Symposium*, and even in some of Plato's early dialogues. In general, however, these elements are overshadowed by others that we are not accustomed to associate with Socrates.

The use of Socrates' name as a vehicle for the expression of an author's ideas should not surprise us. Simon the Shoemaker, one of Socrates' friends, is reported to have invented the Socratic dialogue as a literary genre (DL 2.122–124). In the decades following Socrates' death, this genre was not uncommon, and we come across numerous authors who, like Xenophon and Plato, followed the example allegedly set by Simon. A half-fictional Socrates emerges then as a literary figure, advancing ideas and defending views possibly foreign to those of the actual Socrates. The troublesome issue is, of course, how to separate fiction from fact, which brings us once more to the Socratic problem.

The statement of Diogenes Laertius (3.35), quoted in the previous chapter, is relevant in this respect: "[Socrates], on hearing someone read from Plato's *Lysis*, exclaimed, 'By Hercules, what a number of lies this young man is telling about me!' For he [Plato] has included in the dialogue much that Socrates never said." If Socrates had had the opportunity to read Xenophon's *Oeconomicus*, he might have said the same as he reportedly said about Plato's *Lysis*. The recurrent phrase used by Xenophon, "I once heard Socrates say," lends us little assistance in clarifying the issue because that phrase might not be more than a rhetorical device to lend credibility to his writings. A brief review of Xenophon's life may still give us some assistance.

The date of his birth cannot be fixed with certainty. Diogenes Laertius (2.55) suggests that in 401 BCE he was a middle-aged man, that is, about forty years old, which would yield 441 BCE as the year of his birth. Yet, other dates have been suggested. Little is known about his family background, aside from the name of his father, Gryllus. From his own writings, especially the *Anabasis* and *The Cavalry Commander*, we infer that his family was affluent and aristocratic, and that he served in the Athenian cavalry. He must have received the refined education given in Athens to young aristocrats, indeed the same education he would pass onto his two sons, who attained themselves some fame. His sympathy toward the Spartans, moreover, is an indication of his aristocratic background.

He was certainly associated with the group of Socrates' associates, although the nature of his relationship with Socrates is difficult to assess. Diogenes Laertius, who placed his biography of Xenophon immediately after that of Socrates, speaks of him as one of the chief Socratics (2.47). He describes for us Xenophon's first encounter with Socrates: "The story goes that Socrates met him in a narrow passage, and that he stretched out his stick to bar the way, while inquiring where all kinds of food were sold. Upon receiving a reply, Socrates asked another question, 'And where do men become good and honorable?' Xenophon was fairly puzzled. 'Then follow me,' said Socrates, 'and learn.' From that time onward Xenophon was Socrates' disciple" (DL 2.48).

As with other Athenians, the city's defeat in 404 BCE and the subsequent reign of terror that prevailed for almost one year, must have affected Xenophon in a profound way. There are reports that he served as a knight under the Thirty,[6] as did probably other young aristocrats, and that the overthrow of the tyranny led him to entertain ideas of leaving Athens. The general amnesty still did not ensure a climate of safety for the aristocrats, and it was around that time that he asked Socrates for advice concerning his joining the mercenary army that would invade Persia.

Between 401 and 395 BCE, we find Xenophon engaged in military affairs in Persia and Asia Minor, first under Cyrus and then under the Spartan king Agesilaus. In 399 BCE, he married a woman named Philesia, with whom he had two sons named Gryllus and Diodorus.

Upon his return to Athens, he must have experienced great distress on account of the death of Socrates, who had been executed four years earlier. There is no reason for assuming that he would have been unable to learn about the facts pertaining to the trial and execution. It is true that after Socrates' death, some of his associates, including Plato, left Athens either as the result of their disgust for the regime responsible for the events or because of the climate of intransigence created by the restored democracy.

Still, it would have been easy to gather accurate information. Socrates' trial was an open affair that aroused considerable attention. There must have been numerous witnesses willing to share with Xenophon their recollections. The prosecutors' affidavit was available for inspection at the public registry, where it was kept at least until the second century CE (DL 2.40). Moreover, after Socrates' death, a number of writings had begun to circulate attempting to justify the conviction and execution of Socrates. One of these, a pamphlet attributed to Polycrates, can be partly reconstructed. Thus, information about Socrates and his trial was plentiful in the Athens to which Xenophon returned after his military adventures.

Sometime between 395 and 393 BCE, a decree of banishment was passed against him, forcing him to leave Athens once more, this time permanently. Adequate information about this decree is lacking, although it is suspected that it had to do with his support of the Spartans after the war, as suggested by Diogenes Laertius (2.51). According to Pausanias (5.6), "he was banished by the Athenians for joining Cyrus, who hated their democracy, against the king of the Persians, who was their friend. When Cyrus was at Sardis, he [Cyrus] furnished Lysander and the Spartans with money for their fleet. This is why Xenophon was banished."

Xenophon's banishment seems to have strengthened his ties with Sparta. He admired its constitution and had the highest regard for its people for their simple style of life, their laws and traditions, and their religiosity. It has been said that his predilection for Spartan culture may have shaped the image of Socrates that appears in his writings, which may have resulted in his having misrepresented him. This idea would make sense were it not for the indisputable fact that practically all of Socrates' close acquaintances were at one time or another suspected of Laconism,[7] which is also true of Plato. In his *Birds*, Aristophanes himself stresses the link between Socrates and his associates on the one hand and, on the other, the Spartans. Referring to Socrates and his followers, he writes that "they were all crazy about Sparta. They wore their hair long. They went hungry and were mad. They socratized and carried sticks" (*Birds* 1218).

It is not known how the Spartans felt toward Socrates. What we do know with certainty, however, is how the Spartans felt toward Xenophon. His services were greatly valued by King Agesilaus, from whom he received an estate in the town of Scillus in Elis. Plutarch reports (*On Exile* 603b) that it was in this town that Xenophon lived until an advanced age. It was there, too, that he devoted himself to what was dear to him: family life, hunting, farming, dog and horse raising, and, above all, writing. He died probably in Corinth around 359 BCE, although some historians assign a later date for his death.

Xenophon's Socratic works include the *Symposium*, the *Apology*, and the *Memorabilia*. The authenticity of the *Symposium* and the *Memorabilia* is generally taken for granted. Questions have been raised, however, about the *Apology*, although it is listed by Diogenes Laertius among Xenophon's works. Some argue that its style does not reflect that of his genuine works and should be dismissed as a spurious piece of Socratic propaganda. As in many other cases, however, the issue of its authenticity cannot be resolved to the satisfaction of everybody. We may proceed, therefore, on the assumption that it is a genuine work.

Xenophon's *Symposium* is a work that brings to mind the dialogue of Plato by the same title and with which it can be contrasted. Yet, as one compares their works, it is obvious that we are in the presence of two very different kinds of compositions. In Plato's dialogue, we come upon a sophisticated philosophical work of his mature years, in which the aim is to expound a philosophical doctrine of love that may or may not be historically rooted in Socrates' teachings. The Socrates who speaks in it could be partly a Platonic mouthpiece. In this sense, therefore, Plato's *Symposium* can be compared with Xenophon's *Symposium*, inasmuch as in the latter Socrates appears to assume the character of a literary device employed by the writer in order to express his own ideas.

The Socrates of Xenophon's *Symposium* does not convey a developed idea of love and is not the main participant in a well-structured conversation, as is the case with Plato's *Symposium*. In Xenophon's dialogue, we listen to a casual conversation, more ordinary and realistic than that of the Platonic work. Although love occupies the foreground in both works, any attempt to compare their philosophical contents appears to be fruitless, for the ways in which they approach their subject are vastly different.

Neither is it reasonable to insist on seeing in Xenophon's dialogue an imitation of Plato's work. It has been suggested that Xenophon took from Plato not only the title and the subject matter but even some of the characters, to whom, with the exception of Socrates, he assigned other names. Alcibiades becomes Charmides, Aristophanes turns into Philippus, Callias takes the place of Agathon, and so on. This interpretation rests on the assumption that Plato, not Xenophon, is our original point of reference.

Although it may be impossible to determine the dates of composition of either work, it has often been assumed that Plato's dialogue antedates that of Xenophon and that Xenophon must have been acquainted with the Platonic *Symposium*. It has also been maintained that what Xenophon did in writing his *Symposium* was to contradict or at least correct what he found in Plato's dialogue.

The conversation of the *Symposium* takes place in the house of Callias, the wealthy Athenian with whom we are acquainted from Plato's dialogues (*Theaetetus* 165a, *Protagoras* 311a). The generally accepted literary date of the *Symposium* is 424 BCE, although this presents certain problems. Socrates speaks of himself as "an old man" (2.8), which would make little sense if he was still a man under fifty years of age. Moreover, if Xenophon was born around 441 BCE, his presence in the dialogue is problematic. It would have been inappropriate for a young man to be even a silent spectator at the gathering. Thus, the phrase "I should like to narrate an experience of mine," with which the dialogue begins, would prove to be fictitious. If, on the other hand, a later date for the conversation is allowed, then Socrates' appearance as an old man and Xenophon's presence might seem plausible.

The characters of the *Symposium*, most of whom we know from other sources, are Socrates, who has been invited to join in the banquet as one of those men "whose hearts have undergone the purification of philosophy"; Callias, the general who negotiated the peace with Sparta; Autolycus, a young athlete being honored in the banquet; Lycon, the young man's father, who might be one of Socrates' prosecutors; Niceratus, the son of the famous Nicias, the general; Antisthenes the Cynic, whose devotion for Socrates is boundless; Hermogenes, a friend of

Socrates, mentioned by Xenophon in the *Apology* as his source of information and whom we know from the *Phaedo* (59b); Cristobulus, Crito's son; Charmides, the young oligarch and a relative of Plato; a buffoon named Philippus, who provides much joking and jesting; and a performer accompanied by singers and dancers. Xenophon, although reportedly present, remains silent.

From such characters, we can learn a great deal about Socrates. We observe, for instance, that his humble background did not prevent him from dining with the wealthy and the powerful. With such friends, he obviously had no need to charge fees for his teaching because, as he himself notes in the *Oeconomicus* (2.8), if he ever lacked anything, his friends would drown his humble needs in a flood of abundance.

Antisthenes' presence is significant. It gives the impression of much intellectual intimacy with Socrates, which is supported by statements in the secondary sources that describe him as Socrates' closest and most faithful among his associates. Xenophon himself, it has been argued, was greatly influenced by Antisthenes. Aside from this, moreover, the argument has been repeatedly made that it was Antisthenes and, through him, the Cynic philosophers who captured most accurately the essence of the Socratic presence, which they passed subsequently to the Stoics.[8]

Several themes are explored during the conversation. These include the relationship between knowledge and virtue, the problem of whether virtue can be taught, the nature of physical and spiritual beauty, and Socrates' concept of love. Undoubtedly, neither in arrangement nor in depth are these presented on the level of Plato's *Symposium*. Whereas Plato writes as an extraordinary philosopher and poet, Xenophon does it as a clever reporter.

Xenophon furnishes us with a wonderful description of Socrates' appearance, a description the like of which is not found anywhere else in the sources. In an exchange between the young Cristobulus and the old and ugly Socrates, they argue as to who of the two is the most handsome. Socrates' eyes are said to resemble those of a crab, protruding and bulging, but yet more beautiful because they allow him to see not only straight ahead but sideways (cf. Plato's *Symposium* 221b, *Clouds* 362). His nose, voluminous and flat, is more beautiful because its wide nostrils let him catch scents from all directions (cf. Plato's *Symposium* 215a). As for his mouth, it is said to be bigger and uglier than that of an ass, but still the most beautiful, since, as Cristobulus admits, if the mouth is made to bite off food, Socrates could bite off a far larger mouthful than anybody else. Socrates' belly is voluminous despite his practice of daily exercise. Face and body, then, contrive to make him resemble the Sileni and the Satyrs, those mythological creatures recognizable for their ugly and coarse features.

Beneath such uninspiring characteristics, there is, however, a hidden aspect that can only be discerned by those who pierce into his inner being, namely, his unparalleled spiritual beauty. In him, then, a beautiful soul is wrapped in the humble trappings of an ugly body. This is reminiscent of the words of Alcibiades in Plato's *Symposium* (215a): "He is exactly like the busts of the Sileni, which are set up in the statuaries' shops, holding pipes and flutes in their mouths; and they are made to open in the middle, and have images of gods inside."

Besides the physical description of Socrates, we also learn other biographical details. We hear about his love of good wine and about his enormous capacity to drink great quantities of it without becoming drunk (cf. Plato's *Symposium* 214a). We are told that he was fond of dancing and exercise.

We also learn about the woman he married, reportedly an impatient and ill-tempered wife. Antisthenes asks him a pointed question: "How is it, Socrates, that you don't practice what you preach by you yourself educating Xanthippe, but live with a wife who is the most difficult to get along with of all the women there are, yes, of all that ever were, I suspect, or ever will be?"

To which Socrates replies: "Because I observe, Antisthenes, that men who want to become expert in horsemanship do not get the most docile horses but rather those that are high-spirited, believing that if they can manage this kind, they will easily handle the other. My case is similar. It is with people that I wish to deal and associate. This is why I have her as my wife, convinced that if I can handle her, I will have no difficulty with anybody else I may chance to meet" (*Symposium* 2.10).

Xanthippe's character often appears as a paradigm of impatience, as one can see from the comment of Diogenes Laertius (2.26–36), who recounts how once she scolded and abused her husband. It is difficult to determine the historical value of this and similar reports. In Plato, Xanthippe is mentioned twice (*Phaedo* 60a, 116b), but from his comments nothing can be inferred about her character. In the *Memorabilia* (2.2.1), we witness an incident in which Socrates endeavors to inculcate in his children a sense of respect and affection toward their mother. Yet, aside from these references, nothing more is said by Xenophon or Plato.

Still other aspects of Socrates can be learned from the *Symposium*. We learn about his poverty and his determination to remain poor, and about his opposition to the sophists and low regard for the Homeric rhapsodists. There are comments about his inquisitiveness and his passion for conversation and about his bent toward sexual abstinence. His profound religiosity and his experience of the divine voice or sign are not neglected; neither is the enormous significance of love in his life. "I cannot remember," he says, "a time when I was not in love with someone" (8.2).

Xenophon's *Apology*, a work that cannot be favorably compared with his other works, was written as a pamphlet the purpose of which was to set aright one specific aspect of Socrates' appearance in court. As noted earlier, its authenticity has often been questioned. The date of its composition is uncertain, although it is suspected that it may have been written around 390 BCE. It is by far the shortest of Xenophon's Socratic writings. It belongs to a literary genre developed after Socrates' execution for the purpose of supporting the prosecutors or defending Socrates.

This literary genre, accordingly, assumed two forms: speeches presumably delivered by the prosecutors or apologetic accounts of the trial. How many such pieces were written is not known, but we can assume that there were many. Xenophon himself notes that others had already written about the trial, but except for Plato and Polycrates, we have no knowledge of who those others could have been.

Polycrates' work, written in the form of an indictment, is the only piece of anti-Socratic literature about which there is some information, although hardly anything is known about its author or about his reason for writing against Socrates. Neither Plato nor Xenophon mentions him, although we can assume that they were acquainted with his work. It is also unfortunate that his indictment is not extant in its original form, although its existence is confirmed in sources such as Isocrates, Diogenes Laertius, and Libanius.

On the basis of these and other testimonies, a partial reconstruction of Polycrates' work can be undertaken. As Diogenes Laertius suggests (2.38), this work may have been the indictment read by Meletus at Socrates' trial, although its inclusion of a reference to the rebuilding of the Athenian walls forces us to conclude that Polycrates edited and embellished Meletus's speech. The walls were rebuilt four years after Socrates' trial. Both prosecutors and defendants were expected to read their speeches before the jury, and it is known that Socrates himself could have read a speech prepared for him by Lysias, the renowned orator. Probably he did not. It is even possible, although unlikely, that contrary to what we learn from Plato and Xenophon, Socrates may have remained silent throughout the trial, not unlike Jesus in the presence of Herod (Luke 23:8–9). In Plato's *Gorgias* (521e), he himself, foreseeing his trial, says, "I shall have nothing to say when in court."

The reconstruction of Polycrates' work is based entirely on apologetic authors who sought to defend Socrates. Isocrates, of whom Socrates speaks in complimentary terms in the *Phaedrus* (279a) and who, according to Cicero (*Isocrates* 838f), was deeply grieved at Socrates' death, wrote about Polycrates but only to attack him. He speaks ironically of Polycrates' allegation that Socrates had corrupted Alcibiades: "When your intention was to accuse Socrates, you accidentally defended him. You said that Alcibiades was Socrates' student, although as everybody knew, that was not the case. We all agree that Alcibiades was a great and praiseworthy man. Thus, if the dead could acquire the power of judging what has been said of them, Socrates would be as grateful to you for your accusation as to anyone who has eulogized him."

Libanius, a writer of the fourth century CE, provides a summary of Polycrates' work. From this summary, included in his *Declamations*, however, not much can be learned that is not found in Plato's and Xenophon's testimonies. We are reminded, for instance, that Socrates was accused of irreligiosity (*asebeia*) for worshiping gods not accepted by the state, attempting to unravel the mysteries of the universe, and corrupting or misguiding young people. Of course, as an apologist, Libanius rejects these accusations and endeavors to vindicate Socrates of all wrongdoing and misbehavior.

In Xenophon's *Apology*, the emphasis lies not so much on the vindication of Socrates from the accusation of irreligiosity, but on the need to clear him from an additional charge related to his alleged behavior in court. This new charge involves what some interpreted to be Socrates' arrogant and contemptuous language. The Greek term is *megalegoria* (literally, *talking big*).

Xenophon reminds us that others had already written about Socrates' trial, but he notes their failure to explain Socrates' unusual behavior. Defendants were expected to act humbly before the powerful jurors or at least to behave respectfully toward them. Socrates simply did not. Was it, Xenophon wonders, because he had decided that death was preferable to life and wanted, therefore, to be sentenced to death?

Xenophon insists that in writing his *Apology* it was not his intention to give a complete account of the trial: "More than this, of course, was said by Socrates himself and by his friends who joined in his defense. I have not made it a point to report on the whole trial" (*Apology* 22).

The reference to friends who joined Socrates in his defense is curious. Athenian practice allowed for witnesses for the prosecution and for the defense, and yet, no witnesses are mentioned by Plato or any other source. Xenophon himself notes that Socrates refused to prepare and deliver a formal defense since his entire life had been a preparation for the trial.

Xenophon affirms that the charge of irreligiosity is patently false, as Meletus himself should know, for he has often seen Socrates comply with the customary religious rituals. Concerning Socrates' divine sign or voice, we are reminded that other oracular voices and signs are accepted as genuine divine manifestations and that the gods reveal their will and presence by such means. Why, then, should Socrates' sign or voice be unusual?

Xenophon recounts the story about Chaerephon's visit to the Delphic oracle where he heard about Socrates' unique virtues—freedom, justice, and prudence. Socrates has reflected critically and respectfully on the meaning of the oracle, as a man who since "he began to understand spoken words" has always been moved by great curiosity about all sorts of things. As for the corruption of the youth, how could he, a man who has never been a slave of the desires of the body, who has never sought pay for his teaching, and who has demonstrated great courage and temperance have corrupted anyone?

Surely, the prosecutors and their witnesses must have perjured themselves in their depositions, for they knew and know that he is innocent. In indicting him, therefore, they have indicted themselves. As for Anytus, whose occupation as a tanner renders him so servile, Socrates predicts great suffering and misery because his dissolute son will become a drunkard and will cause him much shame. In the end, despite the wickedness of his accusers and despite his innocence, Socrates cheerfully and calmly accepts the death sentence.

There is little in Xenophon's *Apology* that we could not have learned from his *Memorabilia* or from Plato's *Apology*. What is new, however, is Xenophon's attempt to account for Socrates' language at the trial. How could it have been possible that Socrates, a man of no political or social importance, generally disliked and distrusted by the sort of people who made up the jury, and accused of grave crimes, speak and act as if the jurors and the prosecutors, not he, were the defendants and he were their judge? How could anyone explain so strange a behavior? Was Socrates in reality an arrogant and contemptuous man seeking his undoing? Was he thoughtlessly insulting the jurors, as if begging them to condemn him to death?

His behavior must have appeared unusual. What was expected from defendants was an attitude of humility and remorse, even if they viewed themselves as innocent. Prostrating themselves before the jurors, accompanied by weeping wives and children—that was the expected behavior. In Plato's *Apology* (35a), Socrates speaks of certain defendants, "men of some reputation behaving in the strangest manner when they are on trial, as if they thought that they were going to suffer something terrible if they were put to death, just as if they were immortal if they were not killed." Yet, Socrates behaved in quite a different manner. His suggestion, according to Plato, that the fittest punishment for his crimes was maintenance at the expense of the state is an indication of defiance.

Was this defiance a manifestation of arrogance and disrespect? According to Xenophon, the greatness of his mind does not justify this interpretation, for men of great mind are not arrogant. Thus, we are left with the other alternative. Socrates did not want to remain in the world of the living and had chosen death over life.

It is generally conceded that the prosecutors did not seek Socrates' execution and that their demand for the death penalty was a common legal practice in trials such as his. By asking for the ultimate punishment, what they wanted was to ensure some form of punishment as a fair sentence. Banishment for twenty years might have been such a compromise, but, as we read in Plato's *Apology* (36c), Socrates rejected that option.

What we encounter in Xenophon's *Apology* is not a Socrates who is willing to die for his convictions or a man who expects death to be a transition from this world onto another. Probably, like most Greeks of his time, Xenophon's Socrates must have viewed death as the final moment of human existence—if anything survived physical death, it was only a shadowy ghost of no substance. Most Greeks might have agreed with Homer's lines in which we are told that it is better to be a beggar in the world of the living than a king in the world of the dead. We can assume that the belief in immortality attributed to Socrates in Plato's *Phaedo* was not common among educated Athenians. When in Plato's *Republic* (10.608d), Glaucon shows astonishment on hearing of Socrates' belief in the immortality of the soul, he is probably expressing a prevailing attitude: "Are you not aware [said Socrates] that the soul is immortal and never perishes? [To which Glaucon replies,] No, by Zeus, not I."

We cannot doubt that this answer could have been made by Xenophon himself and by *his* Socrates. Accordingly, from Xenophon's point of view and as far as he understood Socrates, the latter's predicament in court involved one of two avenues, either a humble stance before the jury probably resulting in a sentence of banishment or an uncompromising demeanor ensuring a sentence of death. The former, however, could only promise a life full of aggravations and "the throes of illness," whereas the latter ensured for him a quick and painless death. In either case, moreover, the ultimate fate had to be the same—eternal nothingness. What then could Socrates have chosen other than the death offered by the state? Like other Athenians, he, too, must have feared that time of life, as difficult in those days as it is now, when "my vision will be less perfect and my hearing less keen, and when I will be slower to learn and more forgetful of what I have learned" (*Apology* 6). Thus, it was the natural fear of old age, not the anticipation of another life, that compelled Socrates to behave in court precisely as he did.

This interpretation of Socrates' behavior has often been called absurd and a trivialization of his character. It shows, we are told, a failure on Xenophon's part to understand him, for there must be something demeaning in choosing death over life just to avoid the infirmities of old age. Something more profound, more philosophical should be expected from Socrates.

This may be so. Yet, as in other aspects of the Socratic problem, the issue is complex. We could argue that Socrates' fear of old age is adduced by Xenophon as the main consideration in his choice of death, but this is presented only within the limited scope of his *Apology*. Elsewhere in his other works, nothing is said about it. This suggests that according to Xenophon, it may have been only one of various aspects to be kept in mind. Still, in the *Memorabilia* and the *Symposium*, we discover a Socrates for whom the immortality of the soul—a world beyond this world—plays no role and for whom living in decrepitude and misery would not be a welcomed prospect. Xenophon's Socrates entertains no expectations concerning life after death. Yet, is this Socrates a faithful characterization of the historical man or a superficial rendition of the philosopher who in the *Phaedo* and in the *Republic* looks upon death as the desired transition from this world onto another?

There is also the undeniable circumstance that some of the Socratics not only rejected as false the spiritualistic Socrates of Plato's writings, but also often chose death in order to free themselves from the decrepitude of old age or from the vicissitudes of their lives. The Cynics—who claimed to be descendants of Antisthenes and, through him, of Socrates, had no expectations of surviving their deaths and are known to have often opted for suicide—would have congratulated Socrates for his contemptuous behavior in court and for his preferring death over life. Did they have access to a more genuine Socratic tradition than Plato and the others who constructed a Socrates who never existed? Is the Socrates of Diogenes of Sinope, to whom Plato referred as "a Socrates gone mad" (DL 6.54) closer to the historical man than those to whose images of him we are more accustomed?[9]

We can now move away from Xenophon's sketchy *Apology* in order to comment on his major Socratic work, the *Memorabilia*. This work is a lengthy collection of statements about Socrates presented by the author as his recollections of him, which is what its Greek title conveys.[10] It is divided into four sections or books. The introductory part of the first of these deals exclusively with the indictment of Socrates and gives the impression of having been originally written as a separate apologetic pamphlet.

The *Memorabilia* as a whole can be viewed as an apology, that is, a defense, of Socrates. If even after his departure to Hades, the abode of the dead, his detractors persisted in accusing him, he had to be defended by those who insisted on his innocence, and these included Xenophon, Plato, and others. The overall aim of the *Memorabilia* is succinctly stated at the outset by the author in the form of a question: "By what arguments did those who drew up the indictment against Socrates succeed in persuading the Athenians that his life should have been cut short by the state?" The rest of the work is a sustained effort to show that Socrates was helpful to his associates by his words and example. If we insist on attributing to the *Memorabilia* a more comprehensive aim, we would be disappointed. We would not find in it a cogent philosophical statement of Socrates' ideas. To compare it with any of Plato's works would be futile. Yet, if we approach it with a commitment to remain close to the text and to its purpose, it turns out to be an abundant source of information.

The defense part differs from the other Socratic works of Xenophon in one important respect. While the latter often assume a conversational form and are given some dramatic setting, the former is presented in a simple reporting style, which gives it some historical texture. It begins by quoting from the official indictment, although Xenophon concedes that his quotation is only approximate: "Socrates is guilty of rejecting the gods acknowledged by the state and of bringing in strange deities. He is also guilty of corrupting the youth." This is the substance of the indictment. These accusations also appear in Plato's *Apology* and are repeated by various secondary sources. As we noted earlier, the indictment was physically preserved until at least as late as the second century CE, when it was reportedly seen by Favorinus (DL 2.40). The additional accusations mentioned by Plato, namely, that Socrates was a busybody who investigated things below the earth and in the sky and that he made the weaker argument defeat the stronger (*Apology* 19b) are implicitly contained in the indictment as recorded by Xenophon. Socrates' alleged scientific investigations were somehow related to his irreligiosity, and his sophistical teaching was one of the ways in which he corrupted the youth. Aside from these accusations, there is no information about others, although the indictment is sufficiently vague in order to include other charges. When Aristoxenus accused him of being "an une-ducated and ignorant sensualist," it could have been argued that by having such undesirable traits he was a source of social cor-ruption (Plutarch, *On the Malice of Herodotus* 856d).

In order to deal with these charges, Xenophon adduces evi-dence drawn, he says, from his own recollections and from those of others, to show the senselessness of Socrates' indictment and sentence. An exemplary citizen like Socrates should never have been forced to undergo what he did. Yet, why was he? What explanation could there be for his fate? Was his trial motivated by political considerations, perhaps by his reported dislike for democratic processes and his sympathy toward the Spartans? Were the jurors sufficiently unintelligent and self-serving, as Aristophanes describes them in the *Wasps*, not to have seen through the deceptions of the prosecution? Was Socrates' con-stant appeal to his inner sign or voice, about which Xenophon himself reports, related to the accusation of atheism?

These and similar questions remain unanswered in Xenophon's account. His interest lies in the reasons why Socrates should not have been indicted and sentenced, and for this, he emphasizes his impeccable character. A more righteous citizen, he insists, could not have been found anywhere. His religiosity was evident to anyone who would have cared to observe him: "Socrates never said or did anything contrary to sound religion, and his utterances about the gods and his behav-ior toward them were the words and actions of a man who is truly religious and deserves to be thought so" (*Mem.* 1.1.20). His religiosity, we are told, was demonstrated by his compliance with all the religious practices and rituals expected from the Athenians: "He offered sacrifices constantly and made no secret of it, whether in his home or at the altars of the temples, and he openly appealed to oracles and divination" (*Mem.* 1.1.2).

It is important to bear in mind that the Greeks of Socrates' time were exceptionally religious. Their religiosity in terms of reverence and piety permeated their daily life—reverence understood in the sense of *fearing* the gods and piety in the sense of doing only what is permitted or the proper thing to do. Their religion, however, was far less structured than what is found in nonclassical religions such as Christianity. In these, theological beliefs, often embodied in accepted creeds, play a crucial role and serve as binding mechanisms that hold the believers as one group. The word *religion* itself—from the Latin *religare*—discloses what being religious means, which is to be *bound* by beliefs, rituals, and ethical values.

Among the ancient Greeks, the emphasis was on rituals and practices. Specific beliefs about the gods occupied a secondary place simply because the stories about them were many and varied and were embodied in different traditions that precluded the presence of a firm creed. Furthermore, the absence of a priestly hierarchy in charge of keeping intact a system of beliefs based on holy scriptures contributed to the amorphous character of Greek religion. In fact, there is no Greek word equivalent to what we call religion.

What Greek religion lacked in terms of dogma and hierarchy it made up abundantly in rituals and ceremonies. To be religious meant primarily to be willing to comply with rituals, public prayers, and sacrifices, in which all sorts of polytheistic beliefs and traditions were embodied. There was also the widespread appeal to divination that touched all spheres of public and private life. Divination by the flight of birds, the entrails of animals, fire, mirrors, and other things was the way in which all sorts of questions and issues were resolved. The practice of choosing most public officials by lot was ultimately based on the belief in cleromancy, as it was believed that the gods made their will known through the casting of lots.

It was in this enchanted world that Socrates lived and, if the testimony of Xenophon can be accepted, he was comfortable in it. Yet, a mind as critical as his must have often questioned the effectiveness of divination, as when, according to Xenophon (*Mem.* 1.2.9), he spoke against the choice of public officials by lot. In the ears of those ill disposed toward him, this attitude was a manifestation of irreligiosity. After all, for most people, casting lots was a sacred procedure, not a matter of blind chance.

If we keep in mind the ritualistic and ceremonial nature of Greek religion, we can appreciate Xenophon's emphasis on Socrates' compliance with such common practices. In the *Memorabilia* (4.3.15), we hear Socrates utter this statement: "For you know that to the question, 'How am I to please the gods?,' the Delphic god [Apollo] replies, 'Follow the custom of the state.' I suppose that the universal custom is for people to pay homage to the gods with sacrifices." This recommendation he himself put into practice as he remarks to Dionysodorus in Plato's *Euthydemus* (302c): "I have my own altars and my own religious practices, and family prayers and all that sort of thing, as much as any other Athenian." In what way, then, could he appear to have been irreligious? The answer, according to Xenophon, is to be found in two additional details. The first is related to Socrates' repeated allusions to his divine sign, which he interpreted as emanating from God (*Mem.* I.1.4.1, *Symposium* 8.5), and the second is the curiosity that earned for him the false reputation as a philosopher dealing with the mysteries of nature.

In Xenophon's view, Socrates' experience of his divine sign was the basis for the accusation of introducing new and strange gods. That unusual experience, which accompanied him since childhood (Plato's *Apology* 31d; Plutarch, *On the Sign of Socrates* 580c), was often the subject of his conversations. At times, as Plutarch reports, he would run after his friends to inform them in a loud voice that his sign had come to him. Thus, he was not reluctant to make it public, for which it must have become something well known about him.

Xenophon's account of Socrates' experience is not quite what we find in Plato's testimony. In Xenophon, the sign appears as an internal admonition that sometimes urged Socrates to follow a certain course of action or warned him about future events. It also acted as a restraining or dissuading force that would prevent him from saying or doing certain things. In Plato, however, from whom we have numerous references to it, it is always described as a negative or preventive sign, telling Socrates only what he should not say or do (Plato's *Apology* 31d, *Theages* 128d). Aside from this, however, Xenophon and Plato stand generally in agreement. Both emphasize Socrates' commitment to obey his divine sign and both agree that his experience was the basis for the charge of irreligiosity.

According to Xenophon, this charge is obviously groundless. The sign, he argues, was one of the many manifestations of the presence of the gods. Sometimes they reveal their will by means of birds or other things, while in the case of Socrates, they speak in the privacy of his consciousness. Yet, by whatever means they manifest their presence, it is the same gods that make themselves immanent because "for him who is in their grace the gods grant a sign" (*Mem.* 1.1.9). There was nothing, therefore, strange or unusual about the sign or voice of which Socrates spoke, except that it was a private experience that others neither saw nor heard.

As for the charge that Socrates devoted himself to the investigation of the universe, Xenophon is equally adamant in rejecting it. Never, he affirms, was Socrates concerned with natural science. In fact, he regarded those who deal with such matters as madmen who in their blindness fail to understand that human beings will always be unable to solve the riddle of the universe.

What was it that truly interested Socrates? His conversations, writes Xenophon, "were always about human concerns. He dealt with questions such as how people please and displease the gods, what is the essence of beauty and ugliness, justice and injustice, prudence and moderation, courage and cowardice, and other such matters" (*Mem.* 1.1.16).

What can be said, however, about the charge that he corrupted young people? This charge, already made by Aristophanes, is as mendacious as the others and is a corollary of the charge of irreligiosity. His detrimental influence was the inevitable result of his atheism. Those corrupted by him lost faith in the gods and ended up abandoning all ethical principles. Eventually, they turned out to be depraved people who caused much damage to themselves and to society at large. Surely, they are to blame for their miserable condition, but even more so it is their mentor who was responsible for their having gone astray. It is he, then, who must be forced to pay for their corruption.

But whom did Socrates corrupt? Were they not the young and aspiring aristocrats who one day would cause much misery to the Athenians? The list is long. It includes Critias, Alcibiades, Meno, Charmides, and Phaedrus, most of them members of Socrates' inner circle. For our part, we could add Xenophon and Plato to the list of those corrupted by Socrates.

What did Athens reap from these unprincipled men? In Polycrates' indictment, the charge is made that Socrates taught his associates to despise the common people and that his sympathies were always on the side of the aristocrats. This explains why Anytus, a common man who took part in the overthrow of the aristocrats shortly after the war, played so important a role in the prosecution of Socrates. Is it then not reasonable to say that Socrates himself, despite being a common man, was one of the forces that sustained the antidemocratic movement before and after the war?

In 415 BCE the Athenians were shocked by a blasphemous act of vandalism when they discovered that many of the statues of Hermes, customarily placed in front of houses, had been defaced during the night. Apparently, a gang of irreligious men had perpetrated the crime. Amid the confusion and anger of the following days, it was established that Alcibiades and Phaedrus, two of Socrates' friends, were the leaders of the ravaging gang.

Other examples of the excesses and depravity of some of Socrates' associates can be adduced. Disrespect for religion and the laws, contempt for the common people, political opportunism and voracious greed, indifference toward moral values—these and other undesirable traits can be attributed to some of them on a reasonably firm historical basis. The question is, however, what role did Socrates play in their moral degeneracy? As their teacher and mentor, did he affect them in the same way as the protagonist of Aristophanes' *Clouds* affected his disciples? Can we hold Socrates responsible?

Xenophon endeavors to answer these questions by providing a detailed account of Socrates as a man who was always a perfect master of his emotions and appetites. Gluttony, lust, greed, laziness, selfishness, deceptiveness, and other vices and excesses were foreign to him. In fact, when he detected them in others, he reprimanded them even when by so doing he earned their hatred. We are told, for instance, how angry Critias, Plato's uncle, became when Socrates told him that his mode of life was more suitable for a pig than for a man (*Mem.* 1.2.30). Critias never forgot the remark, and it was for this that when he assumed control of the city after the war, he sought to silence and punish Socrates.

Yet, why did they seek Socrates' company? Xenophon insists that some of them did it only to gain proficiency in language in order to succeed in political affairs. Once they attained what they were looking for, "they sprang away from him and took to politics," for "it was for political ends that they wanted Socrates." He was a means to their ends, and their relationship with him was only one of convenience. As long as they were close to him and under his guidance, they were faithful to his teachings and had the strength to keep their evil passions in check. Once they left him, they returned to their true vicious selves. Socrates and those miserable people were altogether different types of humanity.

Assuming the facts to be as Xenophon describes them, his line of reasoning makes sense. A teacher is never completely responsible for the eventual behavior of his pupils: "What teacher of flute, lyre, or anything else, after making his pupils proficient, can be held responsible if they leave him for another master and then turn out to be incompetent?" (*Mem.* 1.1.27).

These are the salient points of Xenophon's defense of Socrates in the *Memorabilia*. By comparison to Plato's statements in his *Apology*, his words may appear superficial. Yet, if we bear in mind the limited scope of Xenophon's work, their superficiality vanishes. The indictment against Socrates had sought to portray him as an unconventional man whose influence was detrimental to society. Xenophon's Socrates is the very opposite of this characterization. Only by presenting Socrates in a commonplace light as a lawful and honorable citizen can the accusations against Socrates and the jury's verdict be seen as a true travesty of justice.

The rest of the *Memorabilia*, indeed its lengthiest part, embellishes the description of Socrates with details, anecdotes, and occasional dialogues of some philosophical content. There are numerous comments about Socrates' style of life and character, as well as about his family relations. Perhaps the most distinctive aspect persistently emphasized by Xenophon is Socrates' ability and willingness to render himself useful and helpful to those who approached him. This manifests itself in various ways. By his righteous living, he encouraged others to live righteously, and by his sound admonitions, he led them to sound actions and decisions. His presence, as Xenophon repeatedly states, was an inestimable source of good guidance to many.

It is obvious that Xenophon's portrayal of Socrates stands in sharp contrast with that of Aristophanes. The eccentricity and unconventionality of the latter are corrected by the soundness and conventionality of the former. Still, we should note that if they were our only sources, Socrates would have remained in the history of ideas an interesting figure, somewhat challenging and even paradoxical, but certainly not the impressive philosopher we are accustomed to see him as. Undoubtedly, to find something truly great in him and to appreciate the depth and force of the legacy he left as the awakener of the mind and as a turning point in the development of consciousness, it is necessary to turn to Plato.

Yet, with Plato, too, we face the Socratic problem. Is his Socrates closer to the historical reality than what we find in Xenophon? Or is it mostly a grand and complex idealization of the man who impelled him toward philosophy? Is the Socrates of Xenophon a trivialization on the part of someone who failed to understand the greatness of the historical Socrates? Who and what then was Socrates?

As noted earlier, many have opted for a one-sided solution to the problem by relying exclusively on Plato in order to pierce into the Socratic presence. This is quite understandable. Even those who have rejected Plato's philosophical stance have remained impressed by the enormity of his mind and by the compelling representation of the Socrates who speaks throughout his dialogues. Not many have been willing to agree with Diogenes of Sinope, the great Cynic philosopher and a contemporary of Plato, who spoke of Plato's ideas as a waste of time and of his use of Socrates' name to put forth his perverse ideas as an embarrassing act of treason.[11]

Not many either have agreed with the comment made by Hegel, quoted earlier in this chapter, in which we hear that it is in Xenophon's testimony that we can find the real Socrates. Neither has there been much support for the conclusion reached by George Grote, the eminent nineteenth-century historian of philosophy, that "it is to him [Xenophon] that we owe, in great part, such knowledge as we possess of the real Socrates. For the conversations related by Xenophon, though doubtless dressed up and expanded by him, appear to me reports on the main of what Socrates actually said."[12]

As was suggested in chapter 1 and will be reiterated in the subsequent examination of Plato's testimony, it may perhaps be more reasonable to assume that *all* the sources disclose genuine components of the complex and multifaceted presence of Socrates—the same man viewed from different perspectives and at different times. Even Aristophanes' testimony, generally dismissed as a gross distortion, might make some sense if we entertain the possibility that Socrates was indeed not unlike what was witnessed on the comic stage when the *Clouds* was performed, that is, twenty-four years before his death and long before either Xenophon or Plato came to know him.

NOTES

1. G. F. Hegel, *Lectures on the History of Philosophy*, trans. E. S. Haldane, vol. 1 (London: Routledge and Kegan Paul, 1963), p. 414.

2. B. Russell, *A History of Western Philosophy* (New York: Simon & Schuster, 1945), p. 82.

3. E. Zeller, *Outlines of the History of Greek Philosophy* (London: Routledge & Kegan Paul, 1948), p. 99.

4. G. Vlastos, ed., "The Paradox of Socrates," in *The Philosophy of Socrates: A Collection of Critical Essays* (Notre Dame, IN: University of Notre Dame Press, 1980), p. 2.

5. The *Oeconomicus* deals primarily with what the ancient Greeks called *economics*. This word is derived from two Greek words, *oikos* (*house* or *dwelling*) and *nomos* (*usage* or *custom*, hence, *management*).

6. The Thirty were a group of aristocrats who ruled Athens for ten months after the war. Supported by the Spartans and headed by Critias, a relative of Plato, they plunged the city into a reign of terror directed especially at the democrats.

7. Sparta was the main city in the province of Laconia in the Peloponnesus.

8. For a documented study of the relationship between Antisthenes and Socrates, see L. E. Navia, *Antisthenes of Athens: Setting the World Aright* (Westport, CT: Greenwood Press, 2001). The legacy of Socrates inherited and kept alive by the Cynics is discussed in Navia, *Diogenes the Cynic: The War against the World* (Amherst, NY: Humanity Books, 2005).

9. The line of succession that links Socrates to Antisthenes and the Cynics is discussed at length in L. E. Navia, *Classical Cynicism: A Critical Study* (Westport, CT: Greenwood Press, 1996).

10. The Greek title *Apomnemoveymata* literally means 'memories' or 'recollections'.

11. The animosity between Diogenes and Plato is amply reported in many secondary sources such as Diogenes Laertius. For a fair and balanced discussion of Diogenes' vitriolic attacks on Plato, see Navia, *Diogenes the Cynic.*

12. G. Grote, *Plato, and the Other Companions of Socrates,* vol.1 (New York: B. Franklin, 1974), p. 206.

CHAPTER 4
The Creation of Plato

*T*he two previous chapters have given us the opportunity to see Socrates from two very different perspectives. He is portrayed in them either as a dangerous man deserving punishment or as a law-abiding and helpful citizen worthy of praise for his unblemished character. Our attention will now be directed to Socrates as he appears in Plato's testimony, the best known and admired Socrates, and for many the only Socrates worthy of consideration. Whether or not Plato's creation should be regarded in this light, it is indisputable that without this depiction, Socrates, whoever and whatever he was, would have been a minor presence in the history of ideas. Indeed, Socrates the great philosopher is the Socrates of Plato's writings.

For a critical examination of Plato's testimony, it may be useful to comment on his life, specifically, on his relationship with Socrates and on his writings. Much is known about Plato's life, although the task of separating fact from legend is difficult and often disappointing. From the dialogues alone, hardly anything can be learned about their author because he mentions himself only twice. He tells us that he was present at Socrates' trial (*Apology* 34a, 38b) and that he was not with Socrates when he died (*Phaedo* 59b).

There are thirteen letters attributed to Plato. From them, especially from the seventh, there is much that can be learned, although their authenticity has often been questioned. The seventh letter and, to a lesser extent, the second seem to pass the test of authenticity, and it is to them that we can turn to resurrect various aspects related to Plato.

There is abundant material about Plato's life in classical sources. As in the case of Socrates and other Greek philosophers, the oldest surviving biography is by Diogenes Laertius. Unfortunately, our information about this author is deficient. At best, we can say that he was a compiler of ancient anecdotes and opinions who lived in the third century CE. For his eighty-two biographies, he made use of a great number of sources, most of which are not available to us. If they were, our knowledge of ancient philosophy would stand on a firmer foundation.

The anecdotal style of Diogenes Laertius's work has led many scholars to downgrade its value as a serious source of information. Nietzsche, however, whose doctoral dissertation of 1870 dealt with this work, concluded that we can learn from it much more than from all other classical and modern works on ancient philosophy. A philosopher, he insists, is someone who teaches by the example of his life and by every detail of his conduct, not by what he says or writes, which is precisely what we find in Diogenes Laertius's work. He brings to life the subjects of his biographies through stories and anecdotes, which, despite their perhaps dubious character, create a mosaic of living biographical portraits. If used with caution, Nietzsche argues, they succeed in revealing who the ancient philosophers truly were.

The genealogy of Plato makes him a member of an aristocratic Athenian family that included men of distinction such as Solon (640–558 BCE), the famous statesman and lawgiver. His father's name was Ariston and his mother's, Perictione. He had two older brothers, Glaucon and Adeimantus, who were closely associated with Socrates. Potone, his only sister, was the mother of Speusippus, the philosopher who would succeed Plato as the head of the Academy.

Plato was born in Aegina, near Athens, in 427 BCE, when Socrates was forty-two years old. Extraordinary accounts of his birth circulated in antiquity. They tell, for instance, that he was born on the feast of Apollo's nativity and that he was the offspring not of his human father, but of the god himself, through whose intervention his mother became pregnant (DL 3.2). Naturally, a man as impressive as Plato must have been the son of a god. His death is generally placed in 347 BCE, reportedly at a wedding celebrated in the Academy. He was eighty years old.

In his youth, Plato is said to have written poems and dramatic pieces, and, as did other young aristocrats, he saw himself destined to a life of political involvement. Somehow, however, the disappointing aftermath of the war, as shown in the abuse of power on the part of the aristocrats, must have convinced him that a political life was not for him. Still, he must have felt the temptation to work toward reforming the dilapidated Athenian political system when Critias, his uncle, invited him to be part of the tyrannical government of which he was the head. Plato still envisioned the possibility of regenerating the state, as he tells us in his seventh letter: "No wonder that young as I was, I cherished the hope that they [Critias and other aristocrats] would lead the city from an unjust life, as it were, to a condition of justice of which, as they put it, they would be in charge. Indeed, I was keenly interested to see what would come of it" (*Epist.* 7.324d). Nothing good came of it and things took a turn for the worse, as Critias and the others did not hesitate to abuse the power given to them by the Spartans. Among their atrocities and crimes, they sought to involve Socrates, whom Plato calls "an elderly friend of mine, who I should hardly be ashamed to say was the most just man in his

day," in a criminal scheme to bring innocent men to execution
(cf. *Apology* 32c). With so corrupt and unjust a government,
Plato did not wish to be associated.

Yet, when the tyrants were overthrown and a democratic
government was established, conditions did not improve, as was
demonstrated by the execution of Socrates in 399 BCE. This
act, which was in Plato's eyes the climax of political depravity,
convinced him of the uselessness of any sort of political intervention. In such a world, the philosopher cannot but be like "a
man who has fallen among wild beasts, who is unwilling to share
in their misdeeds, and is unable to hold out singly against their
savagery" (*Republic* 6.496d).

After Socrates' execution, Plato saw nothing redeemable in
the Athenian political structure, and, thus, we never again find
him involved in the politics of the city either in action or in
writing. Later on he would dream of remaking the political
world, but this would be far from Athens—in Syracuse—but
even there, he remained convinced of the need to create a completely new canvas for human existence. To him, reforms were
useless.

Plato's aloofness from politics was not only the result of the
disappointing political climate in Athens. Far more significant
was his discovery of Socrates, which happened, it seems, when
he was about twenty years old. His older brothers, Glaucon and
Adeimantus, as well as Antiphon, his half-brother, and others of
his relatives, had already been in the company of Socrates and
were, at least a few of them, part of the Socratic circle.

Diogenes Laertius tells us about Plato's first encounter with
Socrates: "It has been written that once, Socrates dreamed of a
young swan on his knees, which all at once put forth plumage,
and flew away after uttering a loud sweet note. The next day
Plato was introduced as a pupil, and Socrates recognized in him
the swan of his dream" (DL 3.5).[1]

Aside from saying that Plato must have remained after this

encounter a close associate of Socrates, nothing specific can be affirmed about their relationship. If we attach some value to the unfavorable comments made after Socrates' death by others among Socrates' associates, we could conclude that there was nothing special about him, at least in their eyes. Aristippus, for instance, accused him of displaying little concern toward Socrates' fate, as was shown by his absence at the time of the execution (DL 3.36; cf. *Phaedo* 59b). Others denied any close relationship between them, for, they argued, no one well acquainted with Socrates could have attributed to him so many ideas foreign to him.

These allegations are critical in the attempt to evaluate the merit of Plato as a witness of the Socratic presence. If what Antisthenes, Aristippus, and others are said to have alleged has any value, then we might as well conclude that much of what Plato wrote in the name of Socrates is a grand literary creation. Diogenes the Cynic firmly maintained that Plato had literally betrayed Socrates and the spirit of philosophy by inventing lies about him and distorting his ideas. Although Diogenes was not directly acquainted with Socrates, he must have learned a great deal about him from Antisthenes and others in the Socratic circle.

Yet, whatever the relationship between Plato and Socrates could have been, it is undeniable that Socrates' impact on Plato must have been overwhelming. We are justified in seeing in the edifice of Plato's philosophy a monumental structure built as a testimonial to Socrates, even if we conclude that in important respects he moved beyond Socrates and that in others he stood in opposition to him. Regardless of Plato's faithfulness to the historical Socrates, there is no question that it was Socrates who impelled him toward philosophy and that, because of this, he decided to leave for future generations a testimony of his legacy.

Surely, Socrates' influence on Plato does not preclude the presence of other influences perhaps even more decisive than that of Socrates. From Aristotle (*Metaphysics* 987a), we learn of his familiarity with the doctrines of Heraclitus, which were brought to Athens by Cratylus (DL 3.6). Parmenides' ideas were known to Plato through the teachings of philosophers such as Hermogenes and Euclides. Pythagorean traditions, too, must have been part of Plato's philosophical development, especially through the influence of Philolaus, the Pythagorean astronomer who taught in Athens in the last years of the fifth century BCE, as we learn from Cicero (DL 8.6).

After Socrates' death, Plato was exposed to these and other influences, particularly during his sojourn in Sicily and southern Italy, where Pythagoreanism was a powerful philosophical force at that time. His dialogues reveal these influences, for which reason they are an invaluable source of information about Pre-Socratic philosophy. He grasped with unparalleled depth the philosophical contributions of earlier philosophers.

All these circumstances make it difficult to pass judgment on the value of Plato's testimony because what his dialogues reveal is a complex landscape where various philosophical currents are closely interwoven. They all dance magically around the mysterious figure of Socrates, but always under the masterful baton of the dramatic Plato, who remains outside the literary scenes of his dialogues. Often, indeed, when we hear Socrates' voice, we are tempted to suspect that it is Plato who is actually speaking. But how can we be sure of this?

After Socrates' death, Plato traveled extensively for several years. He spent time in Megara in the company of Euclides, the philosopher who, disguised as an old lady, would furtively come to Athens to converse with Socrates—people from Megara were not welcomed in Athens. Apparently, Socrates' execution caused great concern among his associates, some of whom fled to Megara (DL 2.106) After Megara, Plato traveled to Sicily, southern Italy, Cyrene, and Egypt. There is no certainty about the purpose of his trips or about the sequence and length of his travels.

Possibly around 387 BCE, Plato returned to Athens, and it was at that time that he established his famous school in Athens, the Academy. A great deal of scholarship has been devoted to gather information about the origin, structure, and significance of this school. It is known that as a physical location, the Academy had existed and functioned as a meeting place for leisure-loving Athenians long before the time of Plato. Located outside the city, it was a parklike retreat dedicated since remote times to the legendary hero Hecademus, which explains its name. As we read in the *Lysis* (203a), it was frequented by Socrates and his friends. Archaeological excavation in the area has disclosed inscriptions that bear names familiar to us from Plato's dialogues: Charmides, Ariston, Crito, and others. Today, a tour of the site is disappointing because practically nothing remains of the ancient buildings. It functioned as the center of intellectual life in the ancient world for one thousand years until 529 CE, when the Christian fanaticism of Emperor Justinian brought about its demise.

The list of those who were part of the Academy during Plato's time is long and impressive. There were philosophers, mathematicians, astronomers, playwrights, politicians, generals—just about every important person from Athens and elsewhere. Women, too, had access to it—we have the names of two female students: Lastheneia of Mantinea and Axiothea of Phlius. Its most famous student was Aristotle, who spent twenty years there under the tutelage of Plato.

As soon as we move away from these details, we enter into a world of uncertainty. Questions about the Academy's functioning and structure, its orientation and curriculum, and the importance attached to the memory and ideas of Socrates cannot be answered with finality. There are also questions about the relationship between Plato's written works and his oral teachings. It is difficult to determine, moreover, to what extent his dialogues reflect the intellectual climate that prevailed in the

Academy. We can assume that its ideological life and daily activities revolved around the powerful personality of Plato himself, and that he, as its founder, embodied its spirit.

Yet, we would like to go beyond these generalities. Was the Academy a loose association of scholars and prominent people that reflected the informality of Agathon's house in Plato's *Symposium* and Cephalus's home in his *Republic*? Or was it rather a religiously oriented guild similar to the communities of the ancient Pythagoreans with whom Plato had become acquainted in southern Italy? Or was it the classical prototype of our own institutes of advanced studies, where scholars pursue their studies and research in relative independence from one another?

We can assume that it was all these and other things, and that, in the course of time, it underwent changes in structure and direction even during Plato's lifetime. Its religious aspects must have been significant. Its ancient name, the Museum, is related to the fact that it was initially dedicated to the Muses. Given the background of Plato's thought and the scanty information we possess about the daily activities of the school—daily prayers and sacrifices—we may conclude that the worship of the gods must have occupied a special place.

It may have resembled a Pythagorean community with rules governing behavior and adherence to certain philosophical principles. Perhaps, as in the Pythagorean communities, there was the presence of the Master—Plato himself—surrounded by devoted disciples. Besides, as one considers the political activities in which the Academy became entangled, such as an armed expedition to Syracuse, it was more than a school of philosophy.

The subjects studied in the Academy were probably those prescribed by Plato in the *Republic* for the guardians of the state: metaphysics, cosmology, and mathematics. There is a report that an inscription written on the school's entrance forbade those not trained in mathematics to enter. The study of mathematics was for Plato not an end in itself but a means for attaining the beatific philosophical vision of those who succeed in escaping from the cave of ordinary human reality. Next to that inscription, however, people could have noticed the presence of Diogenes the Cynic, reminding them that Plato's teachings were a waste of time (DL 6.24). In Diogenes' view, Plato was a man who talked too much without ever saying anything (DL 6.26).

Plato's work in the Academy must have included three main functions: guiding his disciples, lecturing, and writing. Here, however, we come upon the issue of the alleged gap between his oral teachings and his writings. Some have supported the idea that this gap was wide. What Plato *taught* and what he *wrote* were very different things. Whereas the former was an esoteric and secret doctrine that could not be set down in writing, the latter was intended as preparatory exercises specifically for those who were not part of Plato's inner circle. In a memorable passage from his seventh letter (*Epist.* 7.341c), speaking of true philosophy, he says that "there is no way of putting it into words like other studies" because it transcends language and belongs to an ontological level where communication is useless.

Surely, it is argued, it would be impossible *not* to find in the dialogues hints and traces of the so-called unwritten doctrine, which would somehow allow us to have some understanding of it. In attempts to reconstruct this unwritten doctrine, some have concluded that it must have been a mystical view of reality traceable to Pythagoras and Parmenides, and involving some sort of grand ethical and political project structured along mathematical lines.

A final resolution of these issues will probably never be found. After all, we do have *everything* Plato wrote—which is indeed very rare with any other ancient writer—but we do not have any clear information about what his secret teachings, if any, could have been. Neither can we pretend to know whether Socrates himself had a secret doctrine that he could have passed on to Plato and that never surfaces in the dialogues. It is for this reason that in approaching Plato in our search for Socrates, we must limit ourselves to what can be read, and that is, obviously, Plato's writings.

The oldest classification of these writings belongs to Aristophanes of Byzantium, a scholar of the third century BCE. Three centuries later and on the basis of that classification, a scholar named Thrasylus arranged Plato's dialogues and letters in nine tetralogies or groups of four. This arrangement does not establish a chronology—the order in which they were written—and includes dialogues and letters that later scholarship has dismissed as inauthentic. Thrasylus's tetralogies are as follows:

1. *Euthyphro, Apology, Crito, Phaedo*
2. *Cratylus, Theaetetus, Sophist, Statesman*
3. *Parmenides, Philebus, Symposium, Phaedrus*
4. *Alcibiades I, Alcibiades II, Hipparchus, Anteraste*
5. *Theages, Charmides, Laches, Lysis*
6. *Euthydemus, Protagoras, Gorgias, Meno*
7. *Hippias Major, Hippias Minor, Ion, Menexenus*
8. *Cleitophon, Republic, Timaeus, Critias*
9. *Minos, Laws, Epinomis, Epistles*

The first major attempt to subject Plato's writings to a critical scrutiny was made by Schleiermacher in the nineteenth century, when he endeavored to determine their authenticity and chronology.[2] Since his time, much scholarship has been devoted to this field, but it would be a mistake to affirm that a final solution has been found. At one time or another, practically every one of Plato's writings has been judged inauthentic, and the most diverse chronologies have been defended. Even the *Republic*, probably Plato's most influential dialogue, has not escaped from the suspicion of inauthenticity. It is important to bear in mind, however, that even in the case of those dialogues generally viewed as inauthentic, there is much that we can learn both about Plato and about Socrates, regardless of who their authors could have been.

As noted earlier, much controversy has surrounded the authorship of the Platonic letters. Thrasylus included them in his tetralogies and regarded them as authentic. In modern times, however, they have been dismissed as creations of Hellenistic writers, except for the second and seventh letters, but even these include statements that are troublesome to certain scholars.

There is, for instance, a statement in the second letter (*Epist.* 2.314c) that echoes the passage of the seventh letter quoted earlier, in which Plato maintains that his ideas cannot be expressed in written words (*Epist.* 7.341c). This might convince us, some say, that his genuine writings may be only marginally related to his philosophy. If this cannot be put into written words, he could not have written about it in his dialogues.

Then there is yet another statement in the second letter, in which we are told that whatever Plato ascribed to Socrates in the dialogues is what Socrates actually said, albeit embellished and brought to life: "I have never myself written a word on these matters [philosophy], and neither there is nor will ever be any written treatise of Plato. What now bears the name [of Plato] belongs to Socrates, beautified and rejuvenated" (*Epist.* 2.314c). If this statement is genuine, the Socrates of the dialogues emerges as *the* historical Socrates, while Plato converts himself into a faithful *reporter* of his words and a superb dramatist who knew well how to integrate them into fanciful conversations and scenes. Yet, could this be really so?

The chronology of Plato's dialogues cannot be fully established. Their composition began shortly after Socrates' death until the death of Plato himself in 347 BCE, that is, a period of over fifty years. There are even indications that some of the dialogues were written while Socrates was still alive. Stylometric analysis, which involves the detailed study of Plato's writings—word by word—has yielded some results in determining the sequence of their composition, but the results are never conclusive. Statements found in the secondary sources have also been taken into account, as, for instance, Aristotle's reference to the *Laws* as a dialogue of Plato's old age and Diogenes Laertius's statement that Socrates once heard someone reading from the *Lysis* (DL 3.35)

More fruitful, however, has been the study of the themes presented in the dialogues and the role assigned to Socrates in them. We can assume that Plato moved through complex stages of intellectual development and that he directed his attention to different issues at different times. His dialogues, therefore, would have reflected this circumstance. This may account for the fact that the themes that engage Socrates' attention from dialogue to dialogue are very different.

The themes of Socrates' interest, the style of his participation, and the role assigned to him have been used as tentative indicators for the time of composition for many of the dialogues. For instance, a Socrates exclusively engaged in ethical issues, repeatedly affirming his ignorance, and apparently unable to reach firm conclusions about the subjects of his conversations—such elements, it is said, indicate an early date of composition. A Socrates involved in metaphysical and cosmological issues, assuming an air of certainty about his understanding of them, and expressing himself in lengthy rhetorical statements—these are indications of a later date of composition. A Socrates who is a minor participant in the conversation or a silent witness or not even present at the scene—these are signs of a very late date. On the basis of considerations such as these, a tentative chronology can be established.

We can, therefore, generally classify the twenty-four dialogues of Plato into three groups, early, middle, and late, using the presence of Socrates in them as a major factor for the classification of individual dialogues. It cannot be denied, however, that in this endeavor neither certainty nor finality can be expected. Even the appeal to the dramatic Socrates as a criterion for classifying the dialogues may be based on the questionable assumption that certain dialogues—the early ones—are more Socratic than the middle and late ones. In the early ones, therefore, we would be in the presence of the real Socrates, while in the middle and late, Socrates has transformed himself into a mouthpiece for Plato and into a dramatic personage.

Much has been said about Plato's choice of the dialogue genre as his exclusive medium of expression, and here, as in other issues, controversy and disagreement is what we find. Let it be sufficient to note that this genre was a common form of expression during Plato's time. Others among Socrates' associates, including Xenophon, wrote dozens and dozens of dialogues. In them, Socrates also plays a central role. According to Diogenes Laertius (2.123), the initiator of the dialogue as *the* literary genre to keep Socrates alive after his death was Simon the Shoemaker, actually a real Athenian shoemaker, who is said to have been a close acquaintance of Socrates and who was influential in the development of Cynicism.

It is, moreover, undeniable that if Socrates was what Xenophon and Plato say he was, that is, a man always engaged in conversation, the dialogue is the most adequate medium to re-create his presence. As Xenophon remembers him, he would spend the entire day at the marketplace or in any of the public places endlessly talking with anyone who would care to converse with him. According to Plato, he was even willing to pay to talk with people if he had the means: "I fear that because of my love of people they think that I not only pour myself out copiously to anyone and everyone without payment, but that I would even pay something myself if anyone would listen to me" (*Euthyphro* 3c).

In Plato's *Apology* (23b), we find him approaching all sorts of people, from the humble artisans to the proud aristocrats, in order to engage them in conversation, as if he were possessed by an irresistible obsession, which he calls his "obedience to God." We find him impatient and bored in the presence of people who made lengthy speeches and who were only interested in impressing their audiences. The Socrates of the early dialogues preferred the kind of conversation in which the participants were limited to short questions and answers, and in which the *elenchus*, so essential to his methodology, could be exhibited.[3]

In some of the dialogues, we are introduced to the gap that separates Socrates' mode of speaking from the lengthy speeches preferred by sophists and public orators for whom he had little use (*Apology* 17d). In the *Republic* (1.350d), he does not even allow the talkative Thrasymachus "the freedom of speech" he demanded. For Socrates, long speeches, whether spoken or written, were pointless, since, as he ironically says somewhere, he forgets at the end what was said at the beginning. He engages people in conversation not in order to teach them this or that, or even less to impress them, but to force them to come to grips with the emptiness of their convictions and their lack of intellectual clarity. Literally, he needs to deflate them. His purpose, however, is not to create skepticism or mere confusion. For him, as we read in the *Charmides* (155e), the dialogue is a sort of medicine for the soul, a medicine he is always willing to administer to his philosophical patients. He wants to compel them to turn their eyes inward and thereby to grow in understanding and honesty, and to come closer to the truth.

Regardless of how we resolve the issue of the alleged dichotomy between Plato's unwritten and written doctrines, it is impossible not to see, at least in the early dialogues, that what he attempted to do in transcribing some of the actual conversations of Socrates was to capture in writing the quest for the truth that had animated Socrates. What Socrates did in his unending conversations, Plato sought to do through his dialogues. What had been for Socrates an oral exercise was transformed by Plato into written dialogues. The spoken and heard word became written and seen, but its meaning and purpose remained unchanged.

We can now direct our attention to the portrayal of Socrates that emerges from the dialogues. Its outlines can be best extracted from the early dialogues, although much can still be learned from other Platonic writings. The early dialogues that need to be examined include the *Crito*, the *Euthyphro*, the *Laches*, the *Protagoras*, the *Charmides*, the *Lysis*, and book 1 of the *Republic*. The *Apology* provides for us the most comprehensive statement about Socrates. In these dialogues we can surely find important elements of Plato's interpretation of Socrates' legacy.

Aside from the *Crito* and the *Apology*, what is distinctive in the early dialogues is the perplexing fact that they seem to lead to no definite conclusion about their specific inquiries. In the *Euthyphro*, where Socrates and Euthyphro wrestle with the concept of holiness, the substantive part of the conversation begins with the typical Socratic question, "Tell me, then, what do you say holiness is, and what, unholiness?" (5d). In the end, however, nothing appears to have been accomplished. "We must begin again at the beginning," says Socrates to Euthyphro, "and ask what holiness is" (15e). Obviously, the initial goal had not been reached. We then see how Euthyphro disentangles himself from Socrates' grip by replying, "Some other time, Socrates. Now I am in a hurry and it is time for me to go" (15e). We are, therefore, left in the dark about the correct way of defining holiness.

In the *Laches*, we are in a similar predicament. Here, Socrates wants to know from Laches, "What is that common quality that goes by the name of courage?" (191b). In the end, however, after many futile attempts, nothing seems to have been achieved, and Socrates closes the conversation by urging everyone, including himself, to find a teacher who would truly know what courage is, for neither he nor anyone else knows (201b).

In the *Charmides*, the object of the conversation is to reach a satisfying definition of temperance—we may say moderation in action, thought, and feelings—but here neither the confused Charmides nor the inquisitive Socrates succeeds in coming up with a clear definition. Charmides is finally compelled to confess his ignorance: "Why, upon my word, Socrates, I don't really know whether or not I have temperance. For how could I know it, when even you are unable to discover what this thing is?" (*Charmides* 176a).

In the *Lysis*, Socrates questions two young friends, Lysis and Menexenus, about the meaning of friendship. He ironically suggests to them that they should know it perfectly well, since they regard themselves as friends. How could anyone claim to have a friend without knowing what friendship means? Yet, at the conclusion of the dialogue, the sharp words of the philosopher remind us of the apparent futility of the conversation: "Well, Lysis and Menexenus, today we have made ourselves rather ridiculous, I, an old man, and you, youngsters. Those who have listened to us will spread the report that although we conceive ourselves to be friends—you see, I am also your friend—we have not as yet been able to discover what we mean when we speak about somebody as a friend" (*Lysis* 223a).

In the *Protagoras*, the inconclusiveness of the argument is expressed in a different way. Protagoras, a typical sophist, is described as one who speaks eloquently about what he claims to know and who dispenses to others "food for the soul" (313c). Yet, under Socrates' scrutiny, this food proves to be poisonous because Protagoras does not know himself what it is that he teaches. Protagoras, a man proud of teaching others the noble art of politics, is forced to confront Socrates' view that neither such an art nor indeed any of the virtues can be taught, as evidenced by Pericles' failure to impart his wisdom to his children. However, as the conversation moves along, we are led to a surprising result. Protagoras and Socrates are ready to defend views diametrically opposed to those with which they began. Protagoras is no longer convinced of his ability to teach anything, and Socrates is willing to affirm that virtue can indeed be taught. He brings the conversation to an end by confessing his ignorance and by proposing the continuation of the discussion at some other time. For our part, we are left once more in a suspended state of mind because nothing has been clarified.

This Socratic uncertainty is nowhere given a more compelling expression than in the *Apology*, where it is presented as the kernel of Socrates' wisdom. Apollo, the god of Delphi, let us remember, had declared him to be the wisest human being, but at the end of a long pilgrimage searching for the meaning of the oracle and in the fulfillment of his divine mission, he reaches the conclusion that he is indeed the wisest among all human beings because he knows that he knows little or nothing. Other people, blinded by their ill-founded opinions and their arrogance, do not even know that they know nothing. In recognizing and accepting his ignorance, Socrates has taken the first step in the hazardous search for wisdom, a search in which he does not claim to have attained any success. At the end of his life, he is still ignorant about the meaning of death: "Death can be only one of two things: either the complete extinction of the person if the dead have no consciousness or, as some people say, the removal of the soul from this world to another" (*Apology* 40c).

With the exception of the *Laws*, one of the latest dialogues in which Socrates plays no role, much can be learned about Socrates' life in all of Plato's dialogues. Many of the details provided by Plato are also found in the writings of Xenophon. We learn, for instance, that Socrates was born in Athens and that he was an Athenian citizen. In the *Crito* (50e), the Athenian Laws speak to him as their own child: "Is it not true that since you were born, and since your early years of growth and education, you have been, as much as your ancestors, our child and servant?" His service as one of the prytanes or senators during the trial of the generals of Arginusae in 406 BCE (*Apology* 32b)[4] and his ability to speak in front of the jury are clear indications of his citizenship.[5] Only citizens took part in the government and only they could speak in court.

In the *Gorgias* (495d), his *deme* is said to be Alopece, one of the ten districts or boroughs into which Athens was divided. The names of his parents are given in the *Hippias Major* (298b) and in the *Laches* (180d). Nothing is said about his father's occupation, but we learn that his mother was a midwife: "It is unthinkable that you are not aware of the fact that I am the son of a midwife, a well-built woman named Phaenarete" (*Theaetetus* 149a). Her occupation has a special significance for Socrates. He compares his own occupation with hers. Whereas she, unable to give birth herself on account of her age, helps young women in the process of giving birth, so he, barren of ideas and unable to give birth to any thoughts, is instrumental in aiding others in the difficult task of creating meaningful ideas (*Theaetetus* 149a–51e). Midwifery seems to have been practiced in Athens by women of humble origins, a circumstance that reveals something about Socrates himself. His allusions to his poverty (*Apology* 31c, *Menexenus* 238d) convey to us the picture of a man whose social status was far below that of the aristocrats. He belonged to the working class.

In the *Euthydemus* (297e), we learn about a man named Patrocles, who is said to have been Socrates' half-brother, the son of Phaenarete and of a certain Chaeredemus. In the *Phaedo* (60a, 116a), there are two references to Xanthippe, Socrates' wife, but, as noted in the previous chapter, nothing can be inferred from Plato about her character. The first reference in the *Phaedo* appears in the following passage: "As we came into the prison [says Crito], Socrates had just been released from his chains, and Xanthippe, whom you know, was near him with her little child in her arms. When she saw us, she wept loudly and said, in the typical fashion of women, 'My dear Socrates, after this time you will no longer be able to speak to your friends, nor they to you!' Socrates looked at Crito and asked him to have someone take Xanthippe home. Then, some of Crito's people led her away, as she wept bitterly beating her breast in lamentation."

This scene was magnificently captured by the French painter Jacques Louis David. In his painting, we see the various characters mentioned in Plato's dialogue, including Xanthippe, who is being led away from the prison. To some, this scene is disturbing. It may suggest that the philosopher displayed no affection for his family and that he was more concerned with speaking with his friends than spending his last moments with his wife and child. This interpretation, however, may be the result of projecting into the scene our own preconceptions. It is possible to argue that precisely by sending Xanthippe away, Socrates showed great affection for her and his child because by so doing he was sparing them the pain of seeing him die.

A few details about Socrates' children emerge from the *Apology* and the *Phaedo*. The youngest is said to be young enough to be held in his mother's arms at the time of the father's execution (*Phaedo* 60a). In the *Apology* (34d), Socrates speaks of having three children: "I have three sons, one nearly grown up and two still children." He speaks about his decision not to bring them before the jury in order to avoid using the common argument *ad misericordiam*—asking for pity.

Later on in the *Apology* (41e), he asks the jurors to punish his sons, should they grow up to be the kind of people who value wealth more than virtue and appearance more than reality. In the *Crito* (45c ff.), the sons appear once more, as Crito reminds Socrates that by choosing death, he would be condemning them to the unhappy fate of orphans. The Laws, however, point out to Socrates that his children would not benefit by his unjustly escaping from prison and uselessly prolonging his life a few years.

The date of Socrates' birth can be determined by a reference in the *Apology* (17d) to his being seventy years old at the time of the trial in 399 BCE.[6] The only reference to Socrates' early years also comes from the *Apology* (31d), where he says that his divine sign or voice had accompanied him since his childhood. Beyond this, nothing is known about his childhood from any other sources.

In several passages, we read that Socrates did not travel beyond the immediate vicinity of Athens (*Crito* 52b; *Phaedrus* 227d, 230d; *Phaedo* 99a), except when during the war he served in the Athenian army. He served in Amphipolis in 436 BCE; in Potidaea in 432 BCE, when he is said to have saved Alcibiades' life, demonstrating great courage and endurance (*Symposium* 219e, *Apology* 28e, *Charmides* 153a); and in Delium in 424 BCE (cf. *Laches* 181b, *Symposium* 221a). Nothing is reported by Xenophon about Socrates' military service.

With respect to his education, Socrates states in the *Laches* (186c) that his poverty has made it impossible for him to secure the services of a teacher. In the *Apology* (19c), he declares in no uncertain terms that he has never had any knowledge of or interest in natural philosophy or science. Yet, in the *Phaedo* (96a), we hear something apparently different: "When I was young, I was tremendously eager for the kind of wisdom they call the investigation of nature. I thought it was a glorious thing to know the causes of everything, why each thing comes into being and why it perishes and why it exists." We also hear of his disappointment with the writings of Anaxagoras, a philosopher who wrote about the processes of nature and other such things. "It was a wonderful hope," says Socrates, "but it was quickly dashed" (*Phaedo* 98b).

Anaxagoras, whose ideas are discussed in several of Plato's dialogues, seems to have held a special position in the development of Socrates' thought, although the two philosophers are never depicted in conversation. In the *Phaedo* (97b ff.), we read of how Socrates once heard someone read from a book by Anaxagoras and of how he wasted no time in procuring a copy in order to learn from it the wisdom it promised to impart. What he found in it, however, was disappointing because it failed to address the questions for which *he* needed an answer. It explained the world as if this were merely a physical mechanism devoid of purpose—which is what we generally expect to find from a scientist. Disillusioned with Anaxagoras, Socrates then proceeded to work out his own solution to the problem of why things happen as they do.

It is in this passage from the *Phaedo* that some scholars have discerned the bridge that links Plato and Socrates as well as the first hint about the theory of ideal Forms that Plato would expound in later dialogues. The restlessness of Socrates, his dissatisfaction with science and its mechanistic explanations of the world, and his own inclination to conceive of the world in a teleological and spiritual way—these genuinely Socratic attitudes, well attested to by Xenophon and Plato, as well as by the secondary sources, paved the way, some say, for Plato's own metaphysical development. In subsequent chapters, we will have an opportunity to see whether this interpretation stands the test of scrutiny.

Socrates' friends and acquaintances are distinctly drawn throughout the dialogues, and there are no compelling reasons to believe that any of them are fictitious. In fact, most of them are recognizable historical personages. We come upon the sophists, teachers of the art of speaking, many of whom had come to Athens to educate the youth in ways to attain success. Among them we come upon Protagoras, Gorgias, Thrasymachus, Prodicus, Hippias, Callicles, and others. The dramatic settings may include fictional elements, but the spirit that permeates the conversations probably reflects actual conversations in which Socrates' opposition to the teachings of the sophists is made clearly manifest.

Of the major philosophers of the time, only Parmenides, Zeno, and Cratylus appear in conversation with Socrates. In the *Theaetetus* (183e), he insists that he was personally acquainted with Parmenides: "I met him when I was quite young and he quite elderly, and I thought there was a sort of depth in him that was most commendable." In the *Parmenides*, Socrates' encounter with Parmenides and Zeno is more precisely described: "Zeno and Parmenides once came to Athens for the Great Panathenaea.[7] Parmenides was a man of distinguished appearance. At that time he was well advanced in years, with his hair almost white. He may have been sixty-five years old and Zeno perhaps forty. They were staying with Pythodorus outside the walls in the Ceramicus.[8] Socrates and a few others went there, anxious to hear a reading of the book Zeno had brought to Athens for the first time. Socrates was then quite young" (*Parmenides* 127b–c). In the *Sophist* (217c), there is yet another mention of this encounter, in which Socrates is again described as very young and Parmenides as an old man, precisely as they are described in the *Parmenides*.

Some have alleged that this reported meeting involves an anachronism and is only an invention of Plato. If Diogenes Laertius is correct in maintaining that Parmenides was in his forties around the year 504 BCE (DL 9.23), it may be unlikely that he could have met the young Socrates when he was in his twenties, that is, after 450 BCE. Parmenides would have been approaching one hundred years of age. The accuracy of Diogenes Laertius's report, however, cannot be taken for granted; this leads us to conclude that Socrates' meeting with the famous philosopher from Elea may have taken place after all.

The list of those with whom Socrates is portrayed in conversation in Plato's testimony is long and varied. It includes people from every imaginable background and social status. Surely, the gregarious nature of Socrates led him to make contact with as many people as possible because conversing was his principal and perhaps only occupation. Among his interlocutors, we come face to face with his close associates—Chaerephon, Crito, Phaedrus, Cebes, Simmias, Apollodorus, Glaucon, Adeimantus, Timaeus, Antiphon, Euclides, Hermogenes, and Theodorus, among others. Antisthenes is mentioned only once (*Phaedo* 59b), where he is said to have been present at Socrates' execution.

Besides them, there are aristocrats like Critias, Charmides, Alcibiades, and Nicias, among others. As noted above, the philosophers are represented by the sophists, Parmenides, Zeno, and Cratylus. Aristophanes and Ion represent the poets and the rhapsodists. Sophocles and Euripides, although contemporaries of Socrates, are only mentioned and quoted. Euthydemus and Dionysodorus exemplify the linguistic acrobats of the day, while the pious Euthyphro stands for the religious orthodoxy and Anytus for the advocates of the democracy. The Athenian youth, hungry for power and political distinction, speak through Meno, Polus, and Callicles, and the wealthy foreigners of the Piraeus, the Athenian port, make their appearance in people like Cephalus and Polemarchus. The slaves are not forgotten, as can be seen in the *Meno*, in which Socrates questions at length a young slave.

He converses with these and other people, sometimes monopolizing the conversation, as in the later books of the *Republic* and in the *Menexenus*, and sometimes, as in the *Euthyphro* and other early dialogues, participating in a lively exchange. At times, too, he does not say much, as in the *Critias*, and the *Sophist*. In the *Apology*, the *Crito*, and the *Phaedo*, he is seventy years old, while in other dialogues, as in the *Parmenides*, he is a younger man. He moves comfortably among the highest political and cultural circles of the city and is even closely associated with liberated women like Aspasia, from whom he claims to have learned the art of rhetoric.

His conversations generally revolve around themes and images drawn from the world of artisans and workers. His endless chatter can be heard in the gymnasium, the Lyceum, the homes of the wealthy, the marketplace, under the porticoes of public buildings, or practically anywhere in the city. Rarely, as in the *Phaedrus*, do we find him in the neighboring countryside, where he does not feel at ease, for his real home is the city.

At least in his mature years, Socrates does not seem to have had any kind of employment. It is clear that nothing mattered to him more than the pursuit of philosophy, which assumed for him the form of constant discourse. The business of his life was conversation, to which he devoted himself persistently, neglecting his personal affairs and those of his family. Whether he worked as a statuary during the construction of the temples of the Acropolis or as a mason in his youth, we cannot infer from Plato's dialogues. In them, he is invariably depicted enjoying an unlimited leisure. The generosity of his friends took care of his needs and those of his family.

Plato furnishes us with a clear idea about Socrates' social standing. He was not, at least when Plato knew him, the disruptive and secretive buffoon of Aristophanes' *Clouds*, nor was he the enemy of society, as he was occasionally described in Roman times. According to Plutarch, for instance, Marcus Cato described Socrates in these terms: "Socrates was a mighty babbler who tried to make himself tyrant of his country in order to destroy its customs and entice its citizens into holding views contrary to law and order" (*Cato* 23).

Neither was he in the eyes of the crowd the worthiest and wisest man, as he was for Plato, nor was he the revered master who emerges from Xenophon's writings. In his interaction with others, he reveals himself as someone loved by a few as an irreplaceable friend. They love and eulogize him and look upon him as someone unique, as Alcibiades does in the *Symposium*, but not as someone with whom his friends are unwilling to disagree. In this respect, he does not resemble the Jesus of the Gospels whose very word constitutes for his followers the source of truth.

The love of Socrates' friends, however, was counterbalanced by the dislike and distrust of a group of influential people for whom he represented a threat. In the *Meno* (94e), we witness Anytus's anger for having been publicly humiliated by Socrates, and in the *Republic* (1.336c, 343a), we notice Thrasymachus's exasperation with his quibbling over common words. In their eyes, he was a nuisance, a busybody, and an impertinent fellow, whose pastime was embarrassing and confusing those around him.

Yet, aside from occasional feelings of personal animosity from his opponents, we can assume that they did not see him as a formidable public menace. The comment attributed by Plutarch to Aristoxenus (*On the Malice of Herodotus* 856d), that there was no real harm in him, could be put into the mouth of most of Socrates' opponents. For them, he was an eccentric and annoying man whom the city, in secure and prosperous times, could afford to tolerate, as, indeed, it did. When those times came to an end, however, the Socratic 'problem' took a sinister turn, and then the threats of Anytus in the *Meno* and the anger of Thrasymachus in the *Republic*, no less than the old jokes of Aristophanes, were transformed into the official indictment.

As for the rest, we can assume that most Athenians were not particularly interested in Socrates. Great crowds never gathered around him. His influence was felt solely by a few. The many, the masses, were untouched by his presence even when by accident they came in contact with him. After conversing with him, they went back to their routines, not remembering a single word spoken by him. The gadfly, as he calls himself in the *Apology*, had failed to awaken them from their slumber, which is, of course, expected and understandable. Ordinary people generally have little interest in the sort of questions and issues that agitated Socrates and little capacity even to begin to understand what it was that he was searching. His could have been the statement that Nietzsche makes Zarathustra utter: "They understand me not, for I am not the mouth for these ears. Must one first batter their ears so that they learn to hear with their eyes? Must one clatter like kettledrums and penitential preachers? Or do they only believe the stammerer?"[9]

Plato's account of Socrates' appearance and character is generally in agreement with that of Xenophon. In the *Theaetetus* (143e), we come upon his snub nose and protruding eyes, and in other dialogues other physical characteristics are mentioned. The most impressive description comes from Alcibiades in the *Symposium*, in which from the lips of one of the most influential and dissolute among Athenians we find the most memorable and graphic description of Socrates. Despite his drunkenness, Alcibiades proposes to give a truthful account of the man who has affected him so deeply, the only man in the presence of whom the proud general feels ashamed, for he knows that in reality he is himself the opposite of the philosopher. Socrates is what Alcibiades wished he could have been.

The man, says Alcibiades, is a bundle of paradoxes best described in terms of an analogy. The outer man is ugly and unpleasant to behold, but the inner resembles a god—just like the statues of the monstrous Sileni and Satyrs sold at the statuaries' shops, inside of which one finds figures of the gods.[10] His beauty lies buried within his unappealing body. He resembles the Sileni not only in his ugliness but in his bewitching power. With just a few simple words, he bewitches his hearers and holds them captive. Alcibiades himself has experienced it and has no hope of liberating himself from it. Only Socrates' death might make him free, but, he adds, "I know that even after his death, I would still be his captive."

Alcibiades goes on to describe Socrates' character and habits, revealing a veritable paradigm of excellence and virtue with which Alcibiades contrasts his own shortcomings. He concludes with these words:

> Well, there's a lot more to be said about Socrates, all very strange and all very much to his credit. No doubt there is just

as much to be said about any of his little ways, but personally I think that the most amazing thing about him is the fact that he is absolutely unique. For there is no one like him and I do not think there ever was or will be. You could point to some likeness to Achilles, Brasidas, and the rest of them. You might compare Nestor and Antenor,[11] and so on, with Pericles. There are plenty of such parallels in history, but you will never find anyone like Socrates or any ideas like his ideas in our times or in the past. (*Symposium* 221c)

This description is surely a reflection of Plato's own image of Socrates, probably shared by others among his close friends. In the presence of so overwhelming a personality, they must have been left captivated and helpless. In the *Theages* (130d), the young Aristides claims to have felt Socrates' uncanny spell even by being in the same house with him. Indeed, not only Socrates' words but even his very touch and proximity were sufficient to enrapture those around him.[12]

His influence, as described by Alcibiades, was obviously not the result of his physical appearance, which was anything but pleasant. Thus, the feelings to which he gave rise in others were not those associated with erotic passion. His attractiveness had a very different root. It was the inner man that acted as a powerful magnet, calling forth with an irresistible force those who came within its range. In the inner man, in his spirit, was the secret of his attractiveness, for in him all the virtues praised by the Greeks were eminently present. He was courageous in battle, patient and resigned amid adversities, persistent and consistent in his purpose, kind and generous with those who sought his assistance, restrained and temperate in his desires and emotions, chaste and prudent in his sexual habits, indifferent and oblivious toward the possessions and pleasures coveted by most people, capable of long periods of reflection and concentration, inquisitive and perceptive to the highest degree, concerned solely with the spiritual welfare of others—such, says Alcibiades, was Socrates, and such, we may add, is the portrait of Socrates painted by Plato. Such, too, although less distinctly drawn, is Xenophon's portrait. How, one wonders, could such a man *not* have been the object of love among those who knew him?

There are two aspects of Socrates that deserve special attention, namely, his attitude toward the religious ideas prevalent in his time and the phenomenon of his divine sign or voice. We must concede that the precise nature of Socrates' theological convictions and religious beliefs cannot be stated with certainty. His statements about God and the gods are open to a variety of interpretations that range from the view that in matters of religion he was a humanist for whom the gods were symbols for human aspirations, to the contention that he was as genuinely polytheistic as the most religious among the Athenians. It has also been suggested that beneath his references to the gods, it is possible to detect in him clear indications of an incipient monotheism.

Writing in the second century CE, Apuleius, the author of *The Golden Ass*, argued in his *On the God of Socrates* for a polytheistic interpretation of Socrates' faith. It is undeniable, he insists, that Socrates believed in a multitude of gods and demons and fervently accepted the efficacy of prayer, divination, and sacrifices. There was nothing metaphorical or allegorical in his repeated references and allusions to the gods, particularly to Apollo. He would have never entertained the possibility that beyond the Olympian gods there stood one universal God. Apuleius' insistence on interpreting Socrates' beliefs as manifestations of anthropomorphic polytheism may have been the result of his own desire to keep alive precisely those beliefs. He lived at a time when paganism was beginning its decline under the weight of emerging Christianity. The ancient Greek gods were slowly being devoured by the insatiable Judeo-Christian deity.

Apuleius' interpretation stands in agreement with what many other late and Roman writers maintained. Socrates lived in pagan times, and his beliefs did not radically transcend the parameters of paganism. His gods, many and humanlike, were real and present everywhere. His prayers to them and his faith in the efficacy of prayers, divination, and sacrifices were absolutely genuine.

There is, however, another Socrates—Socrates the humanist—a familiar presence in modern philosophical literature. *This* Socrates did not *truly* believe in gods and demons but talked about such things because of the cultural context in which he lived. He spoke to the overgrown children of his time in the language *they* could understand. He was obviously not an atheist like Theodorus of Cyrene, his contemporary and the most radical atheist of ancient times. Still, he was a humanist who succeeded in transcending the mire of irrational superstitions and beliefs blindly accepted by most people and, to use Kant's phrase, "with an unerring eye for humbug" rising on the wings of reason far above such things. From his flight, he emerged either as a confirmed humanist, oblivious of religion, or as a monotheist, entertaining at least the possibility of the existence of *one* transcendent God.

Every age has reconstructed its own image of Socrates on the basis of its cultural and philosophical preferences and prejudices, even when this has entailed a selective reading—sometimes a misreading—of the primary sources. We then have one more mosaic of representations of him. Was he then an adherent of polytheism or a humanist for whom religion was a collection of myths and for whom human reason was the only judicial court that decides what is real and what is not? Was he, as some Fathers of the Church insisted, a precursor of Jesus amid the dark clouds of paganism? What, then, did he actually believe?

It is important to set aside these interpretations in order to lend an attentive ear to the sources themselves. We must hear and see Socrates in action. In previous chapters, we commented on what Aristophanes and Xenophon wrote in this regard. We found in them two profoundly different accounts. With respect to Plato's testimony, we can now ask, what did Socrates say about the gods and how did he practice his religion? From a critical review of his dialogues, do we walk away with the polytheistic Socrates of Apuleius or the monotheist of Saint Augustine or the atheistic humanist of modern times or the language philosopher of present-day philosophers?

What first strikes us in Plato's dialogues is the frequency and consistency with which religious themes are introduced. God and the gods appear everywhere.[13] God, we are told, cannot cease to exist (*Phaedo* 106e) and is the creator and author of all things good and beautiful (*Sophist* 265b, *Republic* 10.597d). He is absolutely perfect and righteous (*Theaetetus* 176b) and is the immediate source of life, wisdom, and goodness (*Epinomis* 978c, 983b). He governs the world lovingly and providentially (*Statesman* 271d).

The gods, occasionally mentioned as distinguishable from God (cf. *Laws* 10.904a, *Timaeus* 41a), are repeatedly invoked, always reverently and piously. They are said to be imperishable but not eternal and are conceived of as possessing absolute knowledge (*Parmenides* 134c) and as being immune to pleasure or pain (*Philebus* 33b). Even the sun, the moon, and the planets are at times referred to as gods (*Timaeus* 40c, *Apology* 26d), and heroes like Hercules and many others are called children of the gods (*Hippias Major* 293b). Apollo is given a place of special importance and is often referred to simply as "the god." It would indeed be difficult to compile a full list of the references to God or the gods found throughout the dialogues.

More difficult, if not impossible, is to establish a criterion on the basis of which we could separate Socrates' own words from those of Plato. Yet, it might not be unreasonable to assume that at least in what is said about the gods, Socrates and Plato were not distant from each other. Apuleius and along with him many classical authors and commentators seem to be of the opinion that at least in this respect, Plato's statements reflect what Socrates believed.

Socrates' attachment to his religious beliefs is made perfectly clear by Plato. He abides by the prescribed practices and rituals and believes in the existence and providence of the gods (*Apology* 41d). He sees his entire life as a divinely appointed mission (*Apology* 28e), for it was God or the god who guided him to the life of philosophy.[14] His mature life has been shaped by his persistent endeavor to clarify the words of the Delphic oracle concerning his wisdom (*Apology* 20c ff.), and it is his obedience to Apollo that has brought him to the final predicament of his life (*Apology* 37e). To this god, he affirms (*Apology* 29d), he owes greater obedience than to the laws of the state, and in the fulfillment of his religious obligation he would rather die one hundred times than to disobey the god (*Apology* 30a).

This religious piety manifests itself in Socrates' compliance with the expected prayers and rituals of his place and time. In the *Euthydemus* (302c), he declares that, like other Athenians, he has his home altars and performs the accustomed sacrifices. In the *Cratylus* (407d), he speaks of his fear of the gods, and in the *Apology* (41d), he describes his sense of security under their providential protection. The instances in which we find him praying are many. In the *Symposium* (220d), Alcibiades tells us of how, after a long period of ecstatic trance, Socrates said his prayers to the sun and went his way. At the end of his conversation with the young Phaedrus, Socrates offers the following prayer: "Dear Pan[15] and all you other gods who dwell in this place, grant me that I may become beautiful within, and that all outward things I might possess may not war against the spirit within me. May I count him rich who is wise, and as for gold, may I possess so much of it as only a temperate man might bear and carry with him" (*Phaedrus* 279b). As death is about to overtake him, he utters this prayer: "I am allowed or rather bound to pray to the gods that my journey from this world to the other may be prosperous. This is my prayer, then, and I hope that it may be granted" (*Phaedo* 117c). His very last words are an expression of the religiosity that had imbued his life: "Crito, we ought to offer a rooster to Asclepius. See to it and do not forget" (*Phaedo* 118a).[16]

There have been many interpretations of this reported Socratic religiosity. The most common in modern times is that it does not amount to much. Few expect to find a philosopher in a constant state of prayer, for a critical and alert mind just does not go well with a pious attitude. That may or may not be so— it is probably not in the case of Socrates, if what Plato and Xenophon report has any biographical value. A reading of their testimonies and other sources leads to the undeniable reality of Socrates' profound piety, regardless of what value we may or may not attach to it. Take away from him his gods, his spiritual sign, his divinely inspired mission, his prophetic dreams, his ecstatic trances, his prayers and sacrifices, and, above all, his unshakable confidence in the Delphic god, and Socrates becomes an emaciated and skeletal figure of remarkable analytical acumen, but nothing else. He would transform himself into a specimen of analytical philosophy, impressive as an analyzer of language, but a man of no substance.

To suggest that Socrates' prayers and acts of piety were only symbolic and mythical devices through which he sought to gain the attention of his contemporaries, is simply absurd and involves an intentional traducing of the texts themselves, not only those of Plato and Xenophon, but those of later sources. We may not be in sympathy with his religious beliefs, and may not believe in God or gods, but this does not allow us to demythologize the Socratic presence. W. K. C. Guthrie, whose perceptiveness in this and other regards is commendable, put it this way: "Belief in a special, direct relation between himself [Socrates] and divine forces must be accepted in any account of his mentality which lays claim to completeness."[17]

This direct relation between Socrates and the divine can be appreciated in the episode involving the Delphic oracle mentioned by Plato and Xenophon and repeatedly reiterated in the secondary sources. In Plato's account (*Apology* 20c ff.), Socrates tells the jury how his friend Chaerephon, who was already dead by the time of the trial, once journeyed to Delphi, where he inquired from the Pythia whether there was anyone wiser than Socrates. The priestess replied that there was no one, and the perplexing answer was then brought to Socrates. Fully aware of his ignorance, however, he felt puzzled by the oracular answer and, reluctantly at first, proceeded to search for its meaning. Apollo, Socrates believed, could not deceive anyone, and yet he also knew that others were wiser than he. What, then, could be the meaning of the oracle? What did the god mean?

The search for the answer occupied him for the rest of his life, as he went from person to person looking for someone wiser than he. In the end, the solution stood clearly in his mind. He was after all the wisest of men, not because he knew or understood many things, but because he was aware of his ignorance. The others, ignorant too, were deceived by the false appearance of wisdom. He was wiser because he realized that he was not wise, but the others had failed to recognize their ignorance. Only God can be truly wise. Such is the basis of Socrates' pilgrimage and such is the impulse that stands behind his philosophizing.

As noted in the previous chapter, there is in Xenophon's writings an account of the Delphic incident that differs slightly from that of Plato. In the secondary sources, there are still other accounts. In one of them, Apollo orders Socrates to devote himself to philosophy, and, in another, Aristotle is reported to have insisted that it was Socrates, not Chaerephon, who went to Delphi (DL 2.23).

There is hardly any reason to reject *completely* the historical basis of the Delphi incident, although its details will probably never be known with certainty. The least we can say is that *some* connection between Socrates and the oracle must have been real. Certainly, we do not know *when* the oracle about him was given. Neither do we know precisely *what* the Pythia said, for in this regard there are varying reports. Nor can we speak confidently as to *why* the oracle selected Socrates as its choice for the title of the wisest of men.

What could have been the basis of the oracular answers associated with Delphi? This has been the subject of controversy and the opinions are many, ranging from the view that recognizes in them only a sham, to the idea that perhaps at times the Pythia, Apollo's priestess, in a psychedelic state caused by inhaling nitrous oxide (the "mephitic" vapor)[18] or chewing laurel or bay leaves (Apollo's plant) or as a genuine spiritual medium, transcended the parameters of time and space that normally set the limits of human knowledge. Perhaps there was a little of all sorts of things: commonplace answers, unclear pronouncements, lucky guesses, surprising coincidences, knowledge about the pilgrims obtained before their arrival in Delphi, politically arranged responses, and possibly truly inspired spiritual experiences emanating from a psychedelic or a mystical experience. The temporal and cultural gap that separates us from Delphi and the age of oracles is too wide for us to reach a definitive answer about a tradition that lasted more than one thousand years and provided so much guidance for the Greeks.

Plato's *Apology* leaves no doubt about Socrates' reaction to the oracle and about his subsequent course of action: "When I heard about the oracle's answer, I said to myself, What does the god mean? Why doesn't he use plain language? I am only too conscious that I have no claim to wisdom, great or small. So what could he mean by asserting that I am the wisest man in the world? He cannot be telling a lie, for that would not be right for him" (*Apology* 21b). With Socrates, therefore, it is a question of searching for the *meaning* of the oracle, not of testing its truthfulness.

Socrates' religiosity emerges in the clearest light in his experience of the spiritual sign or voice. As noted in the previous chapter, this experience is also reported by Xenophon, but it is in Plato's dialogues that we find the wealthiest information about it. Some passages should be quoted:

> At the moment I was about to cross the river, dear friend, there came to me my familiar sign—which always checks me when I am about to do something or other—and at once I seemed to hear a voice, forbidding me to leave the spot. (*Phaedrus* 242c)

> I happened providentially to be sitting in the place where you saw me, alone in the undressing room, and had just thought that it was time to get up. As I was getting up, however, I had my usual divine sign. So I sat down again. (*Euthydemus* 272e)

> In my own case, the divine sign is hardly worth mentioning—for I suppose it has happened to few or none before me. (*Republic* 6.496c)

> When they come back with extravagant protestations and beg for a renewal of our conversations, sometimes my divine sign, which often comes to me, forbids it. With others, however, it allows me to renew the conversations and they profit abundantly from them. (*Theaetetus* 151a)

> When you were young and your expectations were not yet mature, I would have wasted my time conversing with you, which is, I assume, why the god forbade me to speak with you. Now, however, I have his permission and I will speak with you, for you will listen. (*Alcibiades I* 105e)

> There is something spiritual that, by a divine dispensation, has accompanied me since I was a child. It is a voice that when it comes to me always prevents me from doing something I

may be about to do. It never urges me to do anything. If one of my friends consults me about doing something and I hear the voice, the same thing happens. My friend is not allowed to do what he wanted to do. (*Theages* 128d)

As I have told you on many occasions, I have devoted myself to my philosophical activities on account of the fact that I often experience a divine sign, precisely the one which has been distorted in the official indictment drawn by Meletus. This sign has accompanied me since my childhood. It is something like a voice that prevents me from pursuing certain actions, but never compels me to do anything. (*Apology* 31d)

Gentlemen of the jury—and I feel justified in calling you so— I must tell you something extraordinary. My prophetic voice, which has always accompanied me as a familiar experience, has often prevented me from doing even small things when my course of action would have been inappropriate. Now, however, when I am about to undergo something which most people deem to be the greatest human tragedy, my voice is silent. Neither on my way to the court, nor when I took my place in front of you, nor during my speech, did I hear my divine voice contradict me. At other times, however, it has stopped me even in the middle of a sentence, but at this time, it has been silent and has not stood in my way in anything I have said or done during my trial. (*Apology* 40a)

I am absolutely convinced that it is now better for me to die in order to be freed from all these aggravations. I think that this is why my divine sign has not come to me at this time. (*Apology* 41d)

He [Meletus] says I am a maker of gods and accuses me of inventing new gods and of not believing in the accepted gods. These are his grounds for prosecuting me, he says. [To which Euthyphro replies:] I understand, Socrates. It is because you often say that you experience a spiritual sign. (*Euthyphro* 3b)

Other passages could be adduced, but they would merely reiterate what is conveyed in those quoted above. As one examines them, several characteristics become evident:

- The sign has accompanied Socrates since his childhood as an indication of his special and direct relation to God. Thus, it cannot be interpreted only as the result of his pursuit of philosophy or even as a consequence of the Delphic incident. It is older than both.
- The experience of the sign was completely private, for it was only to him that it announced itself. The private character of the sign, moreover, goes hand in hand with the moments of ecstatic concentration reported by Plato (e.g., *Symposium* 175b, 220c), in which Socrates seems to have lost his awareness of the world around him. We could assume that it was during such moments, although not exclusively, that he was in tune with his unusual experience. It is possible, moreover, that he himself looked upon it as a manifestation of the "divine madness" of which he speaks in the *Phaedrus* (244a).
- The phenomenon of the sign was also characterized by its being widely known because Socrates was not reluctant to talk about it. In the *Apology* (31d), he reminds the jurors of how often he has spoken about it.
- There are several words and expressions used by Plato to refer to Socrates' experience. It was, we are told, a sign (*semeion*) or a voice (*phone*) or an admonition, generally identified as coming from God or the god, presumably Apollo. Occasionally, too, the adjectival word *demonic* is used, which is itself related to the noun *demon* (*ho daimon*). At times, it is described as God or the god manifesting himself.
- Finally, what is most distinctive in Plato's account is the negative or dissuading nature of Socrates' experience. It

acted only as a prohibitive force, and we are repeatedly told that it never urged him to follow a specific course of action.

The spectrum of interpretations of Socrates' experience is indeed wide. It varies in accordance with the interpreters' inclinations. Socrates' experience could have been an ironic device concocted by him in order to make himself famous or gain power over those around him, but it was not a real experience.

Again, it could have been, as a character in one of Plutarch's dialogues insists, a way to make sense of the natural act of sneezing: "When someone sneezed at his right, whether behind or in front, Socrates proceeded to act, but if at his left, he desisted. If he sneezed at the moment when he was about to do something, that was a sign that he should proceed. If it happened while he was doing it, that meant that he should not continue doing it" (*On the Sign of Socrates* 518a). Accordingly, Socrates, a superstitious man, believed that sneezing was an omen from the gods. Perhaps this is why we still say, "God bless you" when someone sneezes.

There is much more, however. Perhaps Socrates suffered from a psychological disorder, possibly auditory hallucinations. He thought he heard voices and thought he saw signs, but these were only present in his disoriented mind. Therefore, he was abnormal, a madman. He lived in the suspended basket of his delusions and lost touch with the reality of normal people. Like others who throughout history have displayed similar symptoms of mental imbalance, he was convinced that the secret voice that spoke to him was more real than the voices of those around him. How crazy can one be! Several writers have reached the conclusion that what the sources disclose about Socrates proves without a doubt that he was mad.[19]

Perhaps Socrates was truly mad. Madness, however, as Diogenes the Cynic—the "Socrates gone mad"—reminds us, is inevitably a relative idea. Anyone who fails to accept the reality of ordinary people, argues Diogenes, is diagnosed as mad. Yet, the fact may well be that it is *they*, the many, who are the crazy ones. The normalcy of the common person could be diagnosed as a form of madness. He may be afflicted by what Machado called "*la terrible cordura del idiota*" ("the terrible sanity of the idiot").[20] Thus, when an important writer such as Lélut concludes that "*Socrate était un fou*" ("Socrates was a madman"), perhaps it is Lélut who has lost his mind.

Then, too, there is the neoplatonic interpretation in which Socrates' experience is none other than the presence of his guardian angel or demon announcing himself to warn and guide him. Plato himself taught that each person is assigned a guardian angel whose task is to lead the soul in safety from this world to another (*Timaeus* 90a, *Statesman* 309c; cf. *Republic* 10.614c, *Phaedo* 113d). Apuleius, a neoplatonist, put it in these terms:

> All of you who hear this divine opinion of Plato, as explained by me, so adapt your minds to whatever you may have to do or to whatever may be the subject of your meditation, as men who know that there is nothing concealed from those guardians either within the mind or external to it. The demon scrupulously takes part in all these matters, sees all things, understands all things, and dwells in the most profound recesses of the mind, that is, in the seat of conscience. He of whom I speak is entirely our guardian, our proper regulator, a searcher into our inmost fibers, our constant observer, our inseparable witness, a judge of our evil actions, a supporter of our good ones. If he is rightfully attended to, carefully examined and devotedly worshiped in the way in which he was worshiped by Socrates in justice and in innocence, he is our support in uncertainty, our monitor in matters of doubt, our defender in danger, and our assistant in need.[21]

In early Christian times, the demons of which Plato and Apuleius wrote were transformed into demonic creatures, that is, into the devil's assistants, spirits who enslave souls and plunge them into the fires of hell, not without having possessed their victims and having made them mad. For demons are responsible for madness (John 8:48). In the eyes of some of the early Fathers of the Church, Socrates was precisely that, a wretched madman possessed by the devil. Only later on, through the agency of Saint Augustine, was he partly exorcised of his demoniacal possession. It is possible, argued Saint Augustine, that Socrates' experience could have been a genuine divine revelation from the true God, albeit an imperfect and obscure one (*City of God* 8.14). God may have also touched the souls of pagans like Socrates, spiritually handicapped human beings, because they did not have access to the only real source of truth—the Christian faith—but who were wise and even holy—like Socrates.

Now then, if neither a ruse concocted by the crafty Socrates nor his invention of new gods nor his misunderstanding of the nature of sneezing nor his having fallen into the clutches of the devil nor his having gone mad nor his imperfect line of communication with the true God, what then could have been the nature of his experience?

For a definitive answer we will search in vain in Xenophon's and Plato's testimonies. The answer is simply not there, nor, we may add, anywhere. The chance of finding it vanished the moment Socrates drank the cup of hemlock early in the spring of 399 BCE. Still, we could *and* will construct a tentative answer, as will be done in the two concluding chapters, where our guiding light will be a comment made by Descartes in his *Discourse on Method*. Reason, he wrote, is the voice of God that secretly speaks to every human being and is the sole method through which the truth can be discerned. Reason, understood as a commitment to critical thinking, may then be what surfaced in Socrates as his enigmatic experience. The fact that his experience was rare, if not unique, as he himself says, is understandable. Most people are only *potentially* rational. Reason lies dormant in them, and it is for this that they cannot hear its whispering voice in the obfuscated recesses of their consciousness.

We can now bring to a close this brief review of Plato's testimony with comments on how reason in the sense of critical thinking surfaced in Socrates, specifically in the context of his stance vis-à-vis the religious ideas of his contemporaries. This stance appears in countless passages from the dialogues, but it is in the *Euthyphro* where we find its clearest appearance.

This dialogue revolves around the idea of piety. This idea, central to the religious beliefs and practices of the time, was constantly invoked by people who, like Euthyphro, claimed to be experts in religious matters—those whom we might call today theologians. They had nourished their expertise in religion by learning from poets like Hesiod and Homer, from whom practically all that was known about the gods was derived. Their tales and moralistic teachings were memorized and endlessly repeated, and questions and issues about the morality of human actions were answered by an appeal to their teachings, not unlike modern preachers who mechanically quote biblical verses in a parrotlike fashion. Those who, like Euthyphro, knew such tales were considered fountains of wisdom. After all, if piety was understood as the essence of righteousness *and* as doing what is pleasing to the gods, knowledge about the gods themselves was indispensable.

Yet, as the inquisitive Socrates questions the simpleminded Euthyphro, furnishing us with the most impressive display of the Socratic method—the *elenchus*—it becomes as clear as daylight that the pious man knows virtually nothing about piety. Despite his protestations to the contrary, his tales are filled with humbug and his definitions are laden with contradictions. Neither his definitions nor his religious tales impress Socrates, who at some point asks him, "Is not this, the reason, Euthyphro, why

I am being indicted, that when people tell such stories about the gods I find it hard to accept them? Do you really believe that these things happened and that there was war among the gods, and fearful enmities and battles and other things of the sort, such as we are told by the poets?" (*Euthyphro* 6a–c). No, Socrates refuses to give his assent to such tales. To believe that the gods were capable of doing everything that is shameful for human beings—murder, deception, theft, adultery, rape—*that* would not be possible for him. His reported religiosity notwith-standing, he cannot believe these and other absurdities. A dosage of critical thinking is all that it takes to make them dis-sipate into thin air as children's tales of no consequence. And if that is so, the definition of piety in terms of doing the will of the gods turns out to be an example of empty talk of no value. Set-ting aside faith and tradition, one must be prepared to appeal to reason as the ultimate judge in such matters, whatever its final verdict may be. Hence, we witness his impatience and restless-ness in regard to religious beliefs that surface over and over again in his conversations.

As noted earlier, it is practically impossible to reach a firm conclusion about the exact nature of Socrates' views about reli-gious issues. All we can affirm, if Plato's testimony is to be trusted, is that Socrates did not feel comfortable with the teach-ings of the poets recited thoughtlessly by many. In the *Apology* (41a), he expresses his hope that, if there is consciousness after death, he would be able to question the poets about their reputed knowledge, just as, we may add, he questioned Euthyphro.

Together with this modest affirmation, we could bring to mind Socrates' consequent refusal to define ethical norms in terms of religious beliefs. The classical passage in which this Socratic stance is found comes once more from the *Euthyphro* (10a), where Socrates says to Euthyphro: "Just consider this question. Is that which is holy loved by the gods because it is holy, or is it holy because it is loved by the gods?" Obviously, if that which is holy is holy because it is loved by the gods, then the basis of morality depends solely on their will, which is never clearly known, or which, even when explicitly revealed, has often commanded abominable actions. If what the gods love is holy because they love it, ethical values are at the mercy of whimsical divine entities. If, however, the gods love what is holy because it itself is holy, then ethical values are independent of their will, and religious beliefs are ultimately of no consequence for the determination of what is right and what is wrong.

Thus, to determine what is right or wrong, it is necessary to search for the proper definition of these concepts and discover their essence, an essence that is independent of divine commands and human opinions. This is, however, a strictly rational undertaking in which only the light of reason, which is accessible through the sort of experience of which Socrates spoke. That light shines sometimes brightly, more often dimly, in the recesses of what Apuleius called conscience. For us to grasp the significance of that light, it is necessary to undertake once more an examination of Plato's testimony. Setting aside its biographical components and other details about Socrates, we must ask, therefore, what philosophical convictions can we attribute to him on the basis of what Plato wrote about him?

An outline of a possible answer to this question, indeed *the* crucial question about Socrates, will be the theme of the two concluding chapters.

As has been stated, the complexity of the Socratic problem makes it impossible to speak with complete confidence about the historical import of any of the sources of information, primary or secondary. This includes Plato's testimony. Undoubtedly, there is much in his dialogues, particularly in the middle and late dialogues, that probably does not belong to Socrates. In this respect, those who literally since his death have insisted that Plato ascribed to him much that he never said or even thought may be right.

Nevertheless, it must have been largely Socrates who impelled Plato on his philosophical journey. We would not be mistaken in assuming that whatever ideas Plato developed in his mature years and whatever he concluded about the nature of reality and human existence owes its genesis to the presence of Socrates. Thus, it is impossible to speak about Socrates' philosophy unless we take into account Plato's ideas. The reverse is also true. At least from the point of view of *our* understanding of Socrates as a monumental philosopher, Plato must be our guide.

Furthermore, if Schopenhauer was correct in affirming that no one can see over his own height and no one can see in another person any more than he already has in himself,[22] then a way out of the Socratic problem can be suggested. It took someone of the intellectual and spiritual height of Plato to capture the enormity of Socrates' mind because of the enormity of his own mind.

NOTES

1. The swan was Apollo's sacred bird (cf. *Phaedo* 85a).

2. F. Schleiermacher, *Introductions to the Dialogues of Plato* (New York: Arno Press, 1973).

3. The word *elenchus* stands for any form of interrogation or questioning in which short answers are expected to pointed questions.

4. The prytanes or senators were members of the council ruling Athens. They were chosen monthly by sortition.

5. Foreigners, slaves, and women were not allowed to address the juries. They had to be represented by a citizen.

6. Socrates' age at the time of his trial is also mentioned in the *Crito* (52e). There are two manuscript variations of *Apology* 17d: one reads that Socrates was seventy years old and the other that he was more than seventy.

7. The Panathenaea was a yearly festival celebrated in Athens on the birthday of Athena.

8. The Ceramicus was an Athenian neighborhood located below the Acropolis, mostly inhabited by artisans and other working people.

9. F. W. Nietzsche, *Thus Spake Zarathustra*, #4 (New York: Modern Library, 1954).

10. The Sileni and the Satyrs were conceived of as spirits of wild life who lived in the woods. Bestial and lascivious in their behavior and ugly in their features, they resembled monstrous horses and goats.

11. Achilles was the famous commander of the Trojan War. Nestor and Antenor were legendary personages also associated with this war. Brasidas (d. 422 BCE) was an important Spartan general. Among the ancient Greeks, men such as these were often mentioned as examples of great virtues.

12. *Theages* is a dialogue of dubious authenticity. Most scholars attribute it to a Hellenistic writer. The reference to the magic touch of Socrates is one of the reasons for doubting its authenticity. Authentic or not, however, it contributes to the portrayal of Socrates created by Plato and by Platonic authors after him.

13. The Greek word for *god* is *theos*. A problem encountered in translating this word into modern languages is that in ancient Greek there was no distinction between capital and small letters. Originally, everything was written in capitals. Furthermore, the definite article *the* (expressed in Greek as *ho*) was often used indiscriminately. Thus, *god* and *the god* in the same sense appear without distinction.

14. See note 13.

15. Pan was originally a rural deity portrayed in the form of a half-man, half-goat that exhibited uncontrolled sexual desires. There is, however, another mythological tradition in which Pan was conceived of as the universal god, the all-god, or the god of all, somewhat reminiscent of what is referred to as God in monotheistic religions like Christianity. Pan's name is related to the Greek word for *all*.

16. Roosters were customarily offered as sacrificial animals to Asclepius, the god of medicine when, through his power, the sick were healed. Socrates' offer at the moment of his life makes sense: Asclepius was about to cure him from the worst disease—life.

17. W. K. C. Guthrie, *Socrates* (London: Cambridge University Press, 1971), p. 84.

18. Nitrous oxide (N_2O), otherwise known as dinitrogen monoxide or laughing gas, is one of the several oxides of nitrogen that, when inhaled, produces insensibility to pain, mild hysteria, and occasionally laughter. Known also as the metaphysical gas, nitrous oxide is said to have been found in volcanic cracks underneath the ruins of Apollo's temple at Delphi, which has led some to explain the phenomena of oracular divination at Delphi in terms of psychedelic intoxication. William James observes that nitrous oxide "stimulates the mystical consciousness in an extraordinary degree. Depth beyond depth of truth seems revealed to the inhaler." James, who experimented with this gas, notes that

> one conclusion was forced upon my mind at that time, and my impression of its truth has ever since remained unshaken. It is that our normal waking consciousness, rational consciousness as we call it, is but one special type of consciousness, whilst all about it, parted from it by the filmiest of screens, there lie potential forms of consciousness entirely different. We may go through life without suspecting their existence; but apply the requisite stimulus, and at a touch they are there, in all their completeness, definite types of mentality which probably somewhere have their field of application and adaptation. (*The Varieties of Religious Experience: A Study in Human Nature* (London: Longmans, Green, and Co., 1929), pp. 378–79.

19. L. Lélut's *Du démon de Socrate. Specimen d'une application de la science psychologique à celle de l'histoire* (Paris: Trinquart, 1836).

20. A. Machado, "Un loco," in *Obras Completas. Poesía y Prosa* (Madrid: Editorial Losada, 1964), p. 140.

21. Apuleius, *The Works of Apuleius* (London: G. Bell and Sons, 1914), pp. 365–66.

22. A. Schopenhauer, *Complete Essays of Schopenhauer*, vol. 2 (New York: Wiley, 1942), p. 67.

CHAPTER 5
Socrates in Aristotle

ristotle's testimony on Socrates is important as a criterion to identify the elements in Plato's writings that can be associated with Socrates and those that may be Platonic extensions of Socrates' thought. Unlike the primary-source authors with whom we have been concerned, Aristotle was not directly acquainted with Socrates, although his relationship with Plato and others among Socrates' associates must have furnished him with significant knowledge about him. This association, no less than his intellectual depth, may be a sufficient ground for reflecting attentively on his testimony. He has been viewed by some as our most important and impartial witness of the Socratic presence.[1]

There are about fifty references to Socrates in Aristotle's extant works. These can be arranged into five groups: grammatical references, references to the Socrates of Plato's writings, direct references to the historical Socrates, observations about the so-called Socratic discourses or dialogues, and statements about Socratic sources other than Plato.

The grammatical references, of course, have no special significance because in them, the name of Socrates is used only as an instance of a proper name for which any other name could be substituted. Such is the case in *Topics* (103a) and *Sophistical Arguments* (160b, 166b). The import of such passages can be gathered from this example from *Sophistical Arguments* (160b): "'He who sits, writes', and 'Socrates is sitting', from which it follows that 'Socrates is writing.'" *Rhetoric* (1356b) and *Metaphysics* (981a) are additional instances of this grammatical usage.

There are fifteen explicit references to the Platonic Socrates in which there can be little doubt that Aristotle meant to say something about the Socrates of Plato's dialogues, whom, in those instances, he identified with Plato himself. Of special interest is the reference to the Socrates of the *Laws*, a dialogue in which Socrates is actually *not* present. As in other Greek texts, Aristotle writes "Socrates" and "the Socrates" interchangeably because the Greek definite article (*ho*, the) is sometimes used and sometimes omitted before proper names.

In these references, we come across statements about Socrates' (that is, Plato's) theory of ideal Forms and its role in the explanation of natural processes. There are numerous comments on the political ideas put forward by Plato in the name of Socrates, especially as these emerge in the *Republic*. In other references, we hear about Socrates' (that is, Plato's) views about music and the importance of these views in the formation of character and about an assortment of other subjects.

Far more significant for our understanding of Socrates, however, are Aristotle's references, in which it is reasonably clear that the subject is the historical Socrates, not the character in Plato's dialogues. Twenty-seven such references can be cited. In none of them, unfortunately, do we encounter much information about the details of Socrates' life, which is not surprising. Aristotle was not a biographer. His comments about his predecessors usually are made in the context of some philosophical discussion in which the assumed aim is to convince us of the correctness of his conclusions. It is generally in this context that he mentions Socrates. These are the references (identified by the symbol •):

- This is the reason why Socrates would only ask questions without answering them. He maintained that he did not know. (*Sophistical Arguments* 183b)

- What is the reason why men who are famous in philosophy, politics, poetry, or the arts invariably have an atrabilious [melancholic] character? Many appear to have been affected in this way, among them Empedocles, Plato, and Socrates, and many other famous philosophers and poets. (*Problems* 953a)

The affliction (*melancholia*) was believed to be the result of an excess of black bile (*melas chole*; in Latin, *atra bilis*, hence its English name). It would cause fits of anger or bad temper or epileptic seizures.

- In his youth, Plato became acquainted with Cratylus' and Heraclitus' idea that all perceptible objects are in a state of change and that there can be no knowledge about them. He accepted these ideas even in his later years. Socrates, however, was concerned with ethical issues and was generally uninterested in the natural world, since his concern was only the identification of the true definitions of ethical terms. He was the first to direct his attention to the problem of definition. Plato accepted this teaching, but argued that the problem did not apply to the objects of sense perception because they are always changing. (*Metaphysics* 987a–b)

Here, in unambiguous language, Socrates and Plato are contrasted. Plato's preoccupation was epistemological and metaphysical, and his recourse was to conceive of transcendent ideal Forms, whereas Socrates remained involved in ethical matters, oblivious of the world of nature and of any world beyond human experience. Aristotle reiterates the same point in the two subsequent passages.

- Socrates turned his attention to the study of ethical virtues and was the first to look into the possibility of defining ethical concepts. Since he was endeavoring to approach this issue in a logical way, it was appropriate for him to inquire into the essence of things, for the essence is always the starting point of logical reasoning. There are two discoveries that can be definitely attributed to him, and these are inductive reasoning and universal definition, both of which are unquestionably the basis of scientific reasoning. Socrates did not view universals or definitions as capable of separate existence, in the fashion of the Platonists who referred to them as ideal Forms conceived of as ideas independent of realities. (*Metaphysics* 1078b)

- Socrates was responsible for the genesis of the theory of ideal Forms on account of his search for universal definitions, but was correct in not conceiving of universals as existing in separation from particulars. (*Metaphysics* 1086b)

- Socrates understood courage as a form of knowledge on account of the fact that experience of particular situations is generally thought to be courage. (*Nicomachean Ethics* 1116b)

- Ironic persons, who undervalue themselves, appear to be more attractive in character, for they give the impression of avoiding ostentation. As in the instance of Socrates, such people care little for things that bring about reputation. (*Nicomachean Ethics* 1127b)

- Socrates was correct in some respects but mistaken in others in maintaining that the moral virtues are forms of practical knowledge. He was wrong in saying that virtue and practical knowledge are identical, but right in his idea that all virtues involve or imply practical knowledge. He viewed all virtues as forms of knowledge. We affirm, however, that all virtues entail some form of practical knowledge, but are not identical with any form of knowledge. (*Nicomachean Ethics* 1144b)

The issue here is Socrates' conviction that it is impossible to do evil while knowing that what is done is evil. Evil is, therefore, the necessary consequence of ignorance, and knowledge becomes the necessary *and* sufficient condition for virtue. Stupid people do stupid things. This conviction is at the heart of Socrates' philosophical mission, for in seeking the enlightenment of people, he expected to render them better persons. In the *Protagoras* (352c), he reminds Protagoras that "knowledge is a fine thing quite capable of ruling a person. If a person can distinguish good from evil, nothing will force him to act otherwise than as knowledge dictates, since wisdom is all the reinforcement he needs." In Aristotle's view, knowledge is a necessary *but not* a sufficient condition for virtue. Hence, Socrates was mistaken. It *is* possible to do evil while knowing that it is evil. It is not true that *only* stupid people do stupid or evil things.

- The question must be raised, how is it possible for a person, whose judgment is correct, to act without self-restraint?[2] According to some, this is an impossibility. In Socrates' view, knowledge is not the sort of thing that can be overpowered and dragged about as if it were a slave. He was, therefore, convinced that there is no such a thing as lack of self-restraint in the presence of knowledge, for nobody, according to him, does anything wrong with full knowledge that what he does is wrong. People do wrong only as a result of their ignorance. Clearly, this idea stands in opposition to the facts revealed by experience. (*Nicomachean Ethics* 1145b)

- The way in which ignorance is dispelled and the person of no self-restraint gains knowledge is similar to that in which

someone who is drunk or asleep recovers his full consciousness. [In reality, the person of no self-restraint does not have
knowledge in the full sense of the term and acts as if in a state
of intellectual confusion, for which reason,] the view maintained by Socrates appears to be tenable. Lack of self-restraint
develops, not in the presence of what can be called full knowledge in the proper sense, but in the presence of apparent
knowledge. [As Socrates maintained,] full knowledge cannot
be dragged about by the emotions. (*Nicomachean Ethics* 1147b)

In the *Protagoras* (352c), Socrates militates against the idea that
knowledge can be pushed around by emotions as if it were
nothing but a slave. Knowledge always can and does control emotions. Aristotle replies that lack of self-control arises when the
person does not know *at the moment* that what he is about to do is
evil. In this reply, he supports to some extent Socrates' conviction.

- Socrates spoke better and more in depth about the nature
  of the ethical virtues [than his predecessors], but was
  unsuccessful in clarifying the issue. He made the mistake
  of equating virtue and knowledge. The fact is that knowledge entails reasoning, and this belongs to the intellectual
  faculty of the soul. In Socrates' view, virtue also resides in
  this intellectual faculty. We can conclude on the basis of
  such a view that, in transforming virtue into knowledge,
  he attempted to eliminate the non-rational aspects of the
  soul, that is, emotion and moral character. Thus, he failed
  to gain clarity in his efforts to elucidate the nature of the
  moral virtues. (*Magna Moralia* 1182a)

- Socrates was in error in insisting on identifying virtue
  with knowledge. Although he believed that nothing exists
  in vain, he eventually succeeded in reducing the virtues to
  something useless. (*Magna Moralia* 1183b)

- According to Socrates, it is not really up to us to be either virtuous or evil, because no one is actually willing to choose evil or injustice over virtue. From this we can apparently deduce that those who are evil or vicious are so only involuntarily [that is, out of ignorance]. Likewise, those who are virtuous or good are so also involuntarily. (*Magna Moralia* 1187a)

"But," Aristotle adds, "this is plainly false" because it implies that no one is good or evil by choice. In the *Meno* (78a), Socrates asks whether anyone wants to be unhappy and unfortunate, and, as Meno replies negatively, the conclusion is reached that nobody desires or chooses evil.

- Socrates was mistaken in his contention that courage is a form of knowledge. (*Magna Moralia* 1190b)

- Socrates' statement that virtue is knowledge is erroneous, as is his idea that brave and just actions are meaningless unless they are done with knowledge and are the result of some rationally conceived goal. (*Magna Moralia* 1198a)

- Socrates the older rejected the possibility of lack of self-restraint while possessing knowledge, and was convinced that no one would ever knowingly choose to do wrong. (*Magna Moralia* 1200b)

Socrates the older refers to Socrates himself. There may have been another Socrates, Socrates the younger, who could have been a student of Plato. Practically nothing is known about him and his very existence has been doubted.

- According to Socrates the older, the goal should always be the knowledge of virtue. His concern was the clarification of justice, courage, and the other virtues. He thought that virtue and knowledge were the same, so that virtue and the knowledge of virtue were attained at the same time. (*Eudemian Ethics* 1216b)

- We can distinguish several types of courage. One is political courage, which is related to shame, and another is military courage, which is related to knowledge, and not, as Socrates thought, to fear. (*Eudemian Ethics* 1229a)

- As in the instance of soldiers, people who face danger with the knowledge given by experience are not really brave. The fact is quite different from what Socrates thought, as for him, courage is knowledge. (*Eudemian Ethics* 1230a)

- There are some who say that we should only love that which is useful, and this can be shown by the circumstance that everybody keeps the useful but casts away the useless, as Socrates the older used to say about spittle, hair, and nails. We throw away what is not useful, as when we dispose of the bodies of the dead, for such bodies are not useful. When such bodies have some use, as among the Egyptians, we keep them. (*Eudemian Ethics* 1235a)

According to Xenophon, Socrates' words are these: "A man's dearest friend is himself. Yet, even in his lifetime, he removes or lets another remove from his body whatever is useless and unprofitable. He removes his own nails, hair, and corns. He lets the surgeon cut and cauterize him, and aches and pains notwithstanding, he feels bound to thank and pay him for it. He spits saliva from his mouth as far as he can, because to retain it does not help him, but harms him" (*Memorabilia* 1.2.54). In the same context, Socrates speaks of the body as something that ought to be disposed of quickly and without ceremony (cf. *Phaedo* 115e).

In *Eudemian Ethics* (1247b), Socrates is reported as having said that wisdom sometimes comes to us by sheer luck. A similar statement is found in Plato's *Euthydemus* (279d): "Wisdom, I suppose, is good fortune. Even a child would know that."

- In the generations of human beings, as much as with the products of the earth, the outcome is not constant. When the roots are healthy, eminent persons are born, but then there is a period of decadence. An intelligent lineage may degenerate towards insanity, as with the descendants of Alcibiades and Dionysius the Elder, or a strong lineage toward stupidity and vulgarity, as with the descendants of Cimon, Pericles, and Socrates. (*Eudemian Ethics* 1247b)

This allusion to Socrates' family, the only one found in Aristotle's works, suggests that his children did not amount to anything and that they grew up stupid and vulgar, which is confirmed by Plutarch (*Cato* 20).

- The officers of the State [according to Socrates] should not be chosen by lot, for that would be like selecting athletes at random instead of by their best qualities for a competition, or like choosing the captain of a ship by lot. In these cases, we would be compelled to select the man chosen by lot, without regard to his knowledge. (*Rhetoric* 1393b)

- We are told that Socrates refused to go to the court of Archelaus[3] because, according to Socrates, it is an insult not to be able to repay favors, as well as not to be able to return offenses. (*Rhetoric* 1398a)

- Once when Plato spoke too dogmatically about a subject, Aristippus reminded him that their friend Socrates never spoke dogmatically about anything whatsoever. (*Rhetoric* 1398b)

This passage is particularly interesting. It reveals the differences among the associates of Socrates with respect to his views and attitudes. These differences seem to have given rise to open animosity. Aristippus, who in the *Phaedo* (59c), is said to have been in Aegina at the time of Socrates' death, disparaged Plato "by saying that [Plato] was not present at the death of Socrates, although he was no farther off than Aegina" (DL 3.36).[4] This animosity was even more pronounced between Plato and the Cynics, especially Antisthenes and Diogenes. Graphic descriptions of it abound in the secondary sources. It was probably based on personal differences, as well as on ideological disagreements born out of their interpretations of Socrates' teachings and example. Of special significance is a brief yet revealing anecdote recounted by Diogenes Laertius (6.53) that deserves to be quoted. It discloses the prevailing climate of disagreement: "As Plato was once talking about ideal Forms and using words like Tablehood and Cuphood, he [Diogenes the Cynic] said to him, 'Table and cup I see, but your Tablehood and Cuphood I cannot see'. 'That is easily accounted for', replied Plato, 'for you have eyes to see the visible table and cup, but not the mind to understand Tablehood and Cuphood'."[5] One cannot help wondering whether Socrates himself had the necessary mind to understand concepts like Tablehood and Cuphood. At least from what we learn from Aristotle, Socrates did not have *that kind* of mind. He had little use for such transcendent ideas. He remained, according to Aristotle and the Cynics, with his feet firmly planted in the world of human experience, where the only tables and cups that exist are those we can see and touch.

- With respect to interrogation (*elenchus*), one should make ample use of it when one's interlocutor has replied in such a way that by merely eliciting from him one more answer, he stands convicted of absurdity. When Meletus, for instance, insisted that Socrates denied the existence of the gods while admitting the reality of his divine sign, Socrates asked him whether spiritual signs were not either the offspring of the gods or something divine. "Yes," said Meletus. "Can there be any person," asked Socrates, "who accepts the existence of the offspring of the gods and not the reality of the gods themselves?" (*Rhetoric* 1419a)

- Our predecessors were unable to discover the appropriate method of dealing with the subject [of definition], because they were uninterested in the idea of essence or in the definition of substance. Even Democritus, who was somewhat close to the solution, was unable to employ it as the only approach to natural philosophy. When he came close to it, it was only by the sheer force of the evidence. During Socrates' time, there was a closer approach, although at that time, people had set aside all inquiries about the natural world, and philosophers had turned their eyes to political philosophy and to the study of useful virtues. (*Parts of Animals* 642a)

There are additional passages in Aristotle's extant works in which he speaks of the so-called Socratic discourses or dialogues. These, however, do not provide any information about Socrates. There is also one passage that deals with sources other than Plato. In it, we learn about a work by Theodectes (375–334 BCE), who was possibly a student of Plato and Aristotle. Nothing else is known about this work, *Apology of Socrates*, aside from Aristotle's reference to it in *Rhetoric* (1399c), where the author rhetorically asks, "Did Socrates dishonor any temple? What gods of the state did he fail to treat reverently?"

By the time Aristotle first came to Athens, that is, around 367 BCE, many of those who had been associated with Socrates must have still been alive. Likewise, many writings about him must have been readily available. Information about him was plentiful in the form of oral reports, as well as in writings. This is especially pertinent in the case of Aristotle, who lived for at least twenty years in the midst of a Socratic circle such as the Academy and who is known to have been an avid reader and a collector of books. The house occupied by him while at the Academy was known as "the house of the reader." Both at the Academy and even more so at the Lyceum, the school he founded, he had at his disposal a wonderful treasure of documents that allowed him to amass the encyclopedic knowledge associated with Aristotelian traditions.

It is, therefore, reasonable to assume that his statements about Socrates, although brief and marginal, are valuable. In mentioning Socrates, he was neither attacking and ridiculing him, as was the case with Aristophanes, nor was he constructing the sort of eulogy we encounter in Xenophon. Least of all, Aristotle was not engaged in developing his ideas as extensions of what Socrates might have thought and said, as, according to some, was the case with Plato.

From a study of Aristotle's references, we can reconstruct his portrait of Socrates, a portrait significantly less comprehensive than what we find in Plato's dialogues and even in the writings of Xenophon. Not for this, however, is the Aristotelian portrait less distinct. This reconstruction can be done by examining those references in which he seems to have had the historical Socrates in mind.

Aristotle's portrait of Socrates discloses only a few features and its scope is narrow. This reflects the character of *all* the historical and biographical passages found in Aristotle's works. In them, seldom, if ever, do we find detailed accounts or descriptive delineations of situations or persons. Aristotle was neither a historian nor a biographer. In mentioning this or that detail about Socrates, it was not his intent to furnish us with a description of Socrates or an account of his ideas. The name of Socrates invariably appears in the context of a larger subject under discussion and always marginally. He appealed to Socrates, no less than to his other predecessors, as a touchstone for testing his own views and theories. Still, Aristotle's testimony may be useful as a litmus test to measure the biographical and historical value of other testimonies, particularly those of Plato and Xenophon.

Aristotle's references to Socrates can be classified in several groups that include comments about his family, observations about his character, notices about his political views, statements about his method and philosophical orientation, criticisms related to his interpretation of the relationship between knowledge and virtue, and assertions regarding the ideological kinship between Socrates and Plato.

The only reference to Socrates' family is found in *Rhetoric* (1390b), where we are told that "in the generations of human beings, as much as with the products of the earth, the outcome is not constant." Sometimes a great and distinguished man can be the father of stupid and vulgar children. According to Aristotle, such was the case with Socrates. As noted earlier, nothing definite is known about his children, except for their names and their approximate ages at the time of his death. Xenophon described Lamprocles, the oldest son, as unruly toward his mother.

We do not know on what basis Aristotle felt justified in speaking about Socrates' children as "stupid and vulgar." It is possible that he could have been acquainted with them because they were younger than Plato and probably lived in Athens during the first four or five decades of the fourth century BCE, when Aristotle was in the city.

There are four statements concerning Socrates' character. In *Problems* (953a), we are told that like other eminent philosophers, he was atrabilious, or melancholic. Nothing of this, however, can be gathered from Plato or Xenophon. Yet, on the basis of their testimonies, it seems evident that Socrates was a man constantly at war with several ingrained character traits that he sought to correct. His physiognomy, coarse and erotic, revealed an emotional and irascible nature, which, like a wild steed, would have easily led him astray, had it not been for his formidable strength of will—or, rather, strength of mind—which allowed him to maintain his character in a state of subjection. His regime of discipline, of which we learn the details in the *Symposium* (220b ff.), was the instrument with which he succeeded in remodeling and refining his inborn personality. In the end, he discloses himself to us as a perfect master of himself who kept his passions and appetites under complete control.

We can assume that just as he subdued his ferocious sexual impulses, hinted at in the *Charmides*, he also conquered his other natural tendencies, including his melancholic bent. In him, if we may borrow Aristotle's language, we find a potentially melancholic man who in actuality was far from being so. The self-restrained and polite Socrates of Plato's dialogues and the relaxed and composed Socrates of Xenophon's writings must be viewed as the finished product of a long struggle toward the complete taming of the natural beast within. Like Saint Paul, with whom the idea of regeneration or rebirth of the old man into a new man is so appropriately associated (Gal. 6:15, where we are told how "the old things are passed away" and how "they have become new"), Socrates, too, could have claimed that he made of himself a new man, not through the liberating power of Christ that brought the transformation in the apostle, but through the overwhelming strength of reason actualized in the daily practice of ethical discipline. The original Socrates—the Socratic *homo vetus*, the old man—could have been, as Aristotle says, atrabilious and irascible, but the final Socrates—the Socratic *homo novus*, the new man—was something altogether different. His inborn physiognomy, as Phaedo's *Zopyrus* tells us,[6] could have disclosed to the perceptive observer a man full of lust and bestiality reminiscent of the Sileni and the Satyrs. Yet, in his innermost being, a more powerful spiritual reality reigned supreme.

There are several references in Plato's dialogues that describe strange fits of listlessness that afflicted Socrates. Of these, nothing is said by Xenophon. In such fits, Socrates would literally lose the world around him and would become motionless and unaware of his surroundings. They were seen by many as manifestations of what was known as "the divine disease," moments when it was thought that a line of communication between the afflicted person and a transcendent divine realm was established. He would be literally *seized* or *possessed* by a force outside of him. For this reason, this condition was known as epilepsy, which literally means 'being taken over' as in a seizure. Aristotle, reflecting Hippocratic traditions, associates it with melancholy, which was caused, it was believed, by an excess of black bile. In Socrates' case, it seems to have manifested in various ways, including in his reported fits of epileptic listlessness.[7] Protruding eyes, such as those of Socrates, as described by Xenophon and Plato, are occasionally viewed as symptoms of this condition.

In *Nicomachean Ethics* (1127b), Aristotle speaks of Socrates as an ironic person. Such people, he tells us, are prone to undervalue themselves in the presence of others, giving the impression of avoiding ostentation and praise. In Plato's early dialogues and occasionally in Xenophon's writings, Socrates' irony or mock modesty appears in the form of his repeated avowal of ignorance about the subjects under discussion. He claims to know little or nothing and hopes to learn from others. His memory is defective and he needs to hear what he is told over and over again. He finds it difficult to follow the thread of the arguments proposed by his interlocutors.

Whether or not Socrates was ironic precisely in the sense in which Aristotle understood it, is a difficult issue to resolve. He might have been honestly self-deprecating and humble, the sort of person who is not unwilling to put down himself and his accomplishments. And so it seems from innumerable passages in Plato's dialogues and statements in the secondary sources. In the

Euthyphro, for instance, Socrates tells us how lucky indeed he is to have come upon Euthyphro at so critical a time in his life—moments before his trial. He is lucky, he insists, because in Euthyphro he has found a golden treasure of wisdom, the wisdom that he himself is lacking. What could this reveal if not sincere self-depreciation and humility?

Yet, it is also conceivable that Socrates' irony could have been an artful device with which he sought to pursue his philosophical mission. Aristotle rightly notes that genuine irony can render a person attractive and likeable. People invariably like those who confess their inferiority because that confirms their own sense of superiority. In the case of Socrates, however, what we discover in the sources is quite different. Instances of anger toward him abound in them. In Xenophon's *Memorabilia*, Charicles accuses Socrates of asking questions when he knows the answer. From *his* point of view, Socrates' confession of ignorance was false and camouflaged arrogance or, at least, snobbishness. Still, what then can *we* say about his irony?

In *Rhetoric* (1398a), Aristotle recounts the story that once, when Archelaus, the king of Macedonia, invited Socrates to his court, he turned down the invitation, saying that it was an insult to invite someone who could not repay the favor. Like Diogenes and other Cynics of later times, he asserted his independence from monarchs and men of power, showing to us his commitment to be self-sufficient in their presence. He displayed toward the king the same disdain shown by Diogenes toward Alexander the Great, Archelaus' ancestor. Once, when Alexander invited Diogenes to come to his presence, the Cynic sent him this caustic reply: "You are too important to need me and I am too independent to need you."[8] On another occasion, when Alexander went to visit Diogenes, he offered him half his possessions if he taught him how to be happy. Barely looking at him, Diogenes, who was warming himself under the sun, mumbled to him, "Just stand out of my light." If the story about

Socrates and Archelaus recounted by Aristotle is genuine, and if the passages in Plato's dialogues in which Socrates' disdain toward those in authority are biographical, there should not be anything surprising in the Cynics' contention that they saw in him a paradigm for their independence and self-sufficiency.

In *Rhetoric* (1398b), we come upon a brief yet revealing statement of Aristotle. We are told that Aristippus of Cyrene, an important associate of Socrates, once reminded Plato that Socrates never spoke dogmatically about anything. To be dogmatic, of course, means to be certain about one's convictions and to be unwilling to accept divergent ideas. The absence of dogmatism is one of the most salient characteristics of Socrates, as he is revealed to us in Plato's early dialogues. He claims to know little or nothing and often acts if he were in a cloud of confusion. As he insists during his trial, it is the recognition of his lack of wisdom that constitutes, if anything, the only wisdom he possesses. He suspends judgment about what others claim to know, laying bare his ignorance. He is a skeptic, that is, a searcher for the truth.[9] If he had attained it, why should he be looking for it? Accordingly, dogmatism was foreign to him, which is precisely Aristippus's point: "Our friend Socrates never spoke dogmatically about anything whatsoever." The one guilty of dogmatism, according to Aristippus, was Plato. But could that be so?

A critical reading of Plato's middle and late dialogues gives us a hint about the veracity of Aristippus's complaint—assuming that such a complaint was actually made and that Aristotle's report is trustworthy. As has been noted, Socrates appears in all of Plato's dialogues, with one exception, the *Laws*. It does not take much effort, however, to realize that as the sequence of the dialogues progresses from the earliest to the latest, the character of Socrates changes slowly yet steadily until he succeeds in shedding his early skepticism and uncertainty, replacing it with an undeniable air of dogmatism and certainty. The Socrates who speaks in the *Phaedo* knows that the soul is immortal, and the Socrates of the *Republic* has arrived at a precise definition of justice. The Socrates of later dialogues knows this and much more. What could have happened to the real Socrates?

Well, if Aristotle's testimony has any value, what happened to Socrates is simply that his presence was taken over by Plato. He was no longer the philosopher who, according to Aristotle, would only ask questions without answering them because he did not have the answers. He transformed himself into a philosopher who was assured of his views and firm in his conclusions, as Plato assuredly was. His seemingly unending search had come to an end. He had at last found the truth. Furthermore, his exclusive preoccupation with ethical and political issues, and his obsession with clarifying the terms involved in them—of which Aristotle wrote in his testimony about him—was expanded to include metaphysical and cosmological matters. In those transformations, however, it is probably not the historical Socrates who changed but Plato himself who asserted his presence as *the* successor of Socrates.

What Plato did is perfectly understandable and, indeed, expected in the development of philosophy. Unlike in religious traditions in which the succession from master to disciple generally takes the form of a repetition of the dogmas learned, in the transmission of philosophical ideas we encounter something altogether different. In philosophy, of course, there are neither masters nor disciples. What a philosopher has taught is taken over by others who subject those teachings to profound transformations and even radical distortions. It has to be so.

In Socrates, possibly more than in other philosophers, we witness a seminal mind that planted its seeds in various kinds of soil, from which idiosyncratic growths emerged. From Antisthenes, a close associate of Socrates, sprang Cynicism, and partly from his influence sprang Diogenes in whom Socrates' mode of life and convictions reappeared but were radicalized and exaggerated. The case is similar with others among the Socratics. This is particularly evident in the eventual development of Plato's thought.

Aristotle may have been correct in asserting in *Metaphysics* (1086b) that Socrates was responsible for the *genesis* of the theory of ideal Forms. He planted the seed, so to speak. In Plato, however, the seed grew like a towering tree as an epistemological and metaphysical interpretation of reality at large. Had Socrates lived long enough to behold such a tree, it is difficult to say what his reaction would have been. He might have congratulated Plato for his depth and perceptiveness and might have even embraced the theory of ideal Forms. He might have, however, agreed with his descendant, Diogenes, who spoke of the theory of ideal Forms as a waste of time and of Plato as a man who talked a great deal without ever saying anything.

If Aristotle's testimony is to be taken seriously, it is difficult not to distinguish the historical Socrates, so beautifully described in Plato's early dialogues, from the Platonic Socrates. It is possible to squeeze the primary and secondary sources to the last drop in order to identify in them the lessons taught by the historical Socrates. These lessons, which constitute the kernel of his legacy, are often the same lessons taught by Plato, but are in some respects very different from them. What remains for us, indeed our major task, is to undertake a reconstruction of Socrates' philosophy, in which we will come face to face with his searching spirit and with the presence of reason, which, as an irresistible force, guided his life and activities. Just as archaeologists succeed in reconstructing a statue out of fragmented and disjointed pieces, so, too, we can try to reconstruct the enigmatic figure of Socrates out of what Aristophanes, Xenophon, Plato, and Aristotle left for us. From them, as well as from various traditions such as Cynicism, we can attempt to grapple with the Socratic problem and extract from them important philosophical lessons that are urgently needed in the world of the twenty-first century, when, it seems, humanity is losing its bearings.

NOTES

1. T. Gomperz, *Greek Thinkers: A History of Ancient Philosophy*, vol. 2, trans. G. C. Berry (London: John Murray, 1905), pp. 64–65.

2. The idea of lack of self-restraint, expressed in Greek by the word *akrasia*, appears in numerous Platonic and Aristotelian passages and is invariably associated with Socrates' denial of the possibility of knowingly doing evil. The common English translation of *akrasia* as incontinence, while technically correct, does not convey the precise sense of its usage in philosophical discussions.

3. Archelaus was king of Macedonia from 413 to 399 BCE.

4. Aegina is an island in front of the Athenian port of Piraeus.

5. Tablehood and Cuphood refer to Plato's ideal Table and ideal Cup, absolute and perfect realities that exist in a transcendent world accessible only through thought, not through sense experience.

6. Zopyrus was a famous Persian physiognomist or face reader, who once visited Athens. After examining Socrates' face, he is said to have exclaimed, "You, sir, are a monster." To which Socrates replied, "What you see, sir, is what I *was*." In chapter 6, we will encounter Zopyrus once more.

7. The sort of epilepsy characterized by fits of listlessness is often referred to as *petit mal*.

8. For a documented discussion of the encounters between Alexander the Great and Diogenes, see L. E. Navia, *Diogenes the Cynic: The War against the World* (Amherst, NY: Humanity Books, 2005).

9. Etymologically, the word *skeptic* refers to someone who is searching, not to someone who is merely in doubt or, still less, someone who has abandoned the search for the truth.

CHAPTER 6
The Search for the Soul

An unexamined life is not worth living, said Socrates at his trial. This, the most often quoted statement from him, sums up the meaning of his philosophy and the essence of his legacy. Death would have been preferable to him, had he not been able to subject himself to constant self-examination.

There are many things that give people the impression that their lives are worth living. It could be pleasure and self-gratification, distractions and entertainments, sports and physical stamina, power and wealth, possessions and security, social recognition and success, the prospect of another life, knowledge and erudition, and, indeed, every other imaginable thing that promises at least a grain of happiness. What makes life worth living varies from person to person, and even in the same person, it is not always the same. Seldom, however, do we come upon a statement as strange as that of Socrates. We can rest assured that there are not many people for whom an unexamined life could forecast a worthless existence.

It seems important, however, to understand the meaning of Socrates' statement before setting it aside as an utterance of a

159

strange philosopher who could not find anything worth doing other than examining himself. What sort of self-examination did he propose? Was it only for himself or for every other human being? What need did he experience that compelled him to dissect himself every moment of his life? Finally, what did he expect to gain from his compulsive self-examination?

We must assume, of course, that Socrates did not have in mind any other kind of life except human life. For him, the world was strictly defined as the human world. The rest was altogether inconsequential and worthy of being ignored. The so-called world of nature, that is, the universe at large, and, here on earth, the multitudes of animals and objects that populate the surface of the planet, all those things left Socrates uninterested and unimpressed. Ultimately, they meant nothing to him, as he says to Phaedrus, for his home, his world, is the city, where people move, live, and have their being.

Clearly, his philosophical orientation was the human world, a world made up of people like himself, each one furnished by nature or by God with the capacity to be aware of themselves and of the world around them. For what distinguishes humans from other living creatures is precisely their power to be conscious of things and to be conscious of their consciousness of themselves and of things.

This reflected sort of consciousness seems to be uniquely human. It is known in psychological jargon as self-consciousness. It empowers human beings with the unique capacity to recognize themselves as the basis on which the consciousness of the world is grounded, and, as if by miracle, it reveals to them their true self. The word used by Socrates for this curious phenomenon is *psyche*, loosely translated as mind or soul. Here, then, resides the true reality of every human being, not in his body or his surroundings, but in the recognition of the *subject*, that is, the consciousness that makes the very existence of the world possible. In its absence, as Schopenhauer puts it, "this very world of ours with all its suns and galaxies is—nothing."[1] It is, therefore, this self-consciousness, this *subject*, that Socrates needed to examine because it is in it that the true and only essence of who we are can be found. His philosophical orientation, accordingly, can be justifiably designated as subjective.

Before him, however, philosophers seem to have had in mind a different orientation, one in which the world at large was the prime, if not the only object of their attention. What engaged the imagination of Socrates' predecessors, beginning with Thales of Miletus in the sixth century BCE, was the universe, the world at large, of which we are a minute part. At first, it began with a search for a universal element or substance that makes up all things. According to Aristotle, they called it the *arche* or the element of the world. It was identified with water, as with Thales, who is supposed to have said that all things are made of water. After him, the *arche* was said to be air, an indefinite element, fire, a combination of elements, and, finally, at the time of Socrates, atoms floating in empty space, as Democritus insisted.

Despite the differences among these early philosophers, one thing remains indisputable, and that was their overwhelming preoccupation with cosmological problems. For them, the fundamental function of philosophy was the explanation of the universe in its totality, a universe in which human beings did not occupy a privileged position. Humanity, in their eyes, was one more manifestation of the enormous natural process (*physis*) that constitutes the universe. In Anaximander, for example, we come upon an early formulation of the theory of evolution, according to which the human species is a transformation undergone by some primitive species: "Living creatures came into being from moisture evaporated by the sun. Human beings originally came from another creature, that is, the fish."

From this viewpoint, human beings were never an object of special interest for those early philosophers who devoted themselves to cosmological pursuits. Among them, we will look in vain for attempts to come to grips with those issues that arise in the context of human existence and that are articulated in ethics, politics, history, and the other social sciences. There is in Diogenes Laertius (2.10) an anecdote about Anaxagoras, an older contemporary of Socrates, that underlines the objectivism that permeated pre-Socratic thought. When asked what the purpose of his life was, Anaxagoras replied, "To study the sun, the moon, and the heavens." If Socrates had been asked the same question, his answer would have been very different. For him, neither the sun nor the moon nor the heavens nor the universe was an object of great importance. The investigation of such things was not only useless but detrimental to the spirit.

It is possible that in his youth Socrates could have been interested in the study of the universe. The comment made in the *Phaedo* (96a–99e) may reflect authentic biographical elements: "When I was young, I had an extraordinary passion for that branch of learning that is called natural science. I thought it would be a marvelous thing to know the causes for which each thing comes and ceases and continues to be."

The secondary sources occasionally state that Socrates was a disciple of Archelaus the physicist, and the Aristophanic Socrates is described as being immersed in the typical issues associated with natural philosophers. Possibly, Aristophanes' description may be related to an early stage in Socrates' life. It is unquestionable, however, that the mature Socrates abandoned such pursuits, as is stated in the *Phaedo*. Like Saint Augustine, he must have said at some point in his life, "I no longer dream of the stars." The mechanistic philosophy of Anaxagoras must have left him with a sense of disappointment because it had failed to answer the questions that *he* deemed significant. Having been finally worn out by his scientific curiosity, he turned his back on the objectivism of his predecessors in order to begin a new journey in the search for wisdom along an altogether different path. In the *Phaedo*, we are led to believe that this new path would eventually guide him to the theory of ideal Forms, but it is difficult not to suspect that in writing this, Plato was unveiling the course that *he himself* followed.

What we can affirm without hesitation is that in his flight from what he viewed as the inconsequential and pretentious investigations of the natural philosophers, Socrates directed his thought inward, that is, toward the hidden recesses of his self. Philosophy, then, turned decidedly toward the *subject* of knowledge, that is, toward consciousness and toward the person. At the end of his life, as he appeared before the jury, Socrates could then unambiguously state that he did not have the slightest desire to know anything about the objects of science and that those who had accused him of being a natural philosopher were uttering false statements.

Socrates' attitude toward natural philosophy is well attested to by Xenophon. In the *Memorabilia*, we find the reasons for it. Socrates argued that as long as human existence remains poorly understood, it makes little sense to be preoccupied with the mysteries of the heavens. We should ignore them. Moreover, the contradictions found in the opinions of the natural philosophers should convince us of the futility of their endeavors. Science, after all, cannot offer any real advantage and, what is worse, can even produce bad consequences in those who pursue it. "In general," writes Xenophon, "with regard to the phenomena of the heavens, [Socrates] condemned our curiosity to learn how the gods had arranged them. He insisted that their secrets could not be discovered by human beings and believed that any attempt to search out what the gods had not chosen to reveal must be displeasing to them" (*Memorabilia* 4.7.6). Xenophon adds, however, that Socrates did not object to the study of the sciences, for instance, mathematics, as long as it could yield useful results for the benefit of people.

The secondary sources are generally in agreement with

Xenophon's report. They often insist on making Socrates responsible for the reorientation of philosophical inquiry in the direction of ethical matters. As noted in the previous chapter, Aristotle describes Socrates as a philosopher who neglected the world of nature as a whole and who was only concerned with ethical matters. The nature of virtue, not the structure of the universe, was Socrates' paramount concern.

From Cicero, we have a revealing statement in this regard: "It is universally agreed that Socrates was the first to divert philosophy from matters wrapped by nature in obscurity, with which all philosophers before him had been concerned. He applied it to ordinary life, directing his inquiries to virtues and vices, and in general to the study of good and evil. He regarded the phenomena of the heavens as beyond human understanding and irrelevant to the good life, even when they are understood" (*Academica* 1.4.15).

Plato's early dialogues confirm what Cicero says. In them, Socrates regards ethical issues as far more significant and critical than the study of the universe. For instance, Euthyphro's indictment of his father for the killing of a servant is a matter of far greater importance than questions about the primordial element of the universe and other such issues. Whereas the former intimately touch the core of human existence, the latter are inconsequential for the right conduct of life.

It must be noted that the emergence of humanistic inquiries during Socrates' time is a cultural phenomenon that cannot be exclusively associated with him. Every person is to some extent a child of his time, and philosophy is partly the reflection of its time and culture. Regardless of his uniqueness, Socrates was no exception. He was born at a critical moment in Athenian history, when the first manifestations of the city's grandeur were emerging and when its culture was about to undergo a profound transformation. Two decades after his birth, Athens was the center of an empire that would first grow vigorously, only to be plunged into an abyss of political and cultural upheaval from which it would never rise, as happens to all empires.

The last twenty years of Socrates' life witnessed a steady decline into decadence and instability. The Athens of Socrates, its influence and power notwithstanding, was a city in a constant state of crisis, not only in a political and military sense but spiritually and morally. In such a world, beset by a long and brutal war, and by the internal convulsions generated by the city's own social and political problems, there must have been little time or energy to become engaged in solving the riddle of the universe. Whether things are made of water or air, whether motion is real or an illusion, or whether there are other inhabited earths in space—these and other questions, typical of pre-Socratic thought, must have lost their original urgency. More pressing issues concerning the problem of human existence rose to the surface and occupied the center of attention. Cosmology and astronomy were replaced by ethical and political inquiries. The object that had engaged the minds of the pre-Socratics—the universe and the nature of reality—gave way to the subject, that is, human existence. How to survive in the steadily deteriorating Athenian world of the second half of the fifth century BCE became the prime concern of the philosophers.

It is at this time that the sophists appeared on the scene. They seemingly brought with them the right answers for which the Athenians, especially the youth, were thirsting. They claimed to be able to instruct their listeners in the art of survival that was so indispensable and had at their disposal the right weapon that any person, living in so disoriented a world, needed—language.

Socrates, too, made his appearance at this time. He raised the same questions as the sophists and, like them, was a true language acrobat. He resembled them. In the eyes of many, he was a sophist. In the *Clouds*, Aristophanes portrays him as a teacher of language, someone who could make a good argument appear bad and a bad argument good. He could convert at will what is right into wrong, wrong into right, and take advantage of others through the use of language. On repeated occasions, his interlocutors in Plato's dialogues accuse him of quibbling over words and of using confusing language to confuse them. For them, Socrates was nothing but a crafty sophist. Who and what, however, were the sophists?

In the endeavor to understand who and what the sophists of Socrates' time were, there are obstacles. For instance, there is the fact that of their numerous writings, not one has survived in its entirety. We have only brief quotations. Furthermore, those who wrote about the sophists, for example, Plato and Aristotle, seem to have been negatively disposed. Their comments have determined to a great extent the bad light in which the sophists have been generally viewed. In Plato, the term *sophist* has negative connotations and is often used in the sense of a pretended or false philosopher.

In its original meaning, *sophist* connoted a wise person, someone who possessed *sophia*, that is, wisdom or understanding. Aeschylus, for instance, refers to Prometheus as a sophist, and Sophocles speaks of great musicians in the same way. In the fragments of Cratinus, the comic playwright, Homer and Hesiod are called sophists; Plato does the same in *Protagoras* (316d). The various lists of the Seven Sages given by Diogenes Laertius (1.40) include men of legendary wisdom, whether theoretical or practical, and they are referred to as sophists. Among the early philosophers, Thales was an example of a sophist because of his reportedly great wisdom. In English, the word *sophistication* reflects the etymological sense once attached to the Greek word *sophistes*.

With the introduction of the word *philosopher*, however, things became a bit more complex. A distinction began to be made between someone who possesses wisdom and someone who searches for wisdom. According to Diogenes Laertius

(1.12), the origin of the word *philosopher* goes back to Pythagoras, who refused to be called a sophist and coined the word *philosopher* to mean, literally, someone yearning for wisdom. God alone, he said, can be called a sophist because only he is truly wise. This is reiterated by Socrates in the *Phaedrus* (278d), where he insists that only God should be referred to as a sophist. For his part, he is merely a philosopher, that is, a lover of wisdom or someone yearning for understanding.

In Plato's dialogues, no less than in certain Aristotelian passages, a clear distinction is made between those who are engaged in philosophy—those who search for wisdom—and those who insist on calling themselves wise—the sophists—who, despite their protestations, have the appearance of wisdom but are not wise. Plato describes the sophists as teachers of wisdom who *appear* to understand what they teach, but who in reality have little or no understanding. They deceive those whom they pretend to teach and use language to manipulate them for their own advantage.

This theme is repeated in countless passages. In the *Sophist*, the typical sophist—a type not easily definable—is a controversialist whose concern is making money through language games. He may appear knowledgeable but is only a peddler of opinions. In the *Hippias Major*, he is described as a salesman of cheap ideas, willing and capable of making a fortune. In the *Protagoras*, his love for money, superficiality, subservience to the stupid rabble, deceptiveness, and other traits are carefully delineated. The sophists, Plato maintains, cannot be compared to the ancient philosophers who were men genuinely concerned with the pursuit of wisdom.

These comments can be found with unusual precision in the *Apology*, because an important component of Socrates' defense is to show the jury that, despite the appearances, he is *not* a sophist. Unlike them, he has never been paid as a teacher and, also unlike them, he does not pretend to be wise. When, at the end of the trial, he asks the jurors to punish his sons if they grow up to be the sort of people who value wealth and who give the impression of being wise, what he is saying is that his sons should be reprimanded if one day they turn out to be sophists.

Whether Plato's description of the sophists is historically accurate is a much debated topic. Aristotle's concurrence with his statements is significant because although he was not directly acquainted with the sophists of Socrates' time, he was probably familiar with their writings. Moreover, unlike Plato, he never assumed the role of an apologist of Socrates. When in the *Metaphysics* (1004b) he affirms that "sophistry seems to be philosophy, but is not," he is undoubtedly making a fair statement about some of the sophists he knew either directly or through their writings.

It is conceivable, however, that the sophistical movement of the late fifth century BCE was not as philosophically superficial or socially detrimental as we may conclude from Plato's testimony. It is worth remembering that the sophists did not stand for one unified set of ideas. In many respects, they differed from one another because they sprang from different philosophical traditions and arrived at different conclusions. Thus, in speaking of the sophistical movement one should have in mind a general cultural development with a more or less defined common denominator. Plato himself was aware of this when he confessed the difficulty of reaching a satisfactory definition of who the typical sophist was.

As we think of the major sophists, that is, individuals like Protagoras, Gorgias, Prodicus, Thrasymachus, and Hippias, we are impressed by the idiosyncratic character of their ideas. Still, certain common themes can be discerned among them. These themes must be understood well in order to appreciate the thrust of Socrates' own philosophy, which was in part a reaction against them. The major themes are the following:

The sophists were generally uninterested in natural philosophy or science. For them, only the human dimension, not the universe, was the problem that demanded a solution. Protagoras's statement that "the human being is the measure of all things, of things that are, that they are, and of things that are not, that they are not" is the key signature for the long symphonic poem composed by the sophists. According to Aristotle, Protagoras's statement means that each person's individual impressions or points of view are always absolutely true. Beyond the person, nothing is true or false. Every individual is the point of reference for all reality. Things are real or unreal, meaningful or meaningless, only in the context of each human presence.

The statement can also be interpreted, as it often is, in a less radical way. We can say that nothing is real or unreal, true or false, apart from human consciousness or awareness in general. It is not that reality and truth depend on each person, but rather on the human experience as whole. It is *we* who create reality and meaning, for apart from the human presence nothing truly exists.

However Protagoras's statement may be understood, one thing is clear. For him, as much as for other sophists *and* for Socrates, a philosopher must turn his attention exclusively to questions and issues that emanate directly from the human consciousness and directly affect human beings. Being or existence has relevance only for and within the human dimension. Everything else is either a total nothingness or at least something with which we should not be concerned. Instead of directing our attention to the world at large, pretending to understand it, we should turn our intellectual sight within ourselves and begin with the question, who and what it is that *we* are.

The investigations of the sophists led them to the realization that language is not only the fundamental tool of human communication but the building material by which human reality is established. Hence, their attention was turned toward the study and analysis of language. They initiated unprecedented studies into the origin of language and were responsible for sophisticated studies in syntax and semantics. Correct diction, the meanings of words, the proper use of names and nouns, the rationale beneath the substantival genders, and other linguistic issues appear in the fragments of their writings and in reports about them. The function of language as the framework of human rationality was clearly identified, as was the importance of language in every sort of political and social activity. In one way or another, the sophists became linguistic experts. They dissected and played with the meanings of words and often converted their expertise into a source of prestige and wealth.

It was inevitable that the sophists' preoccupation with language would find able and clever imitators, language jugglers of questionable philosophical depth. These we meet in Plato's *Euthydemus*, where we are introduced to two linguistic acrobats, Euthydemus and Dionysodorus, who become hopelessly and amusingly entangled in a jungle of verbal quibbles. They make manifest the less consequential aspects of sophistry. In this dialogue, a biting parody of the sophists, Plato sought to show the nonsensical extremes to which the sophistical inquiries into language could lead. When talk is only about talk, little of substance is usually achieved. To any sensible person, that would be nothing but a silly game.

Yet, for some of the sophists, the point was not only to talk about talk but to pierce through the mantle of language into something important about human existence. Just as for Socrates there was something of intense earnestness in the linguistic games in which he entangled characters like Euthyphro and Thrasymachus, so, too, there was for the sophists something of great consequence in their affair with language.

The sophists, too, played with language and quibbled endlessly about words. Yet, their games seem to have had deep philosophical roots and serious ethical and social consequences. Beneath their preoccupation with language, there lurked an adherence to relativism, the outlines of which can be discerned in their ethical ideas. For them, truth, like human language, was a human invention, and, like all human inventions, it was created to serve specific needs and purposes that are never absolute but are valid only at some given time and under some circumstances.

For the sophists, it is not *one* person who is the measure of all things. It is people who *are* the measures of all things, and just as there are immense multitudes of different human beings, so, too, the measures of things are as many as the sands of the sea. On this basis, we can make sense of statements such as "every proposition is equally true and equally false," "every action is equally good and equally bad," "justice is the interest of the stronger," and many others. Nowhere, then, can we locate a stable point of reference, and nowhere is there a privileged point of view. As in a boundless universe where every point is the center, in the world of the sophists the perceptions and opinions of every single consciousness become the ultimate court of judgment. Nothing can be certain, and language proves to be just a game.

It is easy to imagine the uneasiness with which conservative Athenians reacted to so monstrous an idea. Its advocates had to be identified with the "Spectral Shadows" and "the maladies and fevers that plagued our land" of which Aristophanes wrote in his *Wasps* with the sophists and Socrates in mind. The sophists announced to the world, in clear and loud tones, that the Athenian world, with its immortal gods and time-honored virtues, its inviolable laws and immemorial traditions, was, after all, only a passing whim of human culture that rested on unstable foundations.

There are reports that tell us about various sophists who were prosecuted for their teachings. Protagoras and Prodicus, for instance, were charged with the same crime of which Socrates was accused, namely, irreligiosity. This circumstance points to the aura of dangerousness that surrounded the sophists. The ridicule of which they were made an object in the plays of Aristophanes and other comic playwrights was an expression of the animosity ordinary Athenians must have felt toward them. The indictment against Socrates, as we have seen, was in part the result of his apparent association with the sophists. By delving into the intricacies of language and subjecting people's beliefs to questions, he, too, acted as if he wished to unsettle the social structure of the city in the name of a relativism that belonged not to him but to the sophists.

Sophistical relativism, when expressed in linguistic paradoxes in which everything is affirmed and denied, must have sounded in the ears of more solidly minded philosophers as nothing short of rhetorical nonsense. Such, we can assume, must have been Socrates' reaction. He disliked the sophists as much as the conservatives did and, able to follow the tortuous path of sophistical logic, he must have concluded that such logic did not amount to anything. With respect to Protagoras's statement that "the human being is the measure of all things," Socrates observes in the *Theaetetus* (152a) that in speaking thus, the sophist was talking nonsense. Aristotle echoes this when, in *Metaphysics* (1053b), he wrote that "in making so provocative a statement, Protagoras is really not saying anything at all."

Sophistical relativism, moreover, went hand in hand with an all-embracing skepticism, this term understood as the denial of the possibility of any knowledge. The sophists reached the conclusion that there was actually nothing to know about anything. For them, no assertion can be made about the structure of reality because reality is only a changing stream of perceptions, conventions, and interpretations. In Aristotle's view, the sophistical position amounts to this: "If it is equally possible to affirm and to deny anything whatever on any subject, then a given thing will be at once a ship, a wall, and a man. This is the necessary conclusion for those who hold the theory of Protagoras" (*Metaphysics* 1007b).

This skepticism reveals itself in the sophists' attitude toward natural philosophy. In science, there can be no absolute knowledge because all scientific statements are only conventional utterances that are both true and false. It is the same with theological matters and religious beliefs, as Protagoras insists: "As for the gods, I have no way of knowing whether they exist or not, nor, if they exist, what their nature could be. For the obstacles to that sort of knowledge are many, including the obscurity of the subject and the brevity of human life." For this statement, according to Philostratus (*Lives of the Sophists* 494), Protagoras was banished from Athens.

Then there is the sophists' skepticism with respect to ethical values. They reached the conclusion that ethical values are ultimately meaningless because it is impossible to determine what is good or bad, right or wrong. In the *Republic*, Plato allows us to witness a sophist at work, specifically Thrasymachus of Chalcedon, who asks Socrates whether he has a nanny to wipe his running nose. Why? Because Socrates is nothing but an overgrown child. Why? Because he still believes that certain actions are right in themselves and others wrong. He still holds on to certain ethical values and may have imagined himself endowed with what nowadays we would call a conscience. As for Thrasymachus, who has outgrown such silly ideas, he knows that ethical values are crafty rules invented by those in power in order to maintain the masses under control. Morality is only for the weak in body and spirit. The strong are beyond such things. They have understood at last that might makes right and that justice is the interest of the strong. The rest is pious nonsense.

Similar sentiments are expressed by another sophist, Callicles, in Plato's *Gorgias*: "I feel towards philosophers [like Socrates] very much as I do towards those who lisp and play the child. When I see a child, for whom it is proper enough to speak in that way, lisping and playing, I like it and it seems to me charming and cute, and appropriate to the child's age. But when

I hear a grown man lisping and playing the child, I find it ridiculous and unmanly and worthy of a beating" (*Gorgias* 485b).

Callicles' anger is aroused by Socrates' conviction that it is always better to suffer evil than to do evil, and that to do wrong and to escape punishment for wrongdoing is the worst of all possible evils, obviously ridiculous ideas from the point of view of practically everybody. Thrasymachus' reaction is brought about by Socrates' contention that in the political world, those who govern ought to have the interest of the people as their only priority; again, a ridiculous idea among politicians and rulers.

These considerations are useful in the attempt to appreciate the nature of the sophistical movement and, as will become clear subsequently, the gap that separates Socrates from the sophists. If, as the sophists maintained, true knowledge is unattainable and if ethical values depend entirely on social conventions, then the only reasonable attitude would be to act so as to derive for oneself the greatest personal advantage in all social and political affairs. The sophists were experts in the art of success, and language furnished them with the perfect instrument to practice that art. They taught their students what Aristophanes' Socrates taught his stupefied disciples—to speak and to conquer, right or wrong. Rhetorical proficiency—what we might call today public relations—has nothing to do with truth and falsehood or with moral values. It has everything to do with cosmetic manipulation and with the ability to mold opinions and emotions. What, then, was Socrates' response to the challenge embodied in ideas such as these?

In the *Theages* (121d–122a), we witness the anxiety with which a certain Demodocus searches for a sophist to whom he could entrust the education of his son. He does not object to the fees charged by the sophists: "I do not mind so much about the fees and so I have come now on this very business of placing this youth with one of the sophists, or sources of wisdom, as they are held to be." Obviously, Demodocus has made a mistake coming to Socrates, who may *resemble* the sophists in some ways but who is very different from them. He may be as concerned as they with the affairs of human beings and, like them, may be an expert in the use of language. Also like them, he may occasionally challenge the stories about the gods. In reality, however, he is not a sophist. He is not a teacher of anything. His reputation for wisdom is the result of a misunderstanding of what he is. His 'wisdom' consists in his recognition of his own lack of wisdom. Demodocus would do well to look for a true teacher, a real sophist, for *that*, indeed, is not what Socrates is. What then is he?

As noted earlier, the portrayal of the sophists found in Plato's dialogues may be an exaggerated version of what they truly were. Perhaps, some have suggested, in Plato's attempt to clear Socrates of the charges laden on him at the trial, he had to widen the gap that separated him from the sophists. He depicts them as charlatans who profited from the credulity and indolence of the Athenians and who taught lessons in immorality and opportunism. They were people of no conscience. They were challenged by Socrates, who, in the name of moral principles based on reason, exposed their hollowness.

Whether Plato's assessment of the sophistical movement is justified or not, it is likely that at least some of his comments stand on solid historical ground. Even more is the reported gap that separates Socrates from them. He rises from the matrix created by the relativism and skepticism of the sophists, imparting a new sense of optimism and certainty in what concerns human affairs in general and moral values in particular. Despite the outward similarities between them, Socrates belongs to a world very different from theirs, as he insists during his trial. He is not one of them. Yet, what needs to be explored is the way in which he differed from the sophists and, indeed, from other philosophers before his time. What did he discover that others had missed altogether? What secret treasure did he find? How did he succeed in leaving behind the excursions of the natural philosophers who had grappled with the nature of the universe and the chattering of the sophists about the groundlessness of moral values? How did he manage to begin a new chapter in the human quest for meaning?

There have been some for whom this new chapter, allegedly begun by Socrates, is not as impressive and commendable as is often assumed. He differed significantly from the sophists but not in the way in which he is traditionally portrayed. Instead of rising above the moral quagmire supposedly created by sophistical skepticism and nihilism, Socrates fell in a ditch of decadence and mediocrity from which Western culture has been unable to escape. Twenty-three centuries after Socrates' death, Nietzsche confronted once more the Socratic 'problem' and concluded that the real culprit for our cultural decline is Socrates, not the sophistical movement.

The sophists, in Nietzsche's view, were the genuine representatives of the authentic Greek *Weltanchauung*, while Socrates was the embodiment of the degenerate and degenerating decadence that brought about the irreversible demise of the classical world. They stood for a system of values in which strength and vitality were the only ethical determinants, while Socrates preached a plebeian and moralistic philosophy in which it is possible to smell the odor of the rabble. His was a philosophy of resentment and impotent frustration, couched in the language of rachitic malice (*jene Rachitiker-Bosheit*), beneath which there lurked a "buffoon who got himself taken seriously." Indeed, argues Nietzsche, what could be more dishonest, more ridiculous, more un-Greek, than to preach a philosophy based on the senseless equation "reason = virtue = happiness"?

In Socrates, even physiognomy conspired to paint a perfect portrait of decadence and vulgarity:

In origin, Socrates belonged to the lowest class: Socrates was plebs. We know, we can still see for ourselves, how ugly he was. But ugliness, in itself an objection, is among the Greeks almost a refutation. Was Socrates a Greek at all? Ugliness is often the expression of a development that has been crossed, thwarted by crossing. Or it appears as a declining development. The anthropologists among the criminologists tell us that the typical criminal is ugly: *monstrum in fronte, monstrum in animo* [a monstrous face reveals a monstrous soul]. But the criminal is a decadent. Was Socrates a typical criminal? At least that would not be contradicted by the famous judgment of the physiognomist, which sounded so offensive to Socrates' friends. A foreigner [Zopyrus] who knew about faces once passed through Athens and told Socrates that he was a *monstrum*—that he harbored in himself all the bad vices and appetites. Socrates merely answered: "You know me, sir."[2]

The problem with Nietzsche's version of this anecdote is that it differs from that of Cicero, the only ancient account of the incident. The difference is important. In Nietzsche's version, Socrates acknowledges what the physiognomist discovers in his ugly face, whereas in Cicero's version, he tells him that he has transformed himself into the antithesis of his monstrous features. According to Cicero, Socrates' comment to Zopyrus is, "What you see, sir, is what I *was*." Why would Nietzsche alter the anecdote? Was it perhaps to lend validity to his view of Socrates?

The contrast drawn by Nietzsche between the sophists and Socrates is in accord with the glorification of earthly strength and vitality the German philosopher envisions for the triumphant *Übermensch* (Superman) on the one hand, and, on the other, with the vituperation he loads on spiritually inclined types, among whom he classifies not only Socrates but Plato and Jesus. The Nietzschean Superman is the conquering hero, the overpowering warrior, the true anti-Christ, whose kingdom is of *this* world. Like Callicles in the *Gorgias* and Thrasymachus in the *Republic*, the Superman looks upon life as a battlefield in which the only purpose is to conquer and dominate. He knows nothing of another world and views with contempt the despisers of the body. He lives in a state of passionate physical ecstasy and is suspicious of those who have betrayed this world in the name of the "meager, ghastly, and famished" fiction of the soul. The Superman constitutes, according to Nietzsche, the genuine Greek type. Socrates, obviously, is not this type because he stands for something altogether different. In a sense, we could say of him what the Gospel says about Jesus as he stood defeated and humiliated before the imperial Roman procurator: His kingdom is not of this world (John 18:36).

We can now understand the perplexity created by Socrates in Nietzsche's mind. He stood astonished in the presence of the Greek philosopher, ultimately unable to understand the enigmatic Apollonian force that abundantly flowed from the ugliest of men, whose speech was plebeian and pedestrian, and whose features were lascivious and coarse. Who or what was this monster who, like the mythological Marsyas, had stolen the magic of the gods in order to bewitch humanity with the melody of reason and virtue?

Alcibiades, let us remember, also had the same experience, but was able to discern clearly inside the unpleasant physical frame of his friend the hidden semblances of the gods. The sophists, who spoke well Alcibiades' language, who, like him, dismissed the gods and the pious beliefs of ordinary Athenians, and who extolled virtue as strength and preached a life lived beyond good and evil—these sophists, in whom Nietzsche found so much edification and whom he called the real Greeks, left Alcibiades unimpressed and unmoved. He knew them well because he was like them. Yet, he must have thought, they were precisely the ones who smelled like the rabble and were genuine *plebs*. Their rhetorical and social refinement notwithstanding, they were far uglier and decadent than Socrates. In him, Alcibiades recognized something different, something irresistible, which summoned and compelled him to undertake the transformation of his life. Unlike Nietzsche, Alcibiades understood that it was Socrates, not the sophists, who represented the highest achievement of the Greek world.

In Nietzsche's interpretation of Socrates' legacy, we come once more upon the phenomenon encountered in many other cases—an idiosyncratic reaction to his presence. That was what *he* saw in Socrates from his perspective. His language is more condemning than even the lines of Aristophanes' *Clouds*. With Socrates, that is what must be expected. As he himself confesses in the *Euthyphro*, it is impossible to pin him down and say with confidence, *this* is what Socrates was. His lineage, he ironically notes, links him to Daedalus, the legendary sculptor whose statues took on life as soon as they were made and, moving aimlessly, refused to let anyone catch them. Perhaps Socrates spent his life hiding behind a multitude of masks and, as Alcibiades suggests in the *Symposium*, ultimately laughing at those who were bent on unmasking him.

We can still persist in unmasking him at least for the purpose of building for ourselves an image of him of some use in order to make sense of the legacy that is associated with him. For this endeavor, whatever its biographical value could be, we must stay close to Plato's image of him, particularly as this manifests itself in the early dialogues, and to the sober testimony of Aristotle. From them, we can extract several interrelated blocks that can be loosely structured into the edifice of Socrates' philosophical vision. Some of those blocks can be summarized in statements such as these:

- For Socrates, the search for wisdom involves a journey that leads exclusively into the recesses of one's consciousness. At the beginning of this journey, there stands the inscription written on Apollo's temple in Delphi, "Know Thyself."

- This journey inward requires a complete concentration of the mind on those aspects of human existence that are ethically or morally significant, all other things being of no consequence.
- The domain of ethical concerns is one that never involves the individual alone. For this reason, the examination of one's self must be carried out within the structure furnished by human companionship. The search for wisdom, therefore, cannot be a solitary undertaking.
- Language is the fundamental framework of human rationality and is the true bridge that connects one person to another. Accordingly, the Socratic journey assumes initially the form of a carefully contrived analysis of language in which the dialogue serves as the essential instrument for the acquisition of self-knowledge.
- The Socratic dialogue, however, hardly ever unfolds itself as a free-flowing conversation, which is the most common type of human interaction. Its recurrent form is the *elenchus* or interrogation, in which the interlocutor is forced to draw conclusions from his own assertions and in which the deliverance from the initial state of ignorance is sought.
- More specifically, the Socratic dialogue begins as a quest for the correct definition of a moral state or mode of behavior, through which the meaning or definition of an ethical or moral term is sought.
- As the dialogue develops, a variety of formal and informal pedagogical devices are employed, the former being exemplified by the appeal to inductive arguments, that is, leading from particulars to the universal. The latter include devices such as Socrates' irony and his confession of ignorance.

- Socrates' ignorance can be understood in a twofold sense, either as actual ignorance or as ironical ignorance. With respect to certain issues, we can assume that when Socrates confessed his ignorance, it was simply because he did not know the answer to a certain question, for example, one concerning the ultimate meaning of death. At other times, however, his ignorance is a pedagogical device that allows him to elicit answers from his interlocutors.

- Unlike in the case of sophistical skepticism, Socrates' confession of ignorance is not the expression of a final state of mind but an indication of a point of departure. His skepticism, understood here in its etymological sense of searching or being on the lookout, announces his desire to find an answer or a solution. Thus, what for the sophists is an incontrovertible conclusion—knowledge is not attainable—emerges for Socrates as a commitment to make knowledge attainable.

- This is the basis of the Socratic optimism, which can be understood as the conviction that intellectual and spiritual enlightenment *is* a realizable goal. In it, there are no traces of the negativism and nihilism associated with extreme forms of sophistical thought.

- This enlightenment, which as an ideal condition determines the direction of Socrates' philosophical pilgrimage, is the necessary means for the attainment of yet a higher goal, namely, a virtuous life. Thus, while we can affirm that Socrates "thirsted for pure concepts as any mystic ever panted for union with the Godhead,"[3] we must also say that the possession of such pure concepts is the necessary *and* sufficient condition for the actualization of virtue. Understanding for the sake of understanding, knowledge for the sake of knowledge, and theory for the sake of theory make little sense from a Socratic point of view.

- The relationship between knowledge and virtue is such that neither can be conceived in the absence of the other. To know what is good is to do what is good. Ignorance and evil are aspects of one and the same reality.
- Hence, Socrates' educational mission, his *elenchus*, his midwifery—all these must be understood as manifestations of a unified ethical plan. By means of the enlightenment of the mind, he expects to raise himself, as well as others, to a higher plane of ethical existence.
- Enlightenment, however, is not attainable through a process of instruction in which the disciple learns the truth from the teacher. Socratic enlightenment is the result of educational growth ('educational' understood in its etymological sense of *educare*, that is, 'to draw out'). Thus, strictly speaking, Socrates is not a teacher but a source of stimulation. He compels others, as he has compelled himself, to discover the truth within themselves and by themselves.
- In this sense, we are justified in speaking about individualism in the context of his philosophy. As he approaches others, Socrates has nothing to teach. He merely compels them to teach themselves.
- Yet, Socrates' confession of ignorance and his reluctance to speak dogmatically notwithstanding, it is not difficult to discern in him certain firmly held convictions and normative beliefs that he cannot but communicate to others in conversation and through the example of his life. Such convictions and beliefs, with respect to which he does not entertain any doubts, allow us to speak unambiguously of his moral confidence. In certain ethical matters, Socrates is perfectly confident of having reached absolute knowledge.

These statements do not constitute an exhaustive list of the major themes of Socrates' philosophy. They only summarize the most significant among them. We can now comment on the first seven, which disclose in the clearest light the avowed goal of his philosophical enterprise. This goal is none other than the search for the soul, that is, the true essence of the human self.

The conviction that the only path to wisdom is that which leads to the innermost recesses of the mind is of crucial importance. It announces Socrates' program and acts as his guideline. It is his point of departure and his destination. The maxim "Know thyself" is repeated on several occasions in Plato's early dialogues (e.g., *Charmides* 164d, *Protagoras* 342b, *Phaedrus* 230a) and is not forgotten by Xenophon (e.g., *Memorabilia* 4.2.24).

Along with other maxims such as "Nothing in excess," the command "Know thyself" greeted the pilgrims who visited Apollo's temple at Delphi as a reminder engraved on stone that the only wisdom worth looking for is found within each human consciousness. If that wisdom is not found or remains neglected, nothing else can be understood—not even the world that indistinctly discloses itself through sense perception. True wisdom must begin inexorably with the examination of one's self. If we remain ignorant of our own selves, that is, if we do not know who or what we are, how can we make sense of the external world? In the absence of self-understanding, all other types of knowledge are forms of intellectual dissipation and distraction that ultimately amount to nothing. In fact, these are only palliative and toxic patterns of self-forgetfulness that can at most convey the impression of knowledge.

When and why the famous Apollonian call for self-knowledge first emerged in the Delphic tradition we do not know. Its origins go back to legendary times when Apollo was believed to have lived in Delphi as a young god. It was then, according to the tale, that he slew the frightful Python, the gargantuan dragon that lived in the entrails of Mount Parnassus. Like the monstrous Typhon of Cynic traditions, Python's presence meant suffering and death to those unfortunate enough to become its victims. Also like Typhon, it was an unending source of darkness. Just as for the Cynics, Typhon was responsible for the obfuscation and mental obscurity (*typhos*) in which most people live; so, too, Python, in Apollonian traditions, was the creature who caused the human mind to wallow in rottenness and decay (*pythos*).[4] It was this dragon that the young Apollo destroyed. After its death, the inhabitants of Delphi could live once more in peace and tranquility, not groping aimlessly in the darkness of their former days. Now they could see clearly, for Apollo, the god of light, had obliterated the source of darkness.

The story of Python obviously contains much symbolism. It allowed the ancient Greeks to invest Apollo with characteristics antithetical to those of the dragon. Whereas the latter stood for darkness and confusion, the former represented light—the light of the sun—and, more importantly, clarity of mind. Apollo is the enlightener. When he speaks through the lips of the enraptured Pythia, whose very title is reminiscent of the ancient dragon, his words must be accepted as the expression of the truth because, as Socrates reminds us at his trial, Apollo cannot deceive. He cannot say the thing that is not.

An ancient hymn to him expresses this idea with great clarity:

> O Phoebus, from your throne of truth,
> From your dwelling-place at the heart of the world,
> You speak to humans.
> By the decree of Zeus, no lie ever comes from you,
> No shadow to darken the word of truth.
> Zeus sealed by an everlasting edict
> Apollo's honor, that all may trust
> With unshaken faith when he speaks.

Already by the time of the Milesian philosophers, almost two hundred years before Socrates, it was believed that the god's prerogative was to determine who among human beings was truly wise, as we learn from Diogenes Laertius (DL 1.28). There is an ancient legend that recounts how some youths once found a golden tripod while fishing off the coast of Miletus, and how, as a dispute arose as to who should keep the precious object, an appeal was made to the Delphic oracle. "Whosoever is the wisest among humans should possess the tripod," was the answer. It was at that time that Thales became the proud owner of the tripod. After him, and in compliance with the instructions of the god, each one of the seven sages came to own it.

By the time of Socrates, the story of the tripod had become a blurry legend, only remembered through the votive tripods left by the pilgrims at Delphi and by the holy tripod on which the Pythia sat until late classical times. During Socrates' time, Apollo still retained his ancient prerogative of passing judgment on the worth of human wisdom. Thus, the incident in which Socrates was declared to be the wisest among human beings is not, after all, unique. It is a link in a long tradition that antedates Socrates by at least two centuries and would continue into Roman times.

In an earlier chapter, we endeavored to clarify the meaning of the Delphic statement about Socrates' wisdom. We saw how difficult it is to reach a definite conclusion in that regard. The suggestion that the incident must be interpreted only as a Platonic myth, comparable to the story of Atlantis, seems unreasonable, for the Delphic oracle did function as the arbiter of wisdom long before and after Socrates. Moreover, we have Xenophon's version of it, in which we hear Socrates say that "some time ago, when Chaerephon made inquiry at the Delphic oracle concerning me, Apollo answered, in the presence of many people, that no one was more free, more just, and more prudent than I" (*Apology* 14).

Plato's version is more detailed, but it conveys the same sense as that of Xenophon:

You were all acquainted with Chaerephon, who was a friend of mine since I was a child. As you [the jurors] know, he played an important role in the overthrow of the dictatorship of the Thirty and in the restoration of the democracy [in 404 BCE]. He was impulsive in all his undertakings. Some time ago, he made a journey to Delphi in order to submit to the god this question—I beg of you, gentlemen, let me speak without interruption. He asked the god whether there was anyone in the world wiser than I, and the Pythia responded that in fact there was no one. (*Apology* 21a)

In both versions, it was not Socrates who went to Delphi, but Chaerephon, someone about whom not much is known. In Aristophanes' *Clouds*, Chaerephon is portrayed as the most important among Socrates' disciples. Plato and Xenophon appear anxious to lend credibility to the incident by mentioning witnesses other than Chaerephon. Xenophon speaks of the crowd who heard the Pythia's words, while Plato mentions Chaerephon's brother: "His brother, who is here, will vouch for the truth of what I am saying, since Chaerephon himself is dead" (*Apology* 21a).

It is remarkable that in the sources, the jury is said to have reacted vociferously to Socrates' account of the incident. Could it be that the jurors rejected the veracity of Socrates' words, as if he was simply inventing the story? Did they look upon him as an irreverent man for invoking Apollo as a witness? Surely, if the jurors, religious and superstitious as they probably were, had believed that the oracle had declared Socrates to be the wisest man, they would have been reluctant to find him guilty of irreligiosity. Yet, the fact that he was convicted seems to indicate an incredulous attitude on their part, which explains their reaction to Socrates' words.

As for Socrates himself, however, there can be no doubt as to how *he* viewed Apollo's statement. He believed in it and interpreted it as an absolute command deserving his unwavering obedience. At least, that is what he told the jurors. He understood the Apollonian message in terms of an order to search for wisdom, not in the external world that had captivated the attention of the natural philosophers, but in his own self. Wisdom, if attainable, had to be found, Socrates concluded, where Apollo had indicated, that is, in the mystery of the self. Thus, the "Know thyself" became the guiding force of the Socratic pilgrimage.

For us, however, the phrase "Know thyself" remains an unclear injunction of indefinite meaning. Before Socrates' time, others had already endeavored to accomplish this task, and it was through their efforts that the educational power of the Delphic inscription had yielded abundant cultural and philosophical fruit. Pindar, for instance, never ceased repeating it to himself, as he found in it a sense of inspiration when he sought to articulate in his poems the ideals of Greek culture. In the tragedies of Aeschylus, it transformed itself into a categorical imperative to elucidate the limitations inherent in the human condition, and in the tragedies of Sophocles, it embodied the kernel of tragic self-knowledge. The Delphic "Know thyself," according to Werner Jaeger, "deepened and broadened into a comprehension of the shadowy nothingness of human strength and human happiness. To know oneself is thus for Sophocles to know man's powerlessness; but it is also to know the indestructible and conquering majesty of suffering humanity."[5] For the ordinary person, we may assume, it called at least for a moment of reflection and inwardness during which, if only too briefly, the turmoil and confusion of the external world could be silenced and set aside.

For Socrates, the "Know thyself" became the point of departure for a series of reflections and activities, and eventually the essence of his life and philosophy. Still, what specific meaning did he attach to it? What significance did he discern in it? In Aeschylus's *The Persians*, we see clearly that the call for self-knowledge demands a thorough examination of human reality and that this examination leads to the realization that human knowledge, power, and happiness do not amount to much. Like falling leaves and sand castles, human endeavors are inconsequential. For this reason, the gods do not easily forgive arrogance and are forever anxious to punish the pretensions of human beings. For them, *hybris* (arrogant pride) is what the sin against the Holy Ghost is for the Christian God (Matt. 12:31)—an unforgivable offense.

"Thoughts too lofty suit no mortal man," wrote Aeschylus. In Socrates, we discover a theme *apparently* as despairing and pessimistic. True wisdom, he says at his trial, does not belong to human beings but only to God. At the end of his earthly pilgrimage, he, too, like Aeschylus, speaks disparagingly of the ambitions of human knowledge. In calling him the wisest among humans and in making him the heir of the symbolic tripod of knowledge, what Apollo meant was simply that he who, like Socrates, acknowledges his ignorance is truly wise.

If this were the meaning attached by Socrates to the Delphic command, we would be justified in experiencing a sense of frustration in the presence of his philosophy. We would admire him for the persistence of his efforts, for his intellectual integrity, and, above all, for his humility. Still, we could not avoid the temptation of comparing him with genuine skeptical philosophers, for whom the only meaningful option is to suspend judgment on all matters, since knowledge can never be attained. Nothing can ever be truly known, which is the slogan of the sophistical movement.

From Gorgias, one of the most influential among the sophists, we have this declaration of intellectual impotence: "Nothing exists. If anything existed, it could not be known. Moreover, if it could be known, the knowledge of it could not be communicated."

One generation after Socrates, Pyrrho of Elis, the most

famous among the skeptics, gave his complete assent to Gorgias's cryptic words. Since nothing is truly real, and neither knowledge nor language means anything, Pyrrho chose the only reasonable option. He turned his back on the world and remained in silence until his death. Why search for what does not exist? Why seek knowledge that is unattainable? Why continue the human chatter about nothing? Like a disenchanted Quixote, the great skeptic cleansed his mind of all those dragons that had once agitated his imagination and, almost as in an act of philosophical suicide, remained contented and in silence, cultivating the only possession worth having, namely, peace of mind.

Far was Socrates from this state of contentment. Like an ever youthful Quixote, for whom the elusiveness of the dragons of his quest augmented his determination to master them, he found in the emptiness of his mind and of the minds of others an incentive to renew his search. With every new day, this indefatigable knight of ideas would enter the Athenian marketplace and public buildings to engage people in conversation, as if he were a chatterbox. He would pursue his acquaintances through the tortuous streets of the city in the hope of engaging them in a new language joust.

There is something in him that reminds us of a wrestler who finds his satisfaction only in pugilistic contests. His struggle was first with himself—with his self—and then, without discrimination, with the selves of everybody else. Just as he would enter drinking contests in the marketplace to prove to others that he could imbibe the greatest quantity of wine without losing his head, he would speak with others until he left them exhausted. It must have been a draining engagement, which, as he suggests at his trial, left him eventually exhausted but not defeated. His pious hope was that after death, he could continue his wrestling in Hades. The point for us, however, is to understand what it was that Socrates so tenaciously sought to conquer. For what prize was he competing?

We can affirm without hesitation that the coveted prize was the discovery of the soul, the human *psyche* in Socrates' language—*that and nothing else*. That was what Apollo had ordered him to seize and examine because that was what Socrates truly was, and that was and is what every human being has been and is. The "Know thyself" is an imperative to come to grips with the reality of one's soul, for it is here, not anywhere else, that the essence of the human being resides. We have a body and possessions, but that is not what we are. We are fundamentally only one thing: our soul or our self-consciousness.

As we read in *Alcibiades I* (124c), the soul is, according to Socrates, the seat of wisdom and thought, and is that element within us that is closest to God. It is the entity implanted in us by God in order to rule the body. There cannot be any doubt, moreover, that the soul and the self are one and the same thing. "He who orders us to know ourselves is bidding us to become acquainted with our soul," says Socrates to the young Alcibiades.

The value of this statement does not depend on the specific stance we choose vis-à-vis the issue of whether the Socratic concept of the soul is based on the dualism generally associated with Plato, especially in the *Phaedo*. It is true that the soul (*psyche*) had already been invested during Socrates' time with meanings that ranged from the identification with life, any kind of life, to its transformation into a spiritual entity distinct and separable from the body, as exemplified in the beliefs of the Pythagoreans. Given the nature of the Socratic problem, we will probably never come to a definitive conclusion concerning the precise meaning attached by Socrates to the soul.

We could assume that for him the soul and the body are altogether different entities, and that the body is nothing but the prison in which the soul is trapped while in this earthly life. Death, then, would be the moment when the soul is released from the fetters of the physical world, as Socrates insists in the

Phaedrus and the *Phaedo*. The deliverance of the soul, he tells us, is attained when "we ourselves are pure and not entombed in this that we carry about us and call the body, in which we are imprisoned like an oyster in its shell" (*Phaedrus* 250c).

In the *Phaedo*, he speaks of the body as an infection that has contaminated the soul. We are reminded in no uncertain terms that "death is the separation of the soul from the body and that the state of being dead is the state in which the body is separated from the soul and exists alone by itself and the soul is separated from the body and exists alone by itself" (*Phaedo* 64c).

Yet, we could also assume that for Socrates the psychical or spiritual person and the physical person are one and the same, in which case the death of the body is also the death of the soul. Dead bodies have no souls because these no longer exist. They have been plunged into the black hole of nothingness. This assumption, expressing a materialistic understanding of human existence, would rest comfortably on the basis provided by Xenophon's testimony. Like many of his contemporaries, he would have been amazed at the suggestion that after his death, Socrates—the real Socrates—went on existing on a higher plane as a disembodied spirit.

Still, we have to contend with the agnostic tone of the concluding remarks of Plato's *Apology*, where, in very clear words, Socrates confesses his ignorance about the meaning of death: "The state of death is one of two things. Either it is virtually a state of nothingness, so that the dead have no consciousness of anything, or it is, as some people say, a change and a migration of the soul from this to another world" (*Apology* 40c).

We are, therefore, in the presence of three alternatives. Either the soul and the body are one indivisible being and cannot exist apart from each other, or the soul and the body are absolutely different things and the soul can exist apart from the body, or we just do not know anything about this matter. Which could have been Socrates' conviction?

In this regard we must confess our ignorance, just as Socrates often confessed his. If Alcibiades was right when he insisted that no one really knew Socrates, who passed his life laughing at those bent on pinning him down, his conception of the human soul would be a perfect example of our lack of knowledge of him. Nothing we can do would compel him to disclose to us his conviction. He cannot be pinned down. And again, it is possible that in this matter he actually did not know. How, as he suggests at the end of his trial, could he know the meaning of death if he has not yet experienced death?

We can still opt for a makeshift approach and put aside Socrates' understanding of the *nature* of the soul and concentrate our attention on what he might have understood as the *role* of the soul in human existence. The first thought that comes to us in this regard is that, whether immortal or not, the soul is the person's true self and should be, therefore, the only object worth pursuing and caring for. We hear Socrates express this idea with great clarity: "I shall never give up philosophy or stop exhorting you and pointing out the truth to any one of you whom I meet, saying in my accustomed way: 'Most excellent man, are you, who are a citizen of Athens, the greatest of cities and the most famous for wisdom and power, not ashamed to care for the acquisition of wealth and for reputation and honor, when you neither care nor take thought for wisdom and truth and the perfection of your soul?'" (*Apology* 29d).

We encounter the same theme each time Socrates engages others in conversation, whether with Charmides, Alcibiades, or any other Athenian: Forget the world with its glory, honors, and possessions, and direct all your endeavors to the perfection of your soul because, aside from it, nothing ultimately matters. Thus, Socrates' mission has only one goal to achieve, one purpose to accomplish, one task to complete, and that is to instill in his contemporaries his unshakable conviction that only the soul deserves our exclusive attention.

The point is, however, to gain an understanding of the process involved in caring for the soul and the benefit that can be derived from it. The Delphic oracle, as we have seen, enjoined Socrates to strive after self-knowledge because self-knowledge has a regenerative power through which it is possible to reach the high plateau of moral perfection. He who succeeds in knowing himself becomes thereby virtuous, since self-knowledge is the necessary and sufficient condition for the actualization of virtue.

In the *Alcibiades I*, Socrates states that knowing oneself is equivalent to becoming temperate and, we could add, to possessing all the other virtues. Hence, wisdom, understood as self-knowledge and the perfection of the soul, are one and the same thing. Yet, to attain the latter, Socrates insists, we must begin with the former. In order to become virtuous ourselves, we must move along the path that leads to self-knowledge, for he who does not know himself cannot make any improvements in his moral condition.

This is precisely the message conveyed over and over again to the young Alcibiades, as he is about to become entangled in the world of politics. Without self-knowledge, Socrates predicts, he would never become virtuous, and the political state he expects to guide some day would never profit from his presence. Self-knowledge, he is told, is that process in which the soul, itself the seat of wisdom and the source of virtue, turns itself toward itself, as if it were an eye seeking to see itself. In this process of reflected consciousness or introspection, the soul recognizes itself, knows clearly what it is in itself, and learns to distinguish itself from those things that are not essential to it. It discovers that wealth, honor, power, physical beauty, pleasure, and even the knowledge of the world are inconsequential distractions that are hindrances to one's spiritual growth. We must learn to unlearn what we know about them and dispose of them as we do with garbage. They are not even real.

In his endeavor to take hold of the soul, Socrates' search for self-knowledge is not to be construed as a flight of consciousness into its own solitude away from everything and everybody. Such a flight is found in certain Eastern philosophies and in mystic traditions, in which the goal is to bracket away the whole world, human and nonhuman, in order to become immersed in absolute self-abstraction. Here, there is complete silence and isolation, as the world, the not-I, is reduced to a virtual nothingness. Here, too, at the climax of meditation and ecstasy, only pure self-consciousness exists.

With Socrates, however, neither silence nor isolation is his existential mode of life. Aside from those mysterious moments of ecstatic forgetfulness or listlessness of which we spoke earlier, we find him immersed in the world of others. With him, the meaning of the soul is found through dialogue. His ferocious loquacity and his obvious need of human companionship are ample proofs of this. The already quoted lines of Xenophon can be recalled in this regard: "Socrates lived always in the open. Early in the morning, he went to the public promenades and training grounds, and in the forenoon he was seen in the marketplace. He spent the rest of the day where most people were to be met, and he was generally talking to anyone who would listen to him" (*Memorabilia* 1.1.10).

The same description comes to us from Plato's testimony. In the *Apology*, we read that one of the accusations against Socrates was that he was a busybody who could not stop meddling with other people's affairs. In the *Phaedrus*, he assures us that he would follow anyone all over Greece and wherever else he could, just for the benefit of human companionship. Obviously, his soul longed passionately for the human presence. To be, that is, to exist, was for him to be with others and to be a part of their existence.

A life in isolation, such as we find among the desert anchorites of early Christian times, could not have been his mode of existence.

Socrates' need to be with people has two deep and interrelated roots: his avowed eroticism, understood in the sense of an irresistible need for human love, and his conviction that the reflection of his own soul can be best discerned in the souls of others. To see oneself, it is necessary to look into the eyes of others. Nowhere can we find a better and more succinct expression of his eroticism than in that memorable comment reported by Xenophon in his *Symposium*, where Socrates says to Antisthenes that he cannot remember any period of his life when he was not in love with somebody. In Plato's *Symposium*, "love," says Socrates, "is the one thing in the world I understand." The vertigo-producing passion with which he stands in relation to Alcibiades is graphically described by Plato in the same dialogue.

In the *Charmides*, Socrates' erotic nature is magnificently portrayed, as the youthful Charmides makes his entrance into the dramatic scene: Socrates is suddenly at the brink of losing his habitual self-possession, as he "catches fire" at the sight of the young man. In sum, then, Socrates reveals himself as a man capable of experiencing great love, of course, for certain persons more than for others, and as a man for whom love represents the ultimate human experience. The apotheosis of love recorded by Plato in the *Phaedrus* and in the *Symposium* can surely be associated, at least in its origin, with the historical Socrates.

We must bear in mind, however, that the Socratic love is one that transcends the ordinary level of physical relatedness that is customarily what people call love, often expressed in that curious phrase "making love," as if love were like a sausage—a thing that can be *made*. It is not Charmides' body that Socrates craves, nor is the physical Alcibiades the object of his desire. The physical person is nothing but a fragile mask behind which the real person hides, and, thus, when love is directed only at the body, it can only be a perverted and misguided emotion. The only appropriate object of love is the true person, that is, the person's soul, and the genuine consummation of love is not what is sought at the moment when two bodies frantically and thoughtlessly achieve some sort of desperate and illusory union, but only when one soul recognizes itself in the soul of another person. As a soul looks into the eyes of the beloved and sees itself in them as if on a mirror (*Alcibiades I* 133a), it experiences the overwhelming desire to become spiritually one with the other. It discovers in the other soul something that, like itself, is a manifestation of God in this world. Love is, then, the bridge that links one soul to another and is what furnishes us with the only possible source of meaningfulness in human existence. Everything else is secondary and unimportant and only a poor reflection of reality.

As we reflect on Socrates' understanding of love, we realize that for him, it is only in and through human speech that the linking effectiveness of love can be actualized. Language is, therefore, the articulation of love. Through language, the soul learns to understand itself, and by the use of speech, its thinking faculties gain in clarity and precision. It is also in and through language that the soul discerns the reality of other souls because the true person manifests himself through language. "Speak," said Socrates once to a youth, "so that I can *see* you," for what we see with our eyes is only the transitory and negligible physical frame. What we 'see' with our ears can be the genuine expression of the person's inner being.

Thus, language has for Socrates a unique place of importance, almost as if it were something sacred. The sophists also valued language, but, indeed, for other reasons. For them, it was an instrument of communication, a tool of persuasion, and a means for social and political success. It was the kind of thing that can be used for all sorts of purposes, including hiding who we are and what we think, as when we use it to deceive.

For Socrates, however, language is the authentic expression of thought and, if rightly and truthfully used, it is the most genuine manifestation of the soul. Its adulterated and incorrect use reveals a misguided soul and augments the obfuscation in which such a soul lives. Its abuse, moreover, constitutes a formidable obstacle for the attainment of wisdom and, hence, of virtue.

It is for this reason that Socrates' mission initially takes on the form of a pervasive analysis of language. His aim *appears* to be the clarification of words and the discovery of the precise definitions of terms, especially those in which ethical ideas are conveyed. In human speech, he discovered a great deal of confusion and ambiguity. People generally speak as if they understood the meanings of the words they use, but, in reality, all they do is utter sounds that stand in their minds for little or nothing. They repeat what they have heard from others and regurgitate the platitudes they have memorized from books that contain endless concatenations of meaningless phrases. Their intellectual inertia and their pride convince them that they understand what they mechanically say. They even congratulate themselves for their irrelevant wisdom and for their ability to impress listeners who are as clueless as they are about what is being said. As Antisthenes, Socrates' associate, would put it, they would have been better off had they been born mute and deaf.[6] They are truly sick, not in the body, but in the mind, and are urgently in need of medication.

Thus, Socrates' compulsive obsession with the clarification of language is not an end in itself but a means to an end. But what could the end be if not curing people of their intellectual and spiritual disease? This disease can be characterized as a befogging and obscuring of the soul under mantles of poorly understood words such as piety, justice, happiness, friendship, and other ethically relevant terms. Inaccurate language and the misuse and abuse of words are not only the symptoms of that disease but are also contributing causes for its presence in the soul. If those mantles are removed, then it is possible at least for some people to undergo a regeneration. In the *Phaedo*, we hear Socrates say, "You may be sure, my dear Cebes, that inaccurate language is not only in itself a mistake. It implants evil in the human soul" (*Phaedo* 115e).

We can then understand the urgency with which Socrates dealt with language. As physicians cure the ailing body by purging it of detrimental substances, Socrates goes about healing people of their linguistic confusions, assuming precisely the role of what the Cynics would later call a *iatros psyches*, that is, a physician of the soul. In the *Phaedrus*, he confirms for us his 'medical' activities, when he notes that "the method of the art of healing is much the same as that of speaking." Whereas the former makes the body healthy, the latter, if carefully applied, can make the soul aware of itself and, therefore, virtuous.

Surely the analysis of language can be a painful process because it compels a person to confront his own intellectual and spiritual vacuity. The bitter Socratic medicine causes pain and discomfort, and the reaction of the patients is either a speedy flight from their physician, as in the instance of Euthyphro, or an angry stance of resentment and haughtiness, as with Thrasymachus. In either case, it manifests a refusal to look attentively and honestly within oneself and an inability to learn the most elementary of Socrates' lessons, which, to use Dag Hammarskjöld's words, can be stated in these terms: "Respect for the word is the first commandment in the discipline by which a person can be educated to maturity—intellectual, emotional, and moral. Respect for the word—to employ it with scrupulous care and incorruptible love of truth—is essential if there is to be any growth in a society or in the human race."[7]

Probably, in most of those who came in contact with Socrates, the effectiveness of the medicine, applied by him as if they were in urgent need of medical attention, had no positive results. The 'victims' of his interrogations remained mostly unchanged after his intervention and went about their business as if nothing had happened. They had failed to understand the need to respect the word.

There should be no need to reiterate that for Socrates, the analysis of language is something that transcends itself and has a goal far beyond the academic and often sterile compulsion to clarify the meanings of words. It is for him *the* method of his philosophical mission, a mission that involves the task of making the eye of the soul turn and look in the right direction, since in most people, as he tells us in the *Republic*, this eye is accustomed to looking in the wrong direction. Once the soul has been led to recognize its deficiency and confusion, it will inevitably turn itself into the right path.

It must also be pointed out that for Socrates, language is conceived of as a living reality. The language with which he is concerned is *not* the artificial language preferred by sophists, rhetoricians, and scholars, nor, in general, the written word. It is the language of actual and spontaneous conversation, that is, the spoken dialogue. As we have seen, no writings are attributable to him, although it may appear surprising that a man who apparently had so much to say would have chosen not to leave for posterity at least a collection of aphorisms and maxims, especially at a time when writing had already become a common form of expression.

Yet, it is easy to understand Socrates' choice. For him, the written word is rigid and unchangeable, like something dead with which it is impossible to establish a meaningful rapport. At some point he observes that writing "has this strange quality and is very much like painting. Painted images appear to be living beings, but if one asks them a question, they maintain a solemn silence. It is the same with written words. You might think that they could speak as if they had intelligence, but if you question them, wishing to understand what they mean, they go on saying the same thing over and over again" (*Phaedrus* 275d).

It is, therefore, not with books that Socrates deals. His attention is not caught by the words written by those with whom he cannot converse directly, for such words, once written, are like fossilized thoughts that cannot be revived. One may wonder how much he would have wished to engage Anaxagoras and other earlier philosophers in a lively dialogue about their understanding of reality and the reasons why, according to them, things happen as they do. Yet, they were not able to *speak* with him because they were dead. All that he had at his disposal were written scrolls that could not answer his questions. Reading them, moreover, might be comparable to chewing food others had already chewed, as one of Socrates' Cynic descendants would have put it. That sort of food, obviously, would have been neither tasteful nor healthy. Instead of awakening and nourishing the mind, reading may have the tendency of debilitating our thinking capacity.

One can appreciate Socrates' pious hope, of which he spoke at his trial, that perhaps, if death is a migration from this world to another, he might have the opportunity to interrogate those famous men of earlier times, men like Homer and Hesiod, who once claimed to know so much about so many things and who left their wisdom in writings that still dazzle people who read such things. How wonderful, Socrates says, it would be to converse with them, as he does with his contemporaries, in order to know whether their wisdom was real or only an illusion!

The spoken word takes on a variety of forms and serves a multiplicity of purposes. There is, for instance, that most common form of discourse that is made up of strings of fragmented and disjointed utterances by means of which ordinary people endeavor to keep themselves relatively safe from the normal state of total boredom in which they live, and which is called idle talk—talking for the sake of talking. It generally includes all sorts of salutations, social pleasantries, and innocuous remarks about the weather, about one's health, about the latest news, or about a person's most recent experiences. It appears as gossip about things and people, and is equivalent to the chattering of parrots. For many people, it is the structural frame of their social life. It is generally harmless, although it often increases the level of dissipation and distraction in which ordinary minds naturally function. It frequently acts as a barrier to self-understanding. In it, as Schopenhauer insisted, there is hardly ever any listening because people only hear themselves.

Surely, Socrates, who was as human as anybody else, was probably not altogether immune to this kind of language. Judging from Xenophon's *Symposium*, he, too, would be engaged at times in idle talk. In Plato's dialogues, moreover, this idle talk also makes an appearance, but there, it invariably serves the purpose of setting the dramatic scene or functions as a bridge between scenes. Its importance is minimal, which is understandable given Socrates' reported philosophical intensity and concentration of mind.

There is another type of discourse that assumes the form of speeches such as we find in the language of orators, politicians, and preachers. In this kind of language, we often come upon the worst instances of the misuse and abuse of speech and of the ability to stifle the soul. Such language, commonly couched in rhetorical elegance, includes fancy words, long sentences, repetitious phrases, unending paragraphs, and linguistic games, which conspire to create the semblance of meaningful communication, but which, in reality, fail to communicate anything.

The primary aim of this type of language is to convince and move the audiences and to present the speakers in a positive light. In it, neither the speakers nor the audiences have the slightest clue as to what is being said because the very meanings of the words employed are not understood by anybody or are twisted beyond recognition. The speakers themselves, especially among modern politicians, are not even responsible for preparing their speeches. They have at their disposal an army of speech writers—the descendants of the sophists of Socrates' time—whose job is to please and manipulate the mindless crowds. When a politician announces that it is his moral duty to spread democracy throughout the world, we can be reasonably sure that his understanding of concepts like morality, duty, democracy, and world is null. Neither are the people whom he addresses able to understand what he says.

There are instances in Plato's dialogues, including the early dialogues, where we find Socrates engaged in long rhetorical speeches. This can be seen, for example, in the *Menexenus*, the *Gorgias*, and the *Republic*. The *Apology* itself is an outstanding example of the best rhetorical writing, and if it reflects what Socrates said in court, it is also a magnificent demonstration of rhetorical speaking. Still, on the basis of Plato's testimony, nowhere contradicted by Xenophon, we can assume that Socrates was not especially attached to this type of discourse. His preference was on the side of short and pointed exchanges. Long speeches, he tells us, bored him, adding, perhaps ironically, that he could not easily follow them from beginning to end—he would forget at the end what was said at the beginning. It is for this reason that, in the *Republic*, he does not even allow Thrasymachus the luxury of long statements.

The authentic Socratic dialogue is far removed from the free-flowing discourse to which people are accustomed. It is in Plato more than in Xenophon that we come face to face with it. Its content is determined by the requirement imposed by Socrates on his interlocutors to reach a clear understanding of the meaning of a word: "It is the word (*logos*) that I chiefly examine" (*Protagoras* 333c). In Plato's early dialogues and generally in Xenophon's writings, the word has some ethical or moral import. The progress of the discourse follows the path of the Socratic *elenchus*.

The word *elenchus* is present throughout Plato's writings in a variety of contexts. In the *Gorgias* alone, the root *elench* appears over fifty times. In the seventh letter (*Epist.* 7.344b), it is used in the sense of a disputation by the use of question and answer, and in the *Apology* (39b), it simply stands for an account, as when we ask someone to give an account of his life. In the *Sophist* (230d), we are told that the *elenchus* or refutation is the greatest and most effective way to purify the soul, and elsewhere it is said to be some sort of inspection. In general, as the word is used by Plato, its meaning conveys the sense of a refutation or a cross-examination, a meaning that coincides with the Aristotelian use of the word, as in *Sophistical Arguments* (164a).

More specifically, the Socratic *elenchus* takes the form of a refutation in which the interlocutor is compelled to examine and assess a statement made at the beginning of the conversation by eliciting from him further statements, in the light of which his original statement contradicts itself or, at least, appears unsound. In the end, the *elenchus* does not attempt to demonstrate any specific contention. It cleanses the person's mind by showing the emptiness of his conceptions. In a sense, then, it is a carefully contrived argument in which, by posing the right kinds of questions and by forcing the interlocutor to make certain inferences, we succeed in convincing him of his ignorance or confusion with respect to his original assertion. If correctly employed and gratefully received, it functions as a type of *catharsis* or purging of the mind.

Thus, in the *Sophist* (227d), Socrates specifically refers to his method as being cathartic because it involves the removal of evil from the soul. This is accomplished, as noted above, by forcing the person to examine himself through the analysis of his own utterances. As the soul becomes aware in this way of its own ignorance and as it grows more conscious of its own intellectual and spiritual poverty, the expected result is a longing to escape from such a condition. What was once accepted as clear and true knowledge is now seen as a detrimental misconception of true virtue. He who once walked in darkness and depravity is finally cleansed of his old prejudices and errors, which were the chains that held him in a condition of ignorance. For there can be no greater hindrance for the soul than the mistaken conviction that we know something when, in fact, we do not. The path that leads to wisdom and virtue begins with a confession of ignorance.

The first step in this path is, of course, the examination of the language through which the soul reveals itself. It always begins in the same way, that is, with the search of the correct definition of virtue or one of the virtues, as exemplified in the *Euthyphro* and the *Meno*:

> Tell me, Euthyphro, what do you say holiness is, and what, unholiness? (*Euthyphro* 5d)

> What do you yourself [Meno] say virtue is? I do ask you in all earnestness not to refuse me, but to speak out. (*Meno* 71d)

In each case, the definition is set up as the goal of the *elenchus*.

The search for the definition of ethical ideas is, according to Aristotle, Socrates' main contribution to philosophy. As Aristotle notes, the search for the definition is equivalent to an inquiry into the essence of the idea under investigation, and it is the apprehension of such an essence that truly constitutes knowledge. Socrates' conviction, certainly not fully shared by Aristotle, that knowledge is the necessary and sufficient condition for virtue offers then the justification for his insistence on arriving at the correct definition of the virtues. His expectation is that the knowledge of the essence of virtue, articulated in language by means of the correct definition, will necessarily compel the person to act virtuously. Undoubtedly, therefore, this validates Socrates' appeal to the *elenchus*. He did not search for definitions simply to clarify language or to satisfy his curiosity but to bring about the moral regeneration of people.

Even if the identification of knowledge with virtue is challenged, the *elenchus* may still retain some of its intellectual value as an academic endeavor, but its primary function, namely, the moral regeneration of the soul, turns out to be marginal and contingent. For Aristotle, the will, that is the faculty with which we act, does not have to follow the dictates of reason, that is, the faculty with which we know. For Socrates, however, once reason recognizes the good, the will has no option but to obey its dictates.

As noted earlier, the effect of Socrates' *elenchus* was often quite different from what he would have wished. The regeneration of the soul was seldom achieved, and we can rest assured that many of those to whom such an intellectual *catharsis* was administered walked away from Socrates as if nothing had happened. For some, it must have been a source of amusement, and such people must have gone their way with the impression that Socrates did resemble, after all, the character of Aristophanes' comedy.

For others, especially among politicians, sophists, and philosophers, the *elenchus* had to be an occasion for embarrassment in which their arrogance and self-assurance were subjected to public humiliation. In the *Republic* (1.350d), for instance, we stand in the presence of a blushing and angry Thrasymachus, who, "with much balking and reluctance and prodigious sweating," finds it impossible to tolerate the logical siege mounted by the merciless Socrates.

Still for others, as might be expected, the *elenchus* proved to be worth imitating and practicing. As Socrates observed at his trial, it was fashionable for certain ambitious young men to question their elders and superiors in the style they had learned from him. Surely, such imitators augmented the embarrassment created by his questioning and lent support to the accusation leveled against him concerning the corruption of the youth.

There must have been many for whom beneath Socrates' *elenchus* there lurked a deceptive and hypocritical manipulator of language. These people must have suspected that Socrates knew perfectly well the answers to all his questions, which made his confession of ignorance an ironic, if not a sarcastic, game, just as were his references to himself as a midwife. His consistent refusal to let *them* reverse the direction of the *elenchus* back to himself—he would not let *them* ask him questions—was an incontrovertible proof of his insincerity. For them, therefore, the *elenchus* had a contrary effect to that intended by him. It augmented their spiritual and intellectual obfuscation as they became more convinced of their wisdom and righteousness.

Lastly, for still others, but certainly very few, Socrates' *elenchus* proved to be an experience that caused in them a profound sense of bewilderment. Aware of their ignorance and convicted of arrogance, they stood speechless and embarrassed in the presence of the inquisitive philosopher. For them, perhaps, such a painful experience was their first step in the long journey toward self-understanding and the discovery of their souls. Freed from the chains of prejudice and obscure thinking that tie most people as if to the bottom of a cave and touched by the spirit of curiosity and wonder, which, as Aristotle notes (*Metaphysics* 982b), is the true beginning of wisdom, these few people must have been the only ones who eventually profited from the philosophical medicine so liberally administered by Socrates. They were capable of giving birth to meaningful ideas. Meno's memorable statement concerning the effect of Socrates' *elenchus* on him is worth quoting:

> Socrates, even before I met you they told me that in plain truth you are a perplexed man yourself and reduce others to perplexity. At this moment, I feel that you are exercising magic and witchcraft on me and positively laying me under your spell until I am just a mass of helplessness. If I may be flippant, I think that not only in outward appearance but in other respects as well, you are exactly like the flat sting ray that one meets in the sea. Whenever anyone comes in contact with it, it numbs him, and that is the sort of thing that you seem to be doing to me now. My mind and my lips are liter-

ally numb, and I have nothing to reply to you. Yet, I have spoken about virtue hundreds of times and held forth often on the subject in front of large audiences, and very well indeed, or so I thought. Now I can't even say what virtue is. (*Meno* 80a–b)

The success or failure of the Socratic *elenchus* depends, of course, on the type of person who is subjected to it. For its application, Socrates made use of a variety of techniques, if we may be allowed to use this word. Some of these are informal, some formal. Typical of the first group is Socrates' contention that the *elenchus* is *not* an interrogation undertaken as if he were acting on his own. It miraculously happens, as if he were only a medium for it. He often reminds us, as he does to Euthyphro, that the *elenchus* begins and moves toward its inevitable goal regardless of how he himself feels or even thinks about the matter. "The most exquisite thing about my art," he says to Euthyphro, "is that I am clever against my will" (*Euthyphro* 11d). It is not Socrates who asks the questions. It is not he who refutes the definitions of his interlocutors. It is not he who compels them to confess their ignorance and confusion. It is not he who even chooses the people who are to be questioned or the subject of the conversation. It is not he who is seeking the rebirth of their souls. He does not even know how his interrogations would end, nor what effect they will have. If not Socrates, however, who or what is at work during the *elenchus*?

All sorts of answers can be proposed and have been proposed to this, one of the most perplexing aspects of the Socratic phenomenon. As much as with attempts to explain Socrates' divine voice or sign, here, too, all answers appear to fall short of providing a satisfactory solution. Some of the early Fathers of the Church maintained that he was literally possessed by a demon because that is how possessed people speak and act. Others have suspected a psychopathological problem, a touch of madness, we might say, that made him speak in peculiar ways and do strange things.

No wonder those who experienced his presence went on to become so many different types of people, just like the statues made by the legendary Daedalus, which, once made, would not stay still and would assume all sorts of shapes. His followers turned out to be different precisely because he revealed himself in very different ways. Even Meno, the man whom he once left speechless and benumbed and in love with virtue, ended up walking along the path of vice—it was he who betrayed the Greek army into the hands of the Persians at precisely the same time Socrates was being executed.

Thus, with respect to Socrates' claim that the *elenchus* is not *his* doing but is something that somehow is done *to* him, there is obviously no definitive explanation. We could, however, listen attentively to what he says about the matter and come to our own conclusions. What he says *about* it is clear in countless passages of Plato's dialogues and Xenophon's testimony and is not different from what he says about his divine sign or voice. In essence, he claims no responsibility for either. He points his finger away from himself and at God or the Delphic god. His entire life, his philosophical mission, he tells the jurors, has been a fulfillment of his duty to obey a reality beyond himself. He has undertaken the search for the soul, a task that has structured every aspect of his life, in obedience to the directive of that reality. He would have chosen to die many times rather than to be delinquent in his duty. He himself is little or nothing, and knows little or nothing. He even complains at times of his defective memory: "I am a forgetful sort of man, Protagoras, and if someone speaks at length, I lose the thread of the argument" (*Protagoras* 334c; cf. *Meno* 71c).

Socrates claims that if it had been up to him, he would have lived a different kind of life, for who would ever choose poverty and simplicity, asceticism and resignation, of his own accord?

Who would opt for death? Who would spend his life questioning people about moral values and, to use a phrase later on used by Diogenes the Cynic, defacing the currency of his contemporaries, thereby making himself disliked and hated?[8]

For this sort of choices, rarely found among people, one must have a Herculean will and a tremendous lucidity of mind and, above all, an unshakable faith in a transcendent reality that demands obedience. The problem is, of course, that it is practically impossible for us to even begin to sketch what the transcendent reality of the Socratic experience could have been. As noted in an earlier context, nothing definite can be affirmed about Socrates' conception of God or gods—nothing at all.

It might have been a ruse or, rather, partly a ruse, a manifestation of the annoying irony that does not allow us to pin him down. Perhaps it could have been one of those games of which Alcibiades speaks in the *Symposium*. Indeed, often he does not say quite what he means and does not mean what he says. He is literally a bundle of contradictions and byways. He is the ugliest man, yet the most beautiful; the wisest, yet a man devoid of wisdom; the most bestial, yet as chaste as Athena; the poorest, yet the wealthiest; and so on and on.

This irony is present just about everywhere in Plato's dialogues, surfacing here and there in Xenophon's testimony. Repeatedly, it makes him pose as an ignorant man in urgent need of instruction, as when he decides to become Euthyphro's pupil: "The best thing I can do, my admirable Euthyphro, is to become your pupil, and, before the indictment of Meletus comes on, to challenge him and say that I have always thought it very important to know about divine things and that now, since he says that I am doing wrong by acting carelessly and making innovations in matters of religion, I have become your pupil" (*Euthyphro* 5a).

In the *Republic*, Socrates calls Thrasymachus a wise man and asks him to enlighten everybody about the nature of justice, claiming to be himself thoroughly ignorant about this and many other things. The sophist, however, is apparently too clever for Socrates' subterfuge and accuses him of outright hypocrisy: "By the gods! Here we have the well-known irony of Socrates! I knew it and predicted that when it came to replying, you would refuse and dissemble and do anything rather than answer any questions that anyone asked you" (*Republic* 1.337a; cf. *Memorabilia* 1.2.36).

Besides these informal devices, characteristic of the *elenchus*, there are others more formal, including the appeal to inductive arguments, which Aristotle expressly associates with Socrates (*Metaphysics* 1078b). The Aristotelian association of Socrates with the inductive method must not be interpreted to mean that he invented it. We must assume that deduction and induction, as natural reasoning processes, are as ancient as the human species. Aristotle's point is simply that it was Socrates who for the first time used induction in a systematic and methodic way in the search for definitions. With him, induction allows him to gather instances of things and situations to which a certain ethical predicate is customarily given. It soon becomes obvious that a common denominator must exist in order to justify the use of the ethical predicate in the collected instances. As these are further examined, we appeal to various techniques, chief among which are division and composition, which permit us to analyze and synthesize such instances. In the *Phaedrus* (266b), Socrates describes himself as "a lover of these processes of division and bringing together."

Yet, significant as the characteristics of the *elenchus* may be, of far greater importance is the goal that, as a magnet, guided Socrates in the process of questioning people about their ethical convictions. This goal, as we have already emphasized, is the unveiling—the discovery—of the human soul. Nothing is more important, nothing more urgent, than understanding who we are. This is the meaning of that memorable statement that sums up much of what he himself was: "An unexamined life is not worth living."

The most useful tool for the unveiling of the soul was for him the rigorously methodic and painfully honest examination of language—of the things we say—because it is in it and through it that what we think is brought to light and because our thoughts ultimately structure who we are. Language, as we have seen, was for Socrates not merely an instrument of communication or a tool for social success but the true manifestation of the soul.

In a magical way, language creates reality. Light, according to the biblical tale, came into being when God *said*, "Let there be light" (Gen. 1:3). "The word, the *logos*," we are told in another biblical passage, "was in the beginning and was one with the Godhead" (John 1:1). If the word, the *logos*, were to disappear, both light and the world would be plunged into nothingness, because reality emerges and is sustained only in the context of the word, that is, through the agency of language. The world is only in the word and for the word, and is nothing outside of the word.

Twenty-four centuries after Socrates, the creative magic of language was recaptured with great clarity by Martin Heidegger when he wrote: "Words and language are not wrappings in which things are packaged for the commerce of those who write and speak. It is in words and language that things first come into being and are. For this reason, the misuse of language in idle talk, in slogans and phrases, destroys our authentic relation to things."[9] Indeed, Socrates would have added that in idle talk, in meaningless slogans and phrases, reality is itself disintegrated and the soul is reduced to nothing.

Still, Socrates' search for the soul must have been animated by a profound conviction that it is possible to find it and seize it. We noted earlier that despite his apparent skepticism about the things of which he spoke, there must have lived in him certain certitudes that remained unshakable until his death. For these to have been so firmly implanted in his mind, there must have been in him a certain faith, an absolutely unquestionable basis of certainty. What, then, could have been his faith?

NOTES

1. A. Schopenhauer, *The World as Will and Representation*, vol. 1 (Indian Hills, CO: Falcon's Wing Press, 1958), p. 412.

2. F. Nietzsche, *The Twilight of the Idols*, 1889.

3. T. Gomperz, *Greek Thinkers: A History of Ancient Philosophy*, vol. 2, trans. G. C. Berry (London: John Murray, 1905), p. 45.

4. There may be a relationship between the name of the Delphic dragon (Python) and the Greek verb (*pytho*), which conveys the idea of making things rotten.

5. W. Jaeger, *Paideia: The Ideals of Greek Culture*, vol.1, trans. Gilbert Highet (New York: Oxford University Press, 1945), p. 285.

6. For an examination of Antisthenes' theory of language, see L. E. Navia, *Antisthenes of Athens: Setting the World Aright* (Westport, CT: Greenwood Press, 2001).

7. D. Hammarskjöld, *Markings* (New York: Knopf, 1971), p. 112.

8. The Greek word *nomisma* means both currency in the sense of coins and currency in the sense of customs and values. Diogenes is said to have been instructed by the Delphic oracle to challenge or deface the values and customs of his contemporaries.

9. M. Heidegger, *An Introduction to Metaphysics*, trans. R. Manheim (New Haven, CT: Yale University Press, 1964), pp. 13–14.

CHAPTER 7
The Socratic Faith

$\mathcal{T}$he opening words of Kant's *Critique of Pure Reason* can furnish us with a point of departure for this concluding chapter, in which we will attempt to come to grips with the basis of Socrates' philosophy. "Human reason," says Kant, "has this peculiar fate that in one species of its knowledge it is burdened by questions which, as prescribed by the very nature of reason itself, it is not able to ignore, but which, as transcending all its powers, it is also not able to answer."[1]

Understood in a general sense, Kant's statement paints for us a somber and pessimistic picture of the human condition. Beset by urgent and unavoidable questions that cannot be ignored, the mind is unable to answer them because they lie beyond the limits imposed on it by nature. From the point of view of knowledge, then, it remains forever impossible to make any definitive statements about things-in-themselves, that is, about reality. Never will we be able to *know* with certainty anything about the existence and nature of God and the soul, and the reality or lack of reality of the freedom of the will. With respect to these issues, indeed the most important in human existence, we are condemned to grope in darkness because knowledge about them is outside the perimeters of our rational powers.

We must rest satisfied with the *semblance* of knowledge, not actual knowledge, about such matters. Semblance of knowledge, however, is not knowledge and is something that amounts only to passing and subjective opinions of little value. In what concerns knowledge, then, the cave of human existence has ultimately no exit, regardless of what Plato could have said and imagined to the contrary and regardless of what centuries of optimistic philosophical and scientific thought may have sought to demonstrate. Knowledge about reality is an illusion, and we are forever doomed to live in the shadowy dimension of appearances.

If Kant is correct about the human condition and if he had not envisioned the possibility of an escape route out of the cave, we would not be better than Tantalus, the legendary and immortal king who was once punished by the gods for stealing their food and passing it on to humans. His unending punishment could not have been more cruel. Immersed in water up to his chin, as Homer tells us (*Od.* 11.582 ff.), and surrounded by trees laden with luscious fruits, he can neither drink nor eat. When he tries to drink, the water vanishes into nothing as soon as it touches his lips, and when he reaches for the fruits, the wind blows them away. He is, accordingly, condemned to pass eternity forever thirsty and forever hungry, tantalized by things that he must have but cannot reach.

We, too, may be like Tantalus. The crucial questions that demand an answer must forever remain unanswered, and the more we struggle to answer them, the more urgent they appear to us and the more inaccessible their answers are. Indeed, it is not a pretty picture of the human condition! It is as if God, the gods, nature, or the randomness of evolution had played a vicious joke on us by making us want to know and understand, yet depriving us of the power to succeed in our endeavors.

For Kant, however, there is an exit, but this is furnished by *faith*, not by knowledge. Metaphysics, which is ultimately based on reason, promises firm knowledge but delivers none in what concerns subjects such as God, the soul, and the freedom of the will. This can be ascertained by a review of the history of philosophy, in which, as much as in Plato's early dialogues, there is much searching for answers, but no definitive conclusions. In metaphysics, says Kant, "ever and ever again we have to retrace our steps, as not leading us in the direction in which we desire to go. So far, too, are the students of metaphysics from exhibiting any kind of unanimity in their contentions, that metaphysics has rather to be regarded as a battleground quite peculiarly suited for those who desire to exercise themselves in mock combats, and in which no participant has ever yet succeeded in gaining even so much as an inch of territory."[2] The naked appeal to reason yields, therefore, the *expectation* of genuine understanding, not the *attainment* of true knowledge. What true knowledge, for instance, can we gather from the mock combat in which Socrates and Euthyphro are so fiercely engaged, as they struggle with the issue of the basis of moral values? Or between Socrates and Thrasymachus, as they discuss the nature of justice? Or between Socrates and Protagoras, as they consider the problem of knowledge? None, indeed.

Were it not for the escape route made possible by faith, Kant affirms, we would remain in a permanent state of skepticism, not unlike, we might add, the skepticism embraced by some of the sophists of Socrates' time or the indifference with which the Cynics viewed metaphysics. For Diogenes, let us remember, Plato's philosophy was a waste of time.

As we consider the basis of Socrates' philosophy, we can discern in it something reminiscent of the Kantian idea of faith. We say reminiscent because we cannot ignore the gap that separates the German philosopher from Socrates. In some respects, they stand apart. Yet, as has been recognized by many, there is much in Kant, especially during the last years of his life, that sounds like a distant echo of Socrates' voice. Kant's conception of faith furnishes us with an example of this circumstance.

Whereas Kant reaches the conclusion that the most significant issues that confront the mind—God, the soul, and the freedom of the will—can never be answered by means of pure reason, Socrates carries out the examination of his self—the search for the soul—only to arrive at the apparently disappointing result that if he knows more than others, it is because he is conscious of his lack of knowledge. Yet, Socrates is animated by some sort of *faith*, which, as an overwhelming obsession, determines the course of his philosophical journey and saves him from the skepticism into which the sophists had fallen. Like them, he was conscious of his lack of knowledge, but unlike them, he persisted in his quest.

Like Kant, therefore, there is in him the awareness of the *possibility* of attaining certainty. Thus, in him, we discern what Kant would have called faith. It is not altogether far-fetched to suggest that Socrates could have said what many centuries later Kant said: "I have found it necessary to deny *knowledge*, in order to make room for *faith*."[3] It was faith that rescued Kant from agnosticism and it was also faith that sustained Socrates in his search for the soul.

What is essential, however, is to gain some understanding of what sort of faith it was that sustained Socrates. Does it entail the rejection of the possibility of knowledge? Is it an indictment of the pretensions of human reason, which, to use Kant's words, often "ventures out on the wing of the ideas in the empty space of pure understanding,"[4] getting entangled in the webs of its own illusions? Is it a repetition of Protagoras's abandonment of certainty or a reiteration of Gorgias's assertion that nothing can be known? Is it a provisional acknowledgment of intellectual failure that still leaves ample room for possible successes? Is it merely an ironical device behind which there stands a man of firm convictions?

It is possible to make a case for each one of these interpretations. With Socrates, many things are possible. The problem posed by the nature of our information makes it unadvisable to speak with finality about him. In an earlier chapter, we commented on the variety of interpretations of Socrates' philosophy, and there, we could have also added the opinion of an Eastern scholar, according to whom, nobody in the Western world has ever succeeded in deciphering the Socratic message.[5]

Writing early in the fourth century CE, Lactantius, a Christian apologist, was of the opinion that in professing ignorance, Socrates was expressing the fact that he was an ignorant man. He knew nothing of value. Many centuries later, Jeremy Bentham reached the same conclusion. According to him, Socrates was an empty-headed man who spent his time "talking nonsense under the pretense of teaching wisdom and morality." In his moral character, moreover, he was far "below the level of mankind."[6]

It is not difficult to recognize in these and other interpretations clear confirmations of an already mentioned statement of Schopenhauer: "No one can see above his height." Indeed, no one can see in Socrates anything not already present in himself. Lactantius, who converted to Christianity in his mature years and living at a time when the Christians were still being persecuted in Rome, discovered in pagan philosophy the unmistakable presence of the devil. Intoxicated with the evangelical truth he found in biblical texts, he thundered against the pagan ideas disseminated by the devil's emissaries—the philosophers—Socrates among them. He concluded that Socrates was a tempter of innocent souls and an ignorant man posing as an enlightened thinker. He was only honest when he spoke about his lack of knowledge. No attention, therefore, should be paid to him.

As for Bentham, the advocate of utilitarianism in the nineteenth century, what else could he have said about the abstemious and moderate Socrates, who had little regard for the things of the flesh and for the amenities furnished by the material world? What else could he have said in view of his contention that moral values must be based on the *amount* of pleasure—any kind of pleasure—human actions produce? Surely, from such a hedonistic perspective, Socrates could not be anything but an empty-headed man who spent his life talking nonsense about this and that. This was Bentham's learned conclusion about him. Obviously, he could not see above his own height.

The list of interpretations of Socrates' confession of ignorance is literally interminable. In it, one finds every imaginable point of view and every conceivable conclusion, as much as with respect to the interpretations of his divine sign or voice.[7] Perhaps, instead of dwelling on them, it might be wiser to concentrate our attention on what the primary sources and Aristotle say about what could have been the meaning and purpose of Socrates' statement that he knew little or nothing.

Aristotle, as we saw earlier, explicitly mentions Socrates' confession of ignorance: "Socrates would only ask questions without answering them. He maintained that he did not know" (*Sophistical Arguments* 183b).

Yet, Aristotle attributes to him certain convictions, in particular the idea that knowledge is the necessary and sufficient condition for virtue. Thus, on the basis of his testimony, we can conclude that, despite his confession of ignorance, Socrates *knew* at least one thing, namely, that he who knows the good will only do the good and that he who does evil is necessarily ignorant of what he does.

In Xenophon, there are no explicit allusions to Socrates' confession of ignorance. On the contrary, he is a man of great practical wisdom from whom wise counsels can always be expected. Still, emphasis is often put on his search for the essence and conditions of virtue, a commitment that overshadows his practical wisdom. He is not quite a professor of wisdom like the sophists but a philosopher, that is, someone who yearns for wisdom. If, indeed, he yearns for wisdom, it is because he is aware of not possessing it.

As we turn our attention to Plato's early dialogues, where, as we have suggested, the historical Socrates may be more easily found, his skeptical character is more pronounced.[8] It practically eclipses everything else about him. What clear idea of piety does he teach Euthyphro? What positive notion of moderation does he convey to Charmides? What developed concept of justice does he pass on to Thrasymachus in the first two books of the *Republic*?[9]

In these and other instances, Socrates does not communicate any definite knowledge. All his interlocutors could have said to him what, as reported in the *Theages* (130d), Aristides once said to him: "I have never learned anything from you." How could anyone have learned anything from someone who professed to teach nothing and who claimed to know little or nothing? Socrates' conversations begin with a confession of ignorance and end with a similar confession, after which he expresses his desire to go on searching for the answers to his questions:

> Then we must begin again at the beginning and ask what holiness is, since I will not willingly give up until I learn. (*Euthyphro* 15c)

> For my part, Protagoras, when I see the subject in such utter confusion, I feel the liveliest desire to clear it up. I should like to follow up our present talk with a determined attack on virtue itself and its essential nature. (*Protagoras* 361c)

> I tell you, gentlemen—and this is confidential—that we all ought to seek out the best teacher we can find. To leave ourselves as we now are [that is, in ignorance], this I do not advise. (*Laches* 201a)

As we consider Socrates' professed ignorance, a paradoxical interpretation can be suggested. Let us say that he both knew *and* did not know a great deal about the subjects of his inquiries and that he was both willing *and* unwilling to impart his knowledge. He was wise *and* ignorant and was the most effective *and* the least effective of teachers.

To resolve this paradox, we can appeal to his own statements at the trial and those in which he speaks of himself as a sort of midwife. The sense conveyed by Socrates' remarks in the *Apology* concerning his reputation for wisdom is clear. The Delphic oracle ultimately means that he is the wisest human being because he realizes more than others the worthlessness of human knowledge. More specifically, his remarks imply that his ignorance consists more than anything else in his perplexity concerning what virtue is and that his wisdom is manifested in his conviction that virtue is the only thing worth seeking.

Thus, we come upon a way of distinguishing two senses of knowing. Socrates does not know *what* virtue is, but knows *that* virtue is the sole possession we must strive to attain. *This* he knows perfectly well. He also knows that the essence of virtue is knowable, although he does not claim to have attained that knowledge. His ignorance of the essence of virtue explains his unwillingness to advance any definition of his own, whereas his optimism accounts for his indefatigable efforts to arrive at the right definition. For this purpose, as he says in the *Republic* (1.336e), he would leave no stone unturned and no path untrodden to find the gold that will make him immeasurably rich. For this purpose, too, he enlists the assistance of his acquaintances. He cannot enrich them with something he does not have, but he can urge them to seek with him.

At the end of his life, the perplexed Socrates remains as perplexed as he always was. In a sense, he reaches the consummation of his life in a state of temporary disappointment, for which reason he expresses the desire to go on searching for his gold, if, as people say, there is another life after death: "What would one not sacrifice, gentlemen, to be able to question the leader of that glorious army against Troy, or Odysseus, or Sisyphus, or the innumerable other men and women with whom it would be a wonderful experience to be able to talk and argue?" (*Apology* 41c).

Socrates' conception of heaven is not what is sometimes envisioned, that is, a condition of perfect and unending joy and ecstasy in the presence of God. That kind of heaven, one can be certain, would not be for him an appealing prospect. If there is a heaven, he envisions it as a place where his earthly questioning could be prolonged forever and where he could have the opportunity to interrogate the famous men and women of ancient times precisely about the things he interrogated his contemporaries. Perhaps in that heaven, he hopes, he will be able to find the gold that eluded him while in this life.

Despite Socrates' apparent failure to discover the gold of knowledge, he is in possession of a treasure, for he truly knows that virtue alone is what we must understand and possess. This unshakable conviction, repeated by him on many occasions, explains the earnestness and dedication with which he pursues his mission. When he speaks of his willingness to die one hundred times rather than to abandon it, he reveals himself as someone who truly knows the nature of his activity and the direction of his life. Thus, the ignorant and perplexed Socrates, more ignorant and perplexed than any other person, is, after all, a man who knows perfectly well not only the limits of his understanding but also the fact that the pursuit of virtue ought to be the sole goal of his life. His ignorance, therefore, is both real *and* unreal, real with respect to the essence of virtue, but unreal with respect to the indispensable character of virtue in human existence.

No other figure of speech is more adequate to express Socrates' wise ignorance or ignorant wisdom than his description of himself as a midwife. There are no references to it in

Xenophon's and Aristotle's testimonies, and there is only a veiled allusion to it in Aristophanes' *Clouds*. This has led some to conclude that Socrates' midwifery is strictly Plato's invention, perhaps his way to describe his own philosophical birth through the agency of Socrates.

There are, however, no compelling reasons to opt for this interpretation. Silence on the part of any of the sources is not sufficient to set aside what is found in another source. We can accordingly entertain the possibility that Socrates indeed saw himself and spoke about himself as some sort of midwife and that his mother was an actual midwife. In his mother's occupation, he could have found the perfect metaphor for his philosophical mission.

Midwives, let us recall, were traditionally older women who would assist younger women in the process of giving birth. Barren women, strictly speaking, were instrumental in actualizing the fertility of other women, which is precisely what Socrates captures in his metaphor:

> My art of midwifery is in general like that of midwives. The only difference is that my patients are men, not women. My concern is not with the body but with the soul that is in labor. The highest point of my art is the power to prove by every test whether the offspring of a young man's thought is a false phantom or is something alive and real. I am so much like the midwife that I cannot myself give birth to wisdom. The common reproach is true, that, although I question others, I can myself bring nothing to light because there is no wisdom in me. This is because God constrains me to serve as a midwife, but has debarred me from giving birth. (*Theaetetus* 150c–d)

Seen in the context of what has been said about the *elenchus* and against the background of Socrates' confession of ignorance, his art of midwifery clarifies for us the nature of his philosophical stance and the character of his mission. He, who is comparable to a gadfly (*Apology* 30e), a Spartan hound (*Parmenides* 128c), and a stingray (*Meno* 80a), is someone who stimulates the rational faculty in others and helps them in the process of creating ideas. He does not know what virtue is and is unable to instruct others in moral matters. He is not a teacher in the sense of someone who gives instruction.

Yet, he *is* a teacher, a genuine educator, if we understand this term in its etymological sense, that is, someone who leads others out of a condition of ignorance and confusion into a state of real knowledge. This is often a painful process, akin to giving birth. Moreover, just as it is seldom possible for a woman to give birth to another woman's child, likewise in the case of Socrates, it is impossible for him to create ideas for others. Surely, his activity as a midwife is bound to be demanding and dangerous and often disappointing. The instances in which the end result is aborted or a monstrosity are not rare. Sometimes the person in labor gives birth only to a phantom or to a bit of wind (*Theaetetus* 151e). In these instances, he who has expelled from his mind such an abomination is not always happily relieved of it, but feels embarrassed or angry at the midwife: "People have often felt like that toward me and have been positively ready to bite me for taking away some foolish notion they have conceived" (*Theaetetus* 151c).

The persistence with which Socrates carried on his activities as a midwife, despite the frustrating and truncated results of his endeavors, can only be explained by attributing to him an extraordinary degree of intellectual optimism. He was convinced of the possibility of finally grasping the essence of virtue. It is for this reason that in the previous chapter we distinguished the skepticism of the sophists from that of Socrates. The former held on to the conviction that knowledge is unattainable. Their admission of ignorance was a conclusion. For Socrates, however, it is a point of departure because of his belief in the possibility of knowledge at least in what concerns ethical values. For him, intellectual and spiritual enlightenment is a realizable goal.

In Socrates, therefore, we do not find the negativism and nihilism so typical among the sophists. They abandoned all hope of rising to a higher and firmer level of understanding, which had obvious consequences for their conception of ethical values. Just as they no longer believed that knowledge could be the possession of the mind, so, too, they transformed ethical values into fictions and opportunistic inventions. For them, in ethics, as in other areas of human concern, nothing could transcend the realm of transitory opinion.

With Socrates, matters are altogether different. He knows that neither he nor perhaps anyone else has succeeded in liberating himself from the bonds of ignorance. The human condition is, as Plato would make him say in the *Republic* (7.514a ff.), comparable to that of prisoners of an underground cave, whose unfortunate fate is to confuse reality with passing shadows created by a fire inside their miserable abode and kept in motion by clever manipulators, who in the name of politics, religion, science, and tradition control the human herd.

This allegory, the most memorable and influential in Plato's writings, may or may not be associated with the historical Socrates, although it is difficult not to suspect that its genesis was related to him. In the early dialogues, no less than in occasional passages from Xenophon's *Memorabilia*, Socrates speaks of groping in the dark and of searching for the light. This could hardly make any sense unless he was not convinced that the human condition is indeed like that of prisoners who live in darkness and that it is possible to escape from such a condition, as he says in the *Republic* (7.515e), by way of that "rough and steep ascent" that leads to the real world.

Whether the prisoner who in Plato's allegory succeeds in reaching the real world and returns to his former abode in order to bring to his companions the glad tidings is a representation of the historical Socrates is a matter of conjecture. Still, it is not difficult to recognize in him the image of Plato's dear friend.

The liberated prisoner and Socrates die at the hands of those to whom the message from another world is announced. Their message does not reveal *what* that other world is but merely *that* it is. It is a world waiting to be discovered. They do not pretend to be able to release others from their captivity.

Socrates' reluctance to impart knowledge and his refusal to refer to his friends as disciples—they were only his associates or companions (*synontes*)—can now be explained by appealing to Plato's allegory. No human being can take another person out of the realm of darkness and ignorance into the domain of light and wisdom, for intellectual and spiritual liberation is an accomplishment that can only be realized when a person discovers his own soul and succeeds in knowing himself.

Furthermore, the knowledge that is accessible when the world of shadows is left behind is ultimately ineffable. It cannot be described in and through language. It cannot be communicated. Paradoxically, it is through language that we may approach it, but it itself cannot be expressed in words. It must be experienced by each person in the intimacy of his individuality and cannot be taught, for it is, as Plato says, "like a blaze kindled by a leaping spark, and is generated in the soul and at once becomes self-sustaining" (*Epist.* 7.341d).

It is important to emphasize once more that for Socrates, intellectual enlightenment is not an end in itself. Understanding for the sake of understanding, knowledge for the sake of knowledge would have made little sense to him. Gladly, indeed, he would have said of philosophy in general what Aristotle said about ethics, namely, that its sole purpose is not to give us an understanding of virtue but to transform us into virtuous persons, for, otherwise, according to Aristotle, "our inquiry would have been of no use" (*Nicomachean Ethics* 1103b).

For his part, Socrates insisted that philosophical inquiries, if pursued for any purpose other than the moral regeneration of the soul, are misguided and even detrimental. He who claims to know about virtue but is unable to be himself virtuous is, to borrow the language of Saint Paul (1 Cor. 13:1), like "sounding brass or a tinkling cymbal." Had Socrates been able to rephrase the words of the Christian apostle, he would have perhaps expressed himself in these terms: "Although I may speak with tongues of men and gods, and have no virtue, I have become as sounding brass or a tinkling cymbal. Although I may have the gift of prophecy and understand all mysteries, and have all knowledge, and although I may have enough faith to move mountains, and yet have no virtue, *I am nothing*."[10] Indeed, Socrates might have added, in an even closer paraphrasing of Saint Paul's language, that without *love*, "I am nothing," because, as he admits, the only thing he truly knows is love (cf. *Symposium* 177d, *Charmides* 155c, Xenophon *Symposium* 8.2).

The juxtaposition of Socrates and Saint Paul, however, cannot be sustained much further because the chasm that separates them is enormous. The Pauline conviction that knowing what is good is *not* the sufficient condition for being good or doing what is good puts Saint Paul at a great distance from Socrates. If Saint Paul could have incorporated into his frame of mind the Platonic and probably Socratic comparison of the human condition to that of a charioteer who must manage two unequally tempered horses (*Phaedrus* 246a ff.), he would have affirmed that the evil horse, described by Plato as "crooked, heavy, ill put together," can be sufficiently strong to dominate both the other horse and the charioteer. It can convert them into miserable slaves that can be dragged about as if they were nothing (cf. *Protagoras* 352c).

For Saint Paul, the relationship between knowledge and virtue is based on his conviction that the intellect and the will are two independent human faculties that may or may not work in unison. There is in him and, through him, in the Christian conception of human nature, a profound awareness of the moral struggle in which most lives are immersed. We often know what is good, and yet we do what is bad or evil, which validates the Christian concept of sin. To commit a sin, three conditions are necessary: (1) a transgression against one of God's commands; (2) full knowledge that what is done is evil; and (3) the possibility of acting otherwise.

This conception of sin, with its underlying understanding of the relationship between the intellect and the will, is, obviously, not an exclusive Christian doctrine. The theology of Judaism is ultimately based on it, and even among the pagans, there are distinct manifestations of it. Ovid, for example, introduces us to the shattering dimensions of the moral struggle in which a person can be fully aware of what is good and virtuous and yet chooses to do the contrary despite his knowledge: "*Video meliora, proboque; deteriora sequor* (I see what is good and I approve of it. Yet, I do what is evil)" (*Metamorphoses* 7.20).

From Socrates' perspective, however, this conception of human nature is untenable. For him, there is no room for the concept of sin. Evil is never the result of one's conscious determination to do evil with knowledge of what is evil. Evil is the result of the inability of the soul to recognize what is good and, as such, it is nothing but ignorance and mental feebleness. The evil person is evil, not only because his will is corrupted but because his intellect is weak. It is his intellectual weakness that brings about his depravity. Just as evil is the result of ignorance, so are goodness and virtue the result of knowledge, for, as we read in the *Protagoras* (352c), "whoever learns what is good and what is bad will never be swayed by anything to act otherwise than as knowledge bids."

With this assertion, we come to what is perhaps the most important aspect of Socrates' philosophy, the very essence of his thought, which appears to be also an integral component of Plato's own philosophy. This aspect involves the identification of knowledge and virtue. The importance attached to it by Socrates is made manifest by the numerous occasions on which he defended it, by the assertiveness with which he expressed it, and, indeed, by the texture of his activities. Judging, moreover, from Aristotle's testimony, the identification of knowledge and virtue occupied a position of singular importance for Socrates. No other Socratic idea is treated more carefully and at greater length by Aristotle, for whom such an identification entailed a denial of the possibility of *akrasia*.

As noted in our earlier discussion of Aristotle's testimony, this term has been translated in various ways, none of which seems to be fully satisfactory. It has been rendered by words like 'incontinence'—a word often associated with the inability to control physiological functions such as urination—'unrestraint', 'powerlessness', 'psychological weakness', 'moral weakness', 'weakness of the will', and others. Of course, it should be obvious that Socrates' denial of *akrasia* has nothing to do with urination.

Perhaps the least confusing translation is simply *lack of self-restraint*. Fortunately, Aristotle's discussion in the *Nicomachean Ethics* is sufficiently clear to allow us to gain an adequate understanding of this concept, regardless of how it may be rendered in modern languages. Also, there are extended passages in Plato's dialogues, particularly in the *Protagoras*, that shed light on how Socrates understood this concept.

In essence, the problem posed by *akrasia*, according to Aristotle, amounts to this: How is it possible for a person whose judgment is correct to act without self-restraint? In other words, to use Ovid's language, is it possible that we may know the good (*meliora*) and approve of it, and yet choose, against our better judgment, what is evil or morally bad (*deteriora*)? Some people, says Aristotle, view this situation as impossible. It just cannot happen, as Socrates maintained, for he was convinced that there is no such a thing as lack of self-restraint when knowledge, understood in the sense of clarity of mind, is present. Thus, he who does wrong is necessarily someone who lacks knowledge and whose mind is befogged. Again, as noted in chapter 5, clear-headed people do not do evil things. Stupid people do.

A brief examination of Aristotle's critique of Socrates' view may be of assistance in understanding the concept of *akrasia*. With respect to moral character, according to Aristotle, there are three conditions that are to be avoided, namely, viciousness, lack of self-restraint (*akrasia*), and brutishness. The last of these, he notes, is seldom found among civilized people, although it is common among the barbarians.[11] It manifests itself in the sort of behavior that we associate with wild beasts. Savage people are brutish because they behave like animals, and for this reason they can hardly be called human. They have fallen into so low a level of mentality that their behavior cannot even be described as good or bad. They live literally beneath good and evil—like animals.

In the case of viciousness, the situation is different. The vicious person does *not* behave like an animal. His actions are guided by a deliberate purpose, but this purpose is vicious, that is, evil or bad. Fundamentally, then, such a person does not really know what is good, and his viciousness could be attributed to his faulty understanding of the hierarchy of means and ends of human existence. The vicious person, then, pursues goals and becomes engaged in actions, thinking that they are good, whereas, in fact, they are not. Vicious people, therefore, are simply stupid. They identify the good with a moment of pleasure, a piece of gold, some senseless pastime, the acquisition of fame and power, and other such useless things. Perhaps if they *knew* better, they might alter their behavior, and, thus, in *their* case, knowledge could diminish their viciousness.

Lastly, and most important for us, there is the case of the person who lacks self-restraint. Aristotle explains in these terms the difference between self-restraint and its absence: "The person who lacks self-restraint acts under the influence of emotions or passions, whereas the person of self-restraint, who knows that his desires are wrong, is guided by reason in the right course" (*Nicomachean Ethics* 1145b).

The critical question is whether the person who lacks self-restraint really *knows* that what he does is wrong and whether there is in him a certain weakness of character, which Aristotle refers to as softness, by virtue of which his reason is overpowered by his desires and appetites. That such cases abound among people, Aristotle does not doubt, for which reason he says that Socrates' position "plainly contradicts the observed facts." According to Aristotle, we succeed in making sense of the observed facts only if we clarify the sort of knowledge the person of no self-restraint possesses when, under the pressure of his impulses, he opts for immoral modes of behavior. Such a clarification, Aristotle implies, was never undertaken by Socrates, who apparently treated the concept of knowledge as if this were a univocal and simple notion.

For Aristotle, there appears to be two very different kinds of knowing. In the first kind, we may have knowledge and yet fail to apply it to our action, which in his syllogistic analysis amounts to saying that we fall short of applying the minor premise of a moral argument. Stated in plainer language, this is equivalent to saying that the person who lacks self-restraint, while knowing perfectly well that something is universally bad, fails to recognize the fact that the particular action he is about to undertake falls under the universal statement. The fact that the particular action is morally relevant is either not known to him or at that moment his knowledge may be deficient.

The second kind of knowing entails full knowledge of the major premise *and* the minor premise, in which case we are forced to say that the person of no self-restraint knows what is bad in general and what is bad for himself and that, even after reflection, he still does what is bad. But, as Aristotle confesses, such behavior would be no less than extraordinary, which leads him to conclude that "Socrates' view appears to be tenable, for lack of self-restraint develops, not in the presence of what can be called full knowledge in the proper sense of the term, but in the presence of apparent knowledge" (*Nicomachean Ethics* 1147b).

Thus, after a great deal of analysis, Aristotle comes to the conclusion that the person who lacks self-control does not have *full* knowledge *at the time* of the commission of an evil deed. His knowledge of what he does is deficient. This is equivalent to saying that evil deeds are, after all, done in ignorance, which is precisely what Socrates maintained.

Yet, the problem may be more complex. For is it really possible for emotions to befog and muddle the understanding of a person who, while knowing that certain actions are immoral, may still fail to act in accordance with what he understands to be his moral duty? Lack of self-restraint, Aristotle suggests, is comparable to the condition of people who are asleep or intoxicated, which implies that the person who lacks self-restraint is one in whom the reasoning faculty has *temporarily* succumbed under the pressure of emotions or mistaken perceptions. He does not quite understand at that time what the meaning and consequences of his actions are, just as it happens to people who are drunk.

To return to the allegory of the *Phaedrus*, the person who lacks self-restraint is one in whom the unruly or evil horse has overpowered the charioteer and the good horse. Yet, the only explanation for this is to be found in the *weakness* of the charioteer, that is, in his obfuscated vision of the good. His intellectual and spiritual vision is deficient, and his judgment is based on ignorance. Despite appearances, he does not really know. If he had in himself full knowledge of the moral character of his actions, how and why would he choose to act viciously? To do evil with full knowledge would be, as Aristotle is willing to grant, an extraordinary occurrence that defies explanation.

The question is whether full knowledge of the good is a possession that, once acquired, remains permanently engraved in the mind and, as Plato says, is self-sustaining. It can be neither destroyed nor diminished. The person who sleeps or gets intoxicated *temporarily* loses his ability to reason, but can he who has seen and understood the good ever lose his lucidity even for a moment under the pressure of emotions or external circumstances?

Aristotle considers this phenomenon a common occurrence, but Socrates does not even entertain its possibility. From a Socratic point of view, once we have seen and understood the good, and have given to it our total approval (*video meliora, proboque*), we cannot follow the misguided path (*[non] sequor deteriora*). If we did, we can be certain that from the start we really had no clear vision of the good. Thus, the person of no self-restraint and the vicious person prove to be the same. In both, ignorance lies at the root of their evil actions.

Again, the troublesome issue is whether, in the case of *akrasia*, human emotions are at times sufficiently strong to bring about a temporary eclipsing of knowledge. Aristotle's response is affirmative. For Socrates, however, once knowledge has been truly attained and once the eye of the soul has discerned what is good, the strength of emotions and all other factors are permanently neutralized. In him who really knows, the mind cannot be any longer dragged about as if it were a miserable slave (*Protagoras* 352c). Here lies the root of Socrates' intellectual optimism, which, as we will presently argue, is the basis of his moral faith. It is not that he refuses to accept the reality of *akrasia*, if by this term we mean moral weakness or weakness of the will. What he rejects is the possibility of *akrasia* strictly in the sense of *intellectual* weakness.

There is, of course, the issue of whether ignorance is itself a condition that we can actually choose and is, as such, a morally reprehensible option. Is the ignorant person responsible for his ignorance and for his ignorance of being ignorant? The evil person cannot be held directly accountable for his evil deeds, since these are the offspring of ignorance. Yet, from Socrates' perspective, it is possible to blame him for having chosen to remain in a state of ignorance. The ignorant person is one who has chosen not to search within himself for that knowledge, ultimately accessible to all rational beings, that would ensure his deliverance from evil.

In such a person, the eye of the soul is willfully turned in the wrong direction. In his obfuscated mind, knowledge has been replaced by hosts of mistaken ideas and blurry phantoms. He blindly relies on social and political conventions, on popular opinions that are unintelligently voiced by the many (*Crito* 47c), on intellectual clichés that sound appealing but ultimately mean nothing (*Theaetetus* 152a), on mystifying religious beliefs and fantastic tales about God and the gods (*Euthyphro* 6b), and on the persistent allurements of his hedonistic and sensual ambitions that are the motor that maintains most people in frantic motion. Such a person, as we find in the example of Cephalus (*Republic* 1.328b ff.), may have managed to reach an advanced age living in a condition of self-chosen deception. In the eyes of his associates, who are probably as misguided as he is, he may be a person of reputation, social standing, and accomplishments. In fact, however, he is nothing.

His fundamental guilt—his original sin and his tragic flaw—stems from his choice of lifestyle. He has chosen not to think for himself and has turned his back on the command of the Delphic god. Yet, his choice is common and understandable. The commitment to live an examined life is a long and painful process that very few are willing to undertake and in which even fewer succeed. The prisoners of the underground cave are many and are not particularly uncomfortable in their abode. Having always lived in a cave, they are not aware of their unfortunate condition. Those who succeed in escaping along that "rugged and steep ascent" are indeed exceptional, for genuine understanding and mental clarity are possessions that are acquired only after much intellectual effort and spiritual discipline and, to use Plato's words, "after a long period of attendance on instruction" (*Epist.* 7.341c). How and where, however, can anyone secure the first impulse to acquire self-knowledge?

Obviously, self-knowledge cannot be bought at the marketplace, nor can it be learned from anybody. According to Diogenes Laertius (2.48), the young Xenophon was able to tell Socrates where all kinds of foods were sold—in the Athenian marketplace—but not where self-knowledge can be bought. It cannot be found in the writings of Homer and Hesiod or in what people call Holy Scriptures, as Euthyphro and Ion, and along with them so many of their religious descendants, naively imagine. Neither can it be acquired in the delirious world of politics and social struggle, as Critias, Charmides, and Alcibiades, and along with them their innumerable political progeny, pretend. Nor is it obtainable in books or in schools, as the sophists, and along with them their academic descendants, would like to believe. It is not a commodity to be acquired for the asking. If it were so, it might be a common possession.

Self-knowledge, the key that unlocks the door to virtue, is accessible only within a person's own soul. The path that leads to it is narrow, rugged, and steep. This is why most people do not choose to strive in so uninviting a direction. Their intellectual inertia and spiritual barrenness prevent them from doing so. Here is the source of their guilt, that is, in the abandonment of what Socrates viewed as the only solution to the riddle of human existence. This abandonment becomes even more reprehensible when it involves the rejection of the opportunity furnished by the presence of someone like Socrates.

It is for this reason that in the *Apology*, he assumes so severe and almost unforgiving a tone toward those who rejected and condemned him. He had conceived of himself as "a gift of God to the city" and as a providential gadfly sent by God to awaken the slumbering Athenian horse—the Athenians and people in general—from its comfortable and inveterate dreams and deceptions. Yet, the Athenian horse, as he puts it, refused to be awakened and reacted with anger at the pain inflicted by his sting: "I am convinced that God has sent me to the city to perform such a duty, and this is why I go around awakening and reproaching each one of you, looking for you everywhere I can, every single day. I suspect that another person like me will not be sent to you. My recommendation to you is not to condemn me. Yet, you, angry as you are with me, like people who are suddenly awakened from sleep, may follow Anytus' advise and sentence me. In that case, you will slumber for the rest of your lives, unless God in his providence sends another person to sting you" (*Apology* 31a).

When the verdict was heard, it was clear that Socrates' warning had not been heeded. The Athenians had chosen to reject him and had ignored his moral earnestness. He was like a light that shone on the darkness of his contemporaries, a darkness that did not want to accept him, to borrow the language of the Gospels about Jesus (John 1:5). Thus, the guilt of those who rejected him became manifest, as his own words make plain: "Now I wish to prophesy to you who have sentenced me to death, for I have arrived at that time when people are endowed with the gift of prophecy, that is, the time of death. I prophesy to you that after my death the punishment will soon descend upon you, a punishment far more severe than that which you will have inflicted on me. You will have caused my death, hoping in vain to escape from my critical questioning" (*Apology* 39c).

How the prophesied punishment was eventually inflicted on the proud Athenians, who were convinced of having conquered the world through their sophistication, military prowess, and affluence, is a matter of interpretation. Socrates' death coincided with a time when Athens was already moving along the path of decadence. It is also clear that after his execution, the Greek world entered into its final stage of deterioration. In some way, moreover, the prophesied punishment was inflicted on the generations of those who came after Socrates and is still being inflicted twenty-four centuries later. Today, as much as in the past, if not more, self-knowledge is a commodity sought by very few. People continue to live in the deepest recesses of a cave, immersed in a thick cloud of *typhos*, as the Cynics would have put it, that is, in intellectual and spiritual obfuscation, desperately searching for every imaginable thing, except for what Socrates declared to be the only thing worth pursuing. The world remains the same madhouse that Diogenes, who understood well the Socratic message, discerned everywhere. That has been, indeed, the fulfillment of Socrates' prophetic words.

From his perspective, the choice to persist in ignorance of virtue and in ignorance of the ignorance of virtue is morally reprehensible. This choice admits of no excuses. Not even the lack of a formal education nor one's humble social station can be adduced as extenuating circumstances, for even the slaves, as we learn from the *Meno*, have within themselves the seeds that can fructify in self-knowledge. Neither can we appeal to the force of one's emotions, for *akrasia* proves to be only the name of a poor moral subterfuge to cover up one's choice not to pursue the right path.

We can now return to the theme of Socrates' intellectual optimism in order to make a transition to our final set of reflections on his philosophy. This optimism is embodied in two propositions that are clearly vouched for by Plato and Xenophon and by Aristotle: (1) true knowledge, while as yet not attained by any human being, is in principle attainable and is the only worthwhile goal of human life, and (2) self-knowledge is an imperishable possession that, once acquired, is sufficient to guide a person to virtue, nothing being able to obscure it or render it inefficacious.

So stated, then, Socrates' optimism turns out to be the expression of a moral faith. As with other types of firmly held convictions based on faith, those that we find at the heart of Socrates' experience are never subjected to questioning on his part. He may be confused and ignorant about other things, and his ignorance about other ideas may be genuine. With respect to the urgency of searching for self-knowledge and his belief in its redeeming efficacy, however, he entertains no doubts whatsoever. In this regard, he stands in diametrical opposition to the skeptical attitude of the sophists. Like Kant in some respects, he is able to transcend the impasse of philosophical agnosticism by means of the strength furnished by his moral faith. The convictions grounded on his faith stand as unquestionable assertions throughout his elenchical adventures. As if in a vicious circle, his arguments begin implicitly with such convictions and end with their explicit reaffirmation. His premises and conclusions magically merge into one philosophical vision.

It is for this reason that from the point of view of his interlocutors, Socrates gives the impression of always saying one and the same thing. He is often accused of being repetitious, for his message is, after all, simple and clear and fundamentally one and the same. Obviously, for those who do not share his faith, his rhetorical excursions present the texture of linguistic games. Often, too, in the end he proves to be neither especially convincing nor particularly enlightening when he speaks to those whose ears are not attuned to his message.

In the case of those who originally share or at least understand his faith, his message is grasped and appreciated, as can be witnessed by the reaction of people like Plato, Xenophon, and Antisthenes, different as their individual responses may have been. For them and in them, the Socratic message strikes a familiar chord. They are the only ones who can really profit from his presence.

It is futile to inquire into the reasons that may have led Socrates to affirm with so great a determination the two propositions of his faith. Why did he believe in the accessibility of self-knowledge? Why was he convinced that this knowledge inevitably leads to virtue, and virtue to happiness? In posing these questions, we come face to face with the mystery of Socrates, with his innermost individuality, which cannot be fully fathomed by anyone, perhaps not even by Socrates himself.

A statement of Schopenhauer may be of relevance in this context. According to him, it is not that a person chooses his philosophy. The fact is that it is his philosophy that chooses him from the very start of his life. We do not opt for our convictions. Our convictions are mysteriously foisted upon us. For this reason, Schopenhauer maintained that no one can learn anything of value from another person unless he already has in himself at least the seeds of the knowledge that the other seeks to bring to life in him.

Possibly, this may have been the case with Socrates. Those two unshakable convictions that we have identified as the components of his faith were always in him, always even in his childhood, for, as he confesses to the jurors at the end of his life, even as a child he experienced his divine sign. Even then, he heard in the secrecy of his consciousness the voice that would guide him throughout his life. He was born, Schopenhauer would say, with the gift of conscience, a gift often denied to others. His faith, therefore, was part of him from the beginning.

A curious thought arises at this point, a thought that may not have much value but that deserves to be aired at least once. It is sometimes said that a person's name often fits his character, or, the reverse, that his character reflects something inherent in his name. Surely, this may not be more than a superstitious fancy of no significance. Still, at least in the instance of Socrates, we find a peculiar corroboration of that belief.

To be convinced that no one chooses evil knowingly and that once the mind has recognized the good, it cannot be led astray by the will or by any other thing clearly entails the presence of an overwhelmingly strong mind, a mind vigorous enough to control as an imperial magistrate the emotions and other sources of behavior. Thus, evil arises from ignorance, which is itself weakness, not of will, but of mind. A person of *strong* mind, therefore, cannot do evil. People of feeble mind, who are probably the majority, the many of which Socrates speaks in the *Crito*, go through life stumbling from moral mistake to moral mistake, from evil deed to evil deed, just like a blind person running through a maze. Their intellectual weakness and spiritual blindness does not allow them to act otherwise.

Now then, what does Socrates' *name* mean? What is its etymology? It means neither more nor less than what Socrates appears to have been, that is, a man of great strength. The Greek word *sos* conveys the sense of something healthy, sound, whole, and can be used to mean *sure, safe, to a very high degree*, equivalent, in this last sense, to the English word *so*, as in the phrase "Your house is *so* comfortable!" The word *kratos* conveys ideas such as strength, might, prowess, victory, and mastery. The common Greek prefix or suffix *krates* is used to describe someone who has succeeded in conquering, for instance, a city or an opponent. Etymologically, therefore, Socrates' name describes someone who has strength to a very high degree—someone who is a conqueror.

Whatever value there may be in clarifying the meaning of Socrates' name, we may still get a glimpse about his character. One wonders whether the description of the evil horse in the *Phaedrus* may not be a description of Socrates' physical appearance, that is, of his original and natural self. The evil horse is depicted as "crooked, heavy, ill put together, a short neck and a flat nose" (*Phaedrus* 253e), which are precisely the physical features associated with Socrates. Born like a monster, to use Nietzsche's word, he emerged into the world as a bundle of unbecoming features and, worse still, as a cluster of bestial emotions. *That*, as we saw in an earlier context, was what Zopyrus, the physiognomist, discerned in Socrates. *That,* indeed, was what he *was,* as he remarked to Zopyrus. Yet, that was not what he became in the course of his life. He succeeded in remaking himself. But how did he succeed?

The answer is obvious. Socrates was able to subject to complete control his miserable evil horse—his physical frame with all its defects and perverse inclinations—by means of the strength of the good horse—his ability to reason, so that the charioteer—his soul—could at last ascend to the heights of spiritual perfection. His *victory* led him to the optimistic conclusion that every other human being could accomplish so stupendous a feat. Simply stated, he universalized his own private experience, optimistically projecting it onto everybody else. In the end, then, we can say that for *him, akrasia* was an impossibility, which convinced him that it was the same for others. Accordingly, in his discussion of *akrasia,* Aristotle was right and wrong, right with respect to its presence among people in general, yet wrong in the instance of Socrates. The problem is, however, whether the rest of us, whose intellects are irremediably weak, can somehow follow the example set by him.

This example is well illustrated in an anecdote already mentioned in an earlier context, in which we hear how Socrates would enter drinking contests in the marketplace. The purpose was to see who among the participants was able to drink the greatest quantity of undiluted wine without getting drunk. It is said that it was Socrates who would invariably win. While the others would stumble and fall around him, he, as the victor, would walk away as if he had drunk only water. The point of the anecdote, whether genuine or apocryphal, is clear. A drop of wine is sufficient to disorient a feeble mind. Socrates' mind, however, is of Herculean strength, for nothing, not even the greatest quantity of wine, would blur its pristine clarity. An echo of this curious anecdote can be heard in Plato's *Symposium* (223c), where, after a long drinking gathering, Socrates remains perfectly sober despite all the wine he drank. Most of the others are either drunk or have fallen asleep.

The drinking of wine is a subject that often surfaces among the Cynics. Diogenes, for instance, *defined* wine as "the drink of fools,"[12] and Antisthenes, reportedly the closest of Socrates' associates, wrote a book condemning the use of wine, which was the only alcoholic beverage known to the Greeks.[13] Crates of Thebes, a follower of Diogenes, moreover, described his Cynic utopia, Pera, as a happy and peaceful island surrounded by a "wine-colored sea of fog."

Despite the poverty of our information about the Cynics and their writings, one thing can be affirmed without hesitation. They unanimously inveighed against the consumption of wine because of its effects on the mind. It disorganizes our thinking capacity and renders us irrational.

Yet, it was not necessarily against wine that they railed. Wine for them, it seems, was a metaphor for all sorts of things that debilitate the mind, particularly when the mind is feeble and unstable. Emotions, irrational traditions, mistaken perceptions, religious humbug, political rhetoric, myths and deceptions, false expectations, and, in sum, all that keeps the multitudes in motion—all those and other things render the mind powerless, far more than wine could. In the end, then, the Cynics concluded that humanity at large is mostly made up of helpless drunks who live in obfuscation and ignorance. For the Cynics, as much as for Socrates, these are the causes of the deadly disease they called *typhos*. Its only possible cure, if indeed there is any, is a dosage of reason, because it is reason alone that redeems people from stupidity, ignorance, evil, and unhappiness.

Undoubtedly, whatever the relationship between Socrates and the Cynics could have been, their diagnosis and prognosis of the human condition is thoroughly Socratic. Diogenes' favorite advice to thoughtless people was "Hang yourselves," because, as Socrates told his jurors, "an unexamined life is not worth living." Metaphorically speaking, "better to be dead than drunk" could have been the slogan preferred by Socrates and the Cynics.

Socrates' enthronement of reason as the only solution to the human problem allows us to appreciate some of the ethical ideas associated with him. These all flow from his moral faith and are just as unshakable. There is, for instance, the idea that it is only in virtuous living that we can ever hope to attain happiness, as we read in the *Republic* (1.354a–b). There, he stands in opposition to the common belief that a life devoted to righteousness is the surest path to misery and misfortune, a belief emphatically defended by Thrasymachus. The equation reason = virtue = happiness, which, as we saw in the previous chapter, is, according to Nietzsche, the epitome of nonsense and vulgarity, is for Socrates a self-evident truth. In their emotional condition and in their ignorance, people fail to recognize the obvious, namely, that clarity of mind is the necessary and sufficient condition for virtue *and* happiness. Like intoxicated people whose vision is blurry, they cannot think clearly and, therefore, can neither act rightly nor be happy.

Then there is the idea, eloquently expressed in the closing paragraphs of the *Gorgias* (527b), that it is always preferable to suffer evil than to do evil: "We ought to be more careful about doing evil than about suffering evil, and above all we ought to be good and not only appear good, both in our private and in our public affairs."

From the point of view of most people, however, could there be anything more absurd than this idea? Is it not contrary to the most common human response? Who would prefer to suffer rather than to inflict suffering? How would we defend ourselves from the danger often posed by other people? What could be more decadent than to choose to suffer evil rather than to inflict evil? How could we achieve a life of prosperity and happiness by always opting for the role of victims when attacked or abused by others?

According to nature, says Glaucon to Socrates, it is definitely better to commit injustice than to suffer injustice (*Republic* 2.358e). The natural law under which human beings and, indeed, all living beings live obliges us to seek our self-preservation and our welfare even if to do so we may have to hurt or even eliminate those around us. That is simply natural. Turning the other cheek when struck is not.

This appeal to what is natural leaves Socrates unmoved. If, indeed, nature commands us to behave like beasts, we must deny nature in us regardless of the consequences. After all, as he says at his trial, nothing can ever harm a good person either in this life or after death (*Apology* 41d), for evil is the only harmful thing (*Gorgias* 527d). All those things that ordinary people fear and call bad—poverty, sickness, social rejection, persecution, death—are in themselves neither good nor bad and are unrelated to happiness or unhappiness. The good person is not affected by them.

Again, we must ask, what could possibly be more contrary to the facts of experience than this Socratic contention, especially in a world in which the wicked prosper and frolic, in which injustice and depravity are the avenues to great fortunes and sustained pleasures, in which dishonesty, whether in private or in public life, appears to pay tenfold, and in which honor and prestige are easily secured by deception and appearance? If Socrates' ideal life is what ensues from self-knowledge and virtue, it is not surprising that sensible people shun such a life. His goal inevitably leads to an unhappy life and ensures a miserable end—either hanging on a cross or imbibing a cup of hemlock poison. His own definition of philosophy makes perfect sense. Philosophy, as Plato makes him say in the *Phaedo*, is the preparation for death. Yet, how many of us would pursue philosophy for *that* purpose?

That his ideas sound absurd, Socrates does not deny, as he concedes in the *Gorgias*. Neither is he unwilling to admit that by standing firm on his moral convictions, he gives the impression of being less than a real man. Of course, his understanding of what makes and does not make sense and his perception of what is real and unreal are different from those of ordinary people, as he repeatedly states in the *Apology*. If there is anything the jurors must say about him, he insists, it is that he is not like them or like any other person. He is, as Alcibiades notes in the *Symposium*, absolutely unique.

Socrates is aware that in most matters he stands amid the multitude as an aberration, an abnormality, a deranged man who utters nonsense from a suspended basket, a visitor from another world. He acknowledges his peculiarity when he reminds the jurors that they will not easily find another man like him. When he is told by his opponents about the eventuality of an indictment against him, he thinks of himself as a skillful and devoted physician in the presence of a jury composed of children under the leadership of a cook (*Gorgias* 521e). Yet, this does not disturb him because of his conviction that nothing evil can ever happen to a good man. His ignorance may be great in many matters, but he really knows that "to do wrong and to disobey my superior, whether God or man, is wicked and dishonorable" (*Apology* 29b).

As the moment of his death approaches, when the irrevocable sentence has been passed, he faces with equanimity what most people deem to be the greatest of tragedies. If we are to believe Xenophon (*Apology* 33), Socrates faces it with defiant cheerfulness, as an athlete who has just completed a successful race. He is absolutely confident that nothing evil can ever happen to him.

In our earlier account of the testimonies of Xenophon and Plato, we paid particular attention to Socrates' religiosity. We noted that it stands in no opposition to his critical and searching frame of mind. Guthrie's statement on this matter is perceptive: "There is nothing impossible or unprecedented in the union of a keen and penetrating insight into human affairs, and an unerring eye for humbug, with a simple religious piety."[14]

Indeed, it is not always necessary to leave one's brain in the vestibule of a temple, a church, or a mosque as one enters to pray and worship. Intellectual suicide is not always a requirement for holding on to faith because not everything found in religious traditions is necessarily fantasy.

Socrates' religious piety constitutes an accompanying support for his intellectual optimism and moral confidence. It runs smoothly and persistently throughout all his thoughts and activities. It is true that the Socratic religiosity described by Xenophon has tinges of superstitious reverence and reminds us of the attitude found among simpleminded believers endowed with limited intellectual insightfulness, as in the instance of the pious Euthyphro. Yet, from what we learn from Plato, Socrates' faith does not strangulate the power of his mind. He believes, but he also subjects his beliefs to a severe logical examination and lets his reason be the ultimate court of judgment. He reveres the gods but has an unerring eye for the humbug that is often peddled in the name of religion.

It is difficult to reach a conclusion about Socrates' precise stance concerning the religious structure furnished by the polytheism of his time. How clearly and firmly was this stance grounded in the transcendent monotheism that some of the Fathers of the Church insisted on detecting in him? Was he, as some allege, a precursor of Christianity or was his religiosity rooted in the anthropomorphic polytheism of his contemporaries? Or was he at heart an agnostic or even an atheist, who used religiosity as a convenient medium for the expression of his rationalism?

These are questions that cannot be answered with finality. Whether soaring high on the wings of monotheism, as Saint Augustine suggested, or, as Apuleius would have us believe, committed to polytheistic beliefs, one thing must be granted.

From Socrates' point of view, it was his relationship to a super-natural presence, understood here in the sense of God, gods, or the divine, that furnished him with the frame of reference that rendered his life and mission meaningful.

If, as some have insisted, we take away from him his over-whelming faith in that presence, he transforms himself into a clever and dabbling dilettante, comparable to modern language philosophers who deal with words, words, and nothing but words, those who were described by Diogenes as the sort of people who talk a great deal without ever saying anything. Yet, if the testimonies about Socrates are even slightly reliable, Socrates conceived of his calling as a pilgrimage undertaken in strict obedience to a divine command to which he was inex-orably bound even in spite of himself (*Apology* 22a).

This aspect of the Socratic phenomenon cannot be over-looked. It was Socrates' undeviating service to God—whatever this could mean—that reduced him to the apparently lamentable condition in which he found himself at the end of his life, in poverty and without human succor (*Apology* 22c). He did not hes-itate to attribute his social and political vicissitudes to the cir-cumstance, probably as enigmatic to him as it is to us, that he was once chosen for his mission like the liberated prisoner of Plato's cave, who was "made to stand," "dragged up," and "compelled to face the light"—the passive verbal mood is emphasized by Plato (*Republic* 7.515c–e)—to fulfill a dangerous and suicidal task, namely, to arouse human beings from their slumber, to remove from their eyes the scales that had become one with those eyes, and to lift the human spirit from its paltry plane of shadowy exis-tence to a plateau of higher intellectual and spiritual reality.

This explains many otherwise paradoxical manifestations of Socrates' presence such as the statement that he does what he does and is willing to die one hundred times rather than to do anything else, for, in fact, he could not have chosen any other style of life. Through the reality of the divine election, so distinctly manifested in the experience of his voice or sign, he became powerless. His only option was to obey, even when his obedience brought to him a personal calamity. To the jurors, Socrates could have said what the uncompromising Luther once said to the Holy Roman emperor: "Here I stand and I cannot do otherwise." Translated in his own words, Socrates expressed it in these terms: "Gentlemen, I am a loyal and faithful subject of the state, but my first duty is to obey God. As long as I am alive and in possession of my faculties, I shall never abandon philosophy and my commitment of leading you to philosophy and to the truth" (*Apology* 29d).

To insist on interpreting such utterances as mere rhetorical and symbolic gestures entails a disregard of the evidence. It is hardly possible not to discern in them the outlines of the historical Socrates.

As shown in chapter 3, the passages in Xenophon's testimony that stress Socrates' religiosity are numerous. We can recall, for instance, the statements in the *Memorabilia*, where we are told that, according to Socrates, God always knows best what is good for human beings (1.3.2), where God is described as the omniscient and benevolent creator of the universe (1.4.18), or where we discover traces of what in later times came to be known as the moral argument for the existence of God (1.4.19). It has been argued that such passages do not reflect Socrates' views but ideas that belong to other philosophers of his time.

There is, however, nothing to justify a selective reading of the sources and a tossing aside of anything that does not fit our preconceived understanding of Socrates. If what Xenophon and Plato report about him is to be taken seriously, we cannot but conclude that "that serene trust in God which for him was synonymous with faith in the inevitable victory of truth" is indeed the core of his philosophy.[15] All else is of secondary importance. Toward that confidence in his special relationship with God—or a transcendent divine realm—everything in him gravitates.

Socrates succeeds in escaping from skepticism and nihilism by means of his conviction that those questions of which Kant speaks, so urgent for human existence yet so imponderable, are ultimately answerable. If they were not, the Delphic god, who speaks no untruth, would not have commanded him to examine them. If in Kant, knowledge is transcended and overcome by faith, and if in him, faith provides the only escape from the cave of human existence, then in Socrates, an unfaltering trust in the power of reason is guaranteed by yet another faith that manifests itself in his acceptance of the divine command. For is it possible for God to command something impossible?

Socrates looks upon self-knowledge and virtue as the only acquisitions worth seeking, although in actuality neither his efforts nor those of others have succeeded, to borrow Kant's words, in gaining even so much as an inch of territory. He regards self-knowledge as the sufficient and necessary condition for virtue because the Delphic god commanded him to look into himself and to know himself. This knowledge is then conceived of as the only avenue that leads to the regeneration of the soul. His method, his search for ethical definitions, his midwifery, and his confession of ignorance—all these transform themselves into manifestations of an all-encompassing commitment.

One is often tempted to conclude that the paradoxical character of Socrates as a man and as a philosopher is an illusion, a kaleidoscopic deformation of him that arises only in the perception of those who observe him from the outside. For us, Socrates is an enigma and his philosophy is a paradox. His thoughts move aimlessly like the statues of Daedalus. Yet, perhaps in himself and for himself, there is no enigma, no paradox.

When we reduce Socrates' message to its simplest yet most genuine expression, which we have identified as intellectual optimism and moral confidence, it gains in significance for our own time. We could imagine, if he were to be resurrected after twenty-four centuries, how he would look upon our present world. He might conclude that despite so many changes and apparent material progress, little if anything has changed in the human condition. The philosophers still talk about this and that and ultimately about nothing, the sophists still roam the halls of Academia, Euthyphro continues to preach from the pulpit and entertain the masses with senseless talk about God and the gods, the natural philosophers—the scientists—go on pontificating about the universe and peddling their pretended knowledge, the comedians ridicule whoever is different or eccentric, the politicians persist in lying to everybody and milking the public, and the multitudes slumber placidly in the warmth of their hedonism and their illusions, worshiping the empty husks that are known as celebrities. Somehow, at the beginning of the twenty-first century, in the presence of so many impending threats to our survival, we are still as unable as the ancient Athenians to inject some sense of direction in the conduct of our lives. We are still in the hands of morally challenged and mindless politicians, those superb marionette jugglers of Plato's cave, who control the destiny of people and nations. What would the resurrected Socrates say about our political world?

It may be, therefore, useful to conclude these reflections by commenting on Socrates' response to the political conditions of his time, specifically, on his view of the relationship between the individual and the state. The problem can be stated simply. What course of action should be taken by an individual who wants to live well and honorably within a state that is generally depraved and in which corruption and thoughtlessness permeate all activities?

In such a state, what should he do? Should he accept the conclusion reached by Plato, that the political constitution of every state is beyond help and that, accordingly, the only alternative is to withdraw himself from political participation, while dreaming of some utopian republic? If so, should he attempt to transform his utopia into reality? Should he imitate the ancient

Pythagoreans of southern Italy, who one day descended on the cities from their mountain retreats in order to remake by force the corrupted constitutions of the states? Should he, then, turn himself into a revolutionary?

Or should he altogether forsake the political world in order to seek the peace of mind that served as the goal for Epicurus and his followers? Or should he look upon the human world as merely a theatrical play in which each one of us has been given a role, and, therefore, develop within himself the resigned attitude of indifference of Epictetus and the Stoics? The following Stoic recommendation could be his maxim: "Seek not that the things that happen should happen as you wish, but wish that the things that happen be as they are, and you will have a tranquil flow of life" (*Encheridion* 8).

Or, again, should he become defiant, as in the instance of Diogenes the Cynic, and declare war against the world, endeavoring to deface its currency, that is, its laws, traditions, customs, and values? Should he aim, as the Cynics did, to become a citizen of the world, a *cosmopolites*, which ultimately means a citizen of nowhere, and spend his time spitting and hurling insults at people, advising them to hang themselves?[16] In other words, should he become an absolute idiot—using this term in its Greek meaning?[17]

Lastly, should he plunge himself full-fledgedly into the turmoil of political life in order to become, with some luck, a half-decent statesman like Pericles, or, with less luck, a corrupted politician like Alcibiades? Which one of these options, and there seem to be no others, belongs to Socrates? How did he stand ideologically and practically in relation to the Athenian polity?

Much has been written about Socrates' political views, and diverse opinions have been expressed in this regard. In fact, each one of the options mentioned above has been associated with him, and yet, on reflection, none of them should be linked with him, if, of course, by Socrates we mean the Socrates of Plato's early dialogues and the Socrates of Xenophon. *This* Socrates was neither a utopian ideologist nor an Epicurean recluse nor a thundering and rebellious Cynic nor a resigned Stoic nor a political idiot, nor, least of all, a political man in the style of Plato's older relatives such as Critias and Charmides, men who actually played the political game. Socrates was none of these types.

Yet—and here is the paradox—somehow he was *several* of them at once. There is a sense in which each one of those seemingly mutually exclusive options coexisted in him. That he rejected for himself political involvement is evident. The political history of Greece could be written without making a single reference to him. In the *Apology* (32b), he states that the only political office he ever held was that of senator. Also, in the *Apology* (17d), he reminds us that he was unacquainted with the procedures followed in the courts. Ironically, he noted at the start of his trial that he was not even versed in the language used in the courts. He had obviously remained aloof from the workings of the government. In that sense, then, he functioned as a private or nonpolitical person.

Yet, in the *Gorgias* (521d), he refers to himself as the only political man in Athens, for, in his view, only he who is capable of rendering other people political deserves to be called political (*Meno* 100a). The phrase "making other people political" can be understood in the light of his philosophical activities. His goal was to raise the consciousness of the citizens with respect to ethical and social issues. Ethics and politics were for him an indivisible unity because only in the context of the community, the *polis*, can the full development of the individual be realized. A person living in isolation is an abstraction of no significance.

More specifically, however, we can ask what was Socrates' attitude toward the laws and practices of his political world. How did he view the individual's obligations toward the state? He is occasionally characterized as a rebellious man, often willing to stand in opposition to established customs and laws.

This aspect of his presence was exploited by Aristophanes, who depicted him as an antisocial man bent on disrupting the social order by his words and style of life. In the official indictment at the time of his trial, the point is expressly made that he rejected the gods of the state, an accusation that, in a political system established on a religious foundation, amounts to a charge of treason. Furthermore, the accusation involving the corruption of the youth meant that he had taught young Athenians to disobey the laws of the state and flout its customs.

In Plato's *Apology*, no less than in Xenophon's *Apology*, moreover, there is at least the semblance of arrogance and rebelliousness, which manifests itself in Socrates' haughty language (*megalegoria*). He announced to the court his intention to disobey its command, if it required him to abandon philosophy. It was to God, not to men, that he owed his obedience. If anything obstructed the pursuit of his mission, he pledged allegiance to no political structure, Athenian or otherwise. Also, he was outspoken in his caustic criticism of certain Athenian political practices that had the force of established law, practices such as the selection of public officials by lot or sortition, which he regarded as sheer folly. Lastly, he criticized severely prominent politicians, among whom Pericles was no exception. Their inadequacy and corruption, ultimately the offspring of their ignorance, were themes to which he constantly returned in his conversations.

It may thus appear justifiable to speak of Socrates as a rebellious man unwilling to acquiesce with the political and social system. Not content to stand outside the system, he challenged it by open criticism. Among the Cynics, *this* aspect of Socrates would be exploited in an exaggerated form until late Roman times.[18] Beginning with Antisthenes and Diogenes, the Cynics stood defiantly outside the political world, casting aside what they viewed as the fetters of social conventions and restrictions in the name of what they interpreted as *the* only genuine Socratic legacy. Inheriting from Socrates his undeviating commitment to reason, the Cynics transformed the example of his life into the paradigm they sought to imitate. From him, too, they claimed to have inherited the idea of natural law, a law discoverable only through reason and independent of the laws and customs by which people normally live. This idea they would bequeath to the Stoics, who saw themselves as the heirs of Antisthenes and Diogenes.

There is, however, another side to Socrates. He also presents himself to us as a faithful and law-abiding citizen, an aspect of him that, if genuine, would have revolted even the mildest among the Cynics. The most persistent Socratic recommendation heard in the *Memorabilia* with regard to private and public matters is "Follow the custom of the state because that is the way to act righteously." Xenophon's Socrates reveals himself as a man for whom the laws carry an absolute moral weight. He may not be politically active in the community, but he is someone from whom neither rebelliousness nor negativism can be expected. He is not a Cynic. His seemingly arrogant language at the trial, according to Xenophon in his *Apology*, was not born out of contempt toward the state but a manifestation of his desire to die. He hoped for a death sentence.

If our only two sources of information were Plato's *Apology* and Xenophon's writings, we would find ourselves facing an uncomfortable dilemma. We would have to choose between Plato's *apparently* defiant Socrates and the law-abiding and submissive Socrates depicted by Xenophon. A careful review of Plato's testimony, however, does not yield the portrait of a rebellious man in the style of the Cynics, who broke laws and flouted conventions for the purpose of undermining the social fabric. Plato's Socrates is in some respects like the Socrates of Xenophon, that is, a man who respects and honors the laws of the state and who holds dear its customs and traditions.

Yet, there is an important difference. Whereas Xenophon's Socrates appears to obey the laws submissively, Plato's Socrates is repeatedly willing to challenge them, not in actions of disobedience but on the arena of philosophical discussion. He argues about the laws and endeavors to persuade the citizens to alter them whenever they seem unreasonable or unjust. He voices his arguments not in the way politicians and demagogues do, that is, in the midst of the tumultuous meetings of the Assembly. He speaks in private and always to individuals, for it is only in that setting that his *elenchus* can be successfully carried on. When his arguments fail to bring about a change in the laws or when his efforts do not succeed in changing the minds of his hearers, then Socrates obeys the laws.

Socrates' submission to the laws is a theme that occupies the foreground of the *Crito*, a dialogue generally classified as an early dialogue. It takes place in the prison where he is being held awaiting execution. Crito has come to see him with the news that within three days he must die. He has made the necessary preparations for his escape and urges him to do as he suggests, that is, to leave at once. After a short conversation, it is clear what Socrates' decision is. He chooses to remain in prison and to accept his final fate. Why does he opt for what most people would do everything conceivable to avoid? How does he justify his choice?

The reason for Socrates' refusal to accept Crito's offer is eloquently expressed by the personified laws that appear on the scene to speak to him. Escaping from prison and evading punishment, they tell him, would be a shameful act that he must not condone. It would be contrary to the sacred duty of every good citizen of Athens—to obey the laws of the state, who are his real parents and who have nourished, educated, and maintained him since his birth. Now that he is an old man, would he behave like a rebellious little boy toward his venerable parents? Is life so precious that it must be saved at all costs, including by breaking the laws? Righteousness requires him to obey and drink the poison at the appointed time. Indeed, Socrates obeys the laws and dies. He has no other alternative.

We can well imagine Antisthenes' reaction, had he been present at the scene, or, worse still, that of Diogenes. How would they, Cynics in the Socratic tradition, react, since they regarded the state as the greatest enemy of human freedom and the laws as the offspring of the rapacious and mindless many whose opinions, even when embodied in legal documents or judicial verdicts, are never to be taken into account?

Socrates himself reminds Crito that such opinions should be ignored because they spring from ignorance and viciousness. Yet, it is precisely those opinions that he now decides to obey like a little boy in the presence of his parents. What then happened to him? Was it a case of philosophical senility? Was Socrates, as Xenophon insists, simply tired of living and anxious to die? Do the concluding paragraphs of the *Crito* reflect a strictly Platonic idea injected by its author into the historical Socrates, ultimately as an embarrassing distortion of what he was?

He chose to stay in prison and die because the laws so commanded him, despite being convinced of his innocence. His accusers, he knew, were guilty of perjury and the majority of the jurors were swayed by emotions and mistaken impressions. Still, the judicial process was in accord with the laws, and so were the verdict and the sentence. How, then, could he dare to oppose the laws in order to save himself?

It is difficult to determine what in Plato's testimony belongs to Socrates and what to Plato himself, which is one of the roots of the Socratic problem. Whether Socrates' view of the relationship between legality and righteousness is precisely as Plato recounts it in the *Crito* is bound to remain an open question, although it is not easy to accept the description of him as a man who does what he does because it has been prescribed by the laws. Subservient people, who constitute the majority, do precisely that. Like sheep, they obey what the state, the religious authorities, or social pressure command them to do. They generally live in accordance with what they are told and are accustomed to confuse reality with the appearances of the world around them. Their level of self-consciousness is minimal and the presence of conscience in their souls is missing.

Of course, even if Socrates chose to die in obedience to the laws, far was he from the abject behavior of the unthinking masses, for whom obedience is followed out of fear, self-advantage, or, more often, intellectual laziness and obfuscation. As if to distance himself from this common way of acting, he asks Crito, "Why should we pay so much attention to what most people think? The really reasonable people, who have a genuine claim to be considered, will believe that the facts are exactly as they are" (*Crito* 44e). The opinions of the many, therefore, are worthy of no consideration, even when it is the many who establish the laws, as happens in democracies. What, then, about the opinions of the few from whom the laws spring in oligarchies? Should their commands be also disregarded?

Socrates' answer to this question is given with great clarity in the *Apology* (32c–d). He recounts an incident when, after the Athenian defeat by the Spartans five years before the trial, a small group of oligarchs led by Critias, an older relative of Plato, took the reins of the state when the democratic government was disbanded. Acting as the head of the new government and, at that time, as the lawgiver, Critias summoned Socrates and ordered him to take part in the arrest of wealthy foreigners who were to be executed. The government wanted to confiscate their assets. Literally, then, the law had commanded him to take part in the crime. What did he do? Without saying anything—Critias was at that time not interested in arguing about his order and, like all dictators, was completely deaf to all reasoning—Socrates simply ignored his command and went home, putting his own life in jeopardy. Luck had it, he tells us, that Critias's government collapsed about that time and Socrates remained unpunished.

There is also an incident briefly reported in Plato's *Apology* and with more details in Xenophon's *Hellenica* (1.7.16) that deserves consideration. In 406 BCE, just two years before the Athenian defeat, a major naval battle took place near the islands of Arginusae, not far from Miletus. In Athens, practically every able man, citizen or slave, had been drafted for the engagement, and eight generals had been hastily elected by the Assembly.

A battle between a Spartan squadron and a large Athenian fleet took place, and in the end the Athenians were victorious. Yet, their victory turned sour when they were unable to recover from the sea the bodies of their dead and were unsuccessful in capturing the fleeing Spartans. An unexpected storm had prevented them from doing so. When the Athenians came home, they faced the anger of the people because they had not retrieved the dead. A trial by the Assembly was arranged, and six of the generals—the two others never returned—were indicted.

On that occasion, Socrates was a member of the senate. According to the law, each senator would act as the presiding officer of the Assembly for one day. It was on the day Socrates acted in that capacity that the trial of the generals was to take place. Without his consent, no motions could be brought before the Assembly. As the accused generals were brought in, it became clear that the will of the people was for a speedy trial, a conviction, and an execution. The generals—a son of Pericles among them—were to be tried as a group, which was an illegal procedure because the law allowed only for individual trials of each defendant, whether in the Assembly or in the courts.

On that memorable day, as Plato and Xenophon report, Socrates stood firm like a rock before the people and refused to accept the motion because it was in violation of the law. Nothing could sway him, not even the shouts of the Athenian people who unanimously insisted on forcing the issue and threatened Socrates with an indictment for treason. Obviously, his inner voice was louder than the roar of the entire people. In the end, the trial was postponed to the next day and the generals were tried, convicted, and executed.

What we learn from this incident is not different from what we gather from the *Apology* and the *Crito* with respect to Socrates' stance vis-à-vis the laws and, more generally, about his character. The uncompromising philosopher of the *Apology*, the *seemingly* submissive prisoner of the Crito, and the stubborn head of the Athenian Assembly are one and the same person. He is convinced that the laws must be obeyed so long as, in the light of reason, they prove to be righteous. If from his point of view this is not the case, then he must endeavor to challenge the laws through persuasion. If persuasion proves inefficacious, then obedience must follow. Yet, if *he* deems obedience to be an unreasonable option, then he must accept the consequences of his refusal to obey. He must either leave the state and live elsewhere, as he says in the *Apology*, or take refuge in Hades, the kingdom of the dead, as he eventually did. A life of *blind* acceptance to the laws, whether these emanate from the few or the many, would be equivalent to an unexamined life, and an unexamined life is not worth living.

It is, therefore, not altogether far-fetched to assume that Socrates recognized a distinction between the actual laws of the state and a realm of righteousness that may be conceived of as existing independently of such laws. The Cynics, his descendants, certainly recognized this distinction and it is to them that we owe the genesis of the concept of natural law. It was in the name of this natural law, vaguely outlined by them and precisely defined by the Stoics, that they defied, not only in language but in action, the laws and customs of the Greek and Roman worlds. The Cynics pledged allegiance to no state, recognized no nationality, fought for no country, and viewed themselves, each one of them in his own individuality, as absolute monarchs of their lives. They accepted no law other than what their reason certified as a righteous command.

In the case of Socrates, however, it is difficult to speak with assurance about his views in this respect or, in fact, in any other respect. All we have at our disposal are writings *about* him that are not always in agreement with one another. Furthermore, as has been pointed out repeatedly, our knowledge of him reveals a complex and paradoxical philosopher to whom much can be attributed, but only with hesitation.

Concerning his political ideas, that is, his understanding of the relationship between law and righteousness, we can suggest that his keen mind took him to the threshold of the recognition that beyond the political statutes made by human beings there is a higher and universal rational law. Apparently, he did not venture beyond this threshold, but stood on it, looking far into the distance for a clear vision of what he intuitively, yet vaguely, had discovered in himself. The experience of his divine sign or voice, which disclosed itself to him generally as a negative admonition, must have convinced him that far above what society and the state declare to be righteous, that is, customary and lawful, there is another dimension that lies hidden in the recesses of every human soul.

It is probably for this that he incessantly searched for self-knowledge, because this and only this is the path that leads to clear understanding and happiness and, perhaps, as with Kant, to holiness. In a sense, then, Socrates' mission was to point the way without disclosing to others what he himself may have discerned from afar. Perhaps, he himself remained far away from what he sought to discover. As a great explorer of the seas, he saw in the distance the coastline and mountaintops of misty continents into which he was not destined to venture. This explains his optimistic stance toward death, as he reveals it at the end of his trial. If death is, as many claim, a transfer from this world onto another, he might accomplish there what he longed to accomplish while in this world. That, as he says in the *Phaedo*, is the pious hope that has sustained him.

The portrait of Socrates that emerges from the sources is at first sight a collection of disparate and incomplete features of the most complicated nature. Yet, in the light of reflection and without having to disregard completely one single of its varied components, we can still recognize in it a unifying principle that manifests itself in his moral confidence. The paradoxical and seemingly incongruous aspects of his life and thought, so beautifully recognized by Alcibiades in the *Symposium*, so magnificently re-created by Plato throughout his writings, so simply described by Xenophon in his recollections, and so disturbing to the scholars of all times, resolve themselves into a coherent structure, at the basis of which there is a self-sustaining experience that must be described as primordial, fundamental, and ultimately ineffable. It rose to the surface of his consciousness in those strange moments of abstraction and ecstatic forgetfulness of the external world that were so peculiar to him, but that was always present in the recesses of his consciousness.

Socrates emerges, therefore, as an enigma for those who perceive him from the outside. For them, he is a complex of unresolved tensions and insoluble contradictions that refuse to be pinned down in terms of some all-inclusive designation. Seen from the outside and understood from an external point of view, he eludes explanation. Accordingly, his message and the legacy that flows from it are bound to be grasped and interpreted differently by different minds.

He was ugly and even repulsive like the Satyrs and the Sileni, and ill put together like the mythological Marsyas, who once competed with Apollo in the art of enchanting human beings with the sound of the mystical flute. He was, however, spiritually beautiful and ravishing like the statuettes of gods hidden inside monstrous gargoyles. He was discordant and unsettling like the cries of the Dionysian nocturnal revelers, but was soothing and appeasing like the music of the Apollonian flutes of the Orphics.

He was poor like a beggar and uncouth and awkward like a peasant, yet wealthy like the most affluent of citizens and polite and aristocratic like the most refined among gentlemen. He was ignorant and confused like the most unsophisticated among the laborers, yet wise and perceptive like a reincarnation of one of the Seven Sages. He was humble, submissive, and unassuming like a supplicant before a judge and invariably obedient and compliant in the presence of the laws, yet proud, inflexible, and independent, as if he were the only source of legislation.

He was a man of this world, talking always about shoe-makers, shepherds, and masons, and caught in the problems of family life, yet a man whose kingdom was not of this world and whose origin and destiny belonged somewhere else. He was a man always ready to heed human discourse, yet able to lose himself in moments of abstraction and solitude, with ears attuned only to the secret voice of the god who spoke within. He was a quibbler over words and a splitter of phrases, yet a logician whose flawless *elenchus* led inexorably to one and the same conclusion.

He was a sensual man whose physiognomy revealed nothing but bestial desires, yet a restrained and disciplined man always in perfect control of himself. He was an amusing clown and an entertaining buffoon, as only Aristophanes could have adequately depicted him, yet an earnest man around whom there was always a halo of tremendous seriousness and urgency, as only Plato could have described him. He was a rebellious, insolent, and dangerous citizen, whose speech and thought were powerful enough to unsettle the structure of the state, yet he was a solid and balanced citizen, whose behavior was an example of lawfulness, as only Xenophon could have portrayed him.

This is what Socrates was. As a living refutation of himself and, indeed, of the entire human world, and yet as an affirmation of both, he still walks the streets of Athens and the streets of every place where human beings live, move, and have their being. In essence, he was in some measure all that each one of us is and can be.

And yet, at the existential basis of so baffling a summation of humanity, we cannot but see, albeit darkly and indistinctly as if through a distorting glass, the simplest of all possible realities, the reality of experiencing the overwhelming and redeeming power of human reason, which he interpreted, perhaps rightly, as the presence of God within us. As Kierkegaard noted,[19] in the absence of the awareness of *this* reality, it might not even be proper for us to approach Sophroniscus's son, for then, that "ironic and amorous monster and Pied Piper of Athens," as Nietzsche called him, would remain a senseless phenomenon.

The portraits of Socrates that have come down to us through the testimonies may appear discordant and difficult to put together, and today, just as when he lived among the Athenians, he presents himself to us in the garb of an enigma, as an unstable ghost hidden behind a multiplicity of masks. Behind such masks, however, the primordial reality of Socrates—the Socratic presence—is not altogether difficult to decipher.

Above all, the lesson that flows abundantly from that reality, that is, the legacy of Socrates, is perfectly clear, and all that is needed to understand and appreciate it is a receptive and unbiased mind. Socrates was not a language philosopher for whom the analysis of language is the goal of the philosophical activity, and neither was he an existential thinker facing the absurdity of the human condition. He was not a Platonic idealist whose imagination roams freely in ethereal domains of abstract thoughts. Nor was he a Cynic in the style of Diogenes, spitting on people and urinating in the marketplace, convinced that the human world is in a state of total bankruptcy. Nor was he a fanatic man pledging and practicing uncritical adherence to irrational traditions and atavistic customs. Nor was he a materialistic thinker for whom anything that transcends the immediacy of physical existence is devoid of meaning.

No, he was none of these things. He was simply and purely a philosopher, that is, a man committed to the use of reason, moved by a yearning to understand himself and, through his self, the world around him. This overwhelming yearning was ignited and kept aflame in him by the only thing he said he truly knew—love, understood in the sense of a passionate concern for the spiritual welfare of humanity.

To the confused and aimless world in which we live, he teaches that philosophy is not an academic profession for the benefit of linguistic dabblers and ideological preachers but a commitment to a life of reason, through the example of which the young may learn to reorient their lives in a meaningful direction. He teaches that education is not a thoughtless system of mechanical instruction and indoctrination, the aim of which is to satisfy the demands of the slave market and domesticate young people in the ways of the world, but a process of self-growth in which they can learn to be better and happier people through self-examination. He teaches that science is not the embodiment of the truth dogmatically preached by dilettantes as if from a pulpit but an open and honest search for knowledge and an activity that must be compelled to serve the spiritual and physical exigencies of the human condition. For him, if religion is to be meaningful, it must be grounded in an attitude of critical and humble reverence toward a transcendent yet immanent dimension. Socrates would have agreed with Rumi, according to whom true lovers of God, however this term may be understood, have no religion but God himself.[20]

Socrates reminds us that politics is not the unintelligent allegiance to parties, political agendas, flags, slogans, or anthems, through which shrewd manipulators enslave, deceive, and exploit the unthinking masses, who find their satisfaction and joy in following blindly those who control society. For him, politics, if it is to have any value, must be animated by a rational concern for the welfare of humanity, not of this or that country, not of this or that race, not of this or that group, but of the whole human world. He insists that true ethics is not the study of ethical utterances and usages in which analytical experts, like the ancient sophists, excel, but a way of life committed to moral convictions that make sense in the light of reason.

Socrates' message, then, is that human life is not just a senseless concatenation of fleeting moments devoted to the pursuit of pleasure, wealth, power, knowledge, or success but a task to be structured and completed by each one of us, just as a great artist strives to realize his supreme creation. This is what Socrates teaches and this is the meaning of his presence. This is his legacy. In a world such as ours, in which we are prone to worship the empty gods of material success and affluence, of appearance and accommodation, of military and technological strength—in this world of irrationality and dismal spiritual poverty, whose advancement over that of the ancient Greeks is anything but real, Socrates' legacy may be difficult to accept and even more difficult to actualize. Yet, do we really have any other choice?

NOTES

1. Kant, *Critique of Pure Reason* (London: Macmillan, 1961), p. 7.
2. Ibid., p. 21.
3. Ibid., p. 29.
4. Ibid., p. 47.
5. A. R. Wadia, "Socrates, Plato, and Aristotle," in *History of Philosophy, Eastern and Western*, vol. 2, ed. S. Radhakrishnan et al. (London: Allen & Unwin, 1952), pp. 46–75.
6. J. Bentham, *Deontology, or the Science of Morality*, vol. 1 (London, 1834), p. 39.
7. For extensive bibliographical comments on Socrates' confession of ignorance, see L. E. Navia, *Socrates: An Annotated Bibliography* (New York: Garland, 1988).
8. The word *skeptic* is derived from the Greek verb *skeptomai*, a word that conveys the sense of searching or inspecting.

9. The first two books of the *Republic* are generally regarded as an early dialogue used subsequently as an introduction to the rest of the work.

10. This is, of course, an altered quotation of the passage where Saint Paul speaks of love (*agape, caritas*) as the only essential human possession (1 Cor. 13:2).

11. Among the ancient Greeks, the term *barbarian* generally designated any person who was not Greek.

12. L. E. Navia, *Diogenes the Cynic: The War against the World* (Amherst, NY: Humanity Books, 2005), p. 181.

13. For a discussion of Antisthenes' condemnation of wine, see L. E. Navia, *Antisthenes of Athens: Setting the World Aright* (Westport, CT: Greenwood Press, 2001), pp. 110ff.

14. W. K. C. Guthrie, *Socrates* (London: Cambridge University Press, 1971), p. 163.

15. T. Gomperz, *Greek Thinkers: A History of Ancient Philosophy*, trans. G. C. Berry, vol. 2 (London: John Murray, 1905), p. 57.

16. According to Diogenes Laertius (6.63), it was Diogenes the Cynic who first used the word *cosmopolites*, a word that literally means a citizen (*polites*) of the universe (*kosmos*). For a discussion of the Cynics' rejection of the idea of nationality, see Navia, *Diogenes the Cynic*, pp. 152ff.

17. The word *idiot* is derived from the Greek *idiotes*, a word that originally conveyed the sense of someone who was unconcerned by social and political affairs and who lived a private life.

18. For a documented account of the history of classical Cynicism, see L. E. Navia, *Classical Cynicism: A Critical Study* (Westport, CT: Greenwood Press, 1996).

19. S. Kierkegaard, *Philosophical Fragments or a Fragment of Philosophy*, trans. D. P. Swenson (Princeton, NJ: Princeton University Press, 1944), p. 93.

20. Mowlana Jalaluddin Rumi (1207–1273) is the greatest Sufic poet of Persia.

Bibliography

Adkins, A. W. H. "Clouds, Mysteries, Socrates, and Plato." *Antichthon* 4 (1970): 13–24.

Afnán, R. M. *Zoroaster's Influence on Anaxagoras, the Greek Tragedians, and Socrates.* New York: Philosophical Library, 1969.

Alastos, D. *Socrates Tried: Drama Reconstruction.* London: Zeno Publishers, 1966.

Allen, R. E. "Law and Justice in Plato's *Crito*." *Journal of Philosophy* 69 (1972): 562–66.

———. "A Note on the Elenchus of Agathon, *Symposium* 199c–201c." *Monist* 50 (1966): 460–63.

———. "Plato's Earlier Theory of Forms." In *The Philosophy of Socrates: A Collection of Critical Essays*, edited by G. Vlastos. Notre Dame, IN: University of Notre Dame Press, 1980, pp. 319–34.

———. *Plato's Euthyphro and the Earlier Theory of Forms.* London: Routledge & Kegan Paul, 1970.

———. *Socrates and Legal Obligation.* Minneapolis: University of Minnesota Press, 1980.

———. "The Socratic Paradox." *Journal of the History of Ideas* 21 (1960): 256–65.

Amelung, W. "Notes on the Representations of Socrates and of Diogenes and Other Cynics." *American Journal of Archaeology* 31 (1927): 281–96.

Amory, F. "Socrates: The Legend." *Classica et Mediævalia* 35 (1984): 19–56.

Anderson, A. "Was Socrates Unwise to Take the Hemlock?" *Harvard Theological Review* 65 (1972): 437–52.

Anderson, M. *Barefoot in Athens.* New York: William Sloane, 1951.

Anderson, R. "Socratic Reasoning in the *Euthyphro.*" *Review of Metaphysics* 22 (1969): 421–81.

Anselment, R. A. "Socrates and Clouds—Shaftesbury and a Socratic Tradition." *Journal of the History of Ideas* 39 (1978): 171–82.

Anton, J. P. "The Secret of Plato's *Symposium.*" *Diotima* 2 (1974): 27–47.

———. "The Ultimate Theme of the *Phaedo.*" *Arethusa* 1 (1968): 94–102.

Baily, D. "A Caricature of Socrates." *American Journal of Archaeology* 78 (1974): 427.

Baker, A. "Socrates." In *Prophets for an Age of Doubt.* London: Centenary Press, 1934.

Baker, W. W. "An Apologetic for Xenophon's *Memorabilia.*" *Classical Journal* 12 (1916–1917): 293–309.

Bakewell, C. M. "The Unique Case of Socrates." *International Journal of Ethics* 20 (1909): 10–28.

Barefoot in Athens (a motion picture based on M. Anderson's novel *Barefoot in Athens*). Princeton, NJ: Films for the Humanities, #FFH775D.

Baring, M. *Xantippe and Socrates* (a drama in five acts). *Diminutive Dramas.* Boston: Houghton Mifflin, 1911.

Barnes, J. "Socrates and the Jury, Part I." *Proceedings of the Aristotelian Society*, sup. 54 (1980): 193–206.

Bedell, G. *Philosophizing with Socrates: An Introduction to the Study of Philosophy.* Lanham, MD: University Press of America, 1980.

Bedu-Addo, J. T. "On the Abandonment of the Good in the *Phaedo.*" *Apeiron* 13 (1979): 104–14.

Belfiore, E. "Elenchus, Epope, and Magic." *Phoenix* 34 (1980): 128–37.

Benjamin, W. "Socrates." *Philosophical Forum* 15 (1983): 52–54.

Benson, A. C. "Socrates the Athenian." In *Men of Might: Studies of Great Characters.* London: E. Arnold, 1921.

Bentley, R. *Socrates*. London: George Bell & Sons, 1883.

Berger, H. "Plato's Flying Philosopher." *Philosophical Forum* 13 (1982): 385–407.

Berland, K. J. H. "Bringing Philosophy Down from the Heavens: Socrates and the New Science." *Journal of the History of Ideas* 47 (1986): 299–308.

Bertman, M. A. "Socrates' Defence of Civil Disobedience." *Studium Generale* 24 (1971): 576–82.

Beverslu, J. "Socratic Definition." *American Philosophical Quarterly* 11 (1974): 331–36.

Bicknell, P. J. "Sokrates' Mistress Xanthippe." *Apeiron* 8 (1974): 1–5.

Blank, D. "Socrates vs. Sophists on Payment for Teaching." *Classical Antiquity* 4 (1985): 1–49.

Bleckly, H. *Socrates the Athenian*. London: Trench, 1884.

Blum, A. F. *Socrates: The Original and Its Images*. London: Routledge & Kegan Paul, 1978.

Blumenthal, H. "Meletus the Accuser of Andocides and Meletus the Accuser of Socrates." *Philologus* 117 (1973): 167–78.

Boutroux, É. "The Search for a Science of Morality." In *The State Versus Socrates: A Case Study in Civic Freedom*, edited by J. D. Montgomery. Boston: Beacon, 1954, pp. 197–202.

Brann, E. "The Offense of Socrates: A Re-reading of Plato's *Apology*." *Interpretation* 7 (1978): 1–21.

Brickhouse, T. C., and N. D. Smith. "Irony, Arrogance, and Truthfulness in Plato's *Apology*." In *New Essays on Socrates*, edited by E. Kelly. New York: University Press of America, 1984, pp. 29–46.

Brumbaugh, Robert S. "Plato and Socrates." In *Plato for the Modern Age*. Westport, CT: Greenwood Press, 1979, pp. 29–50.

———. "The Trial of Socrates." In *Six Trials*, edited by R. S. Brumbaugh. New York: Thomas Y. Crowell, 1969, pp. 9–23.

Burger, R. "Socratic Irony and the Platonic Art of Writing: The Self-Condemnation of the Written Word in Plato's *Phaedrus*." *Southwestern Journal of Philosophy* 9 (1978): 113–26.

Burnet, J. *The Socratic Doctrine of the Soul*. London: H. Milford, 1916.

Burnyeat, M. F. "Socrates and the Jury." *Proceedings of the Aristotelian Society*, sup. 54 (1980): 173–92.

———. "Socratic Midwifery, Platonic Inspiration." *Bulletin of the Institute of Classical Studies of the University of London* 24 (1977): 7–16.

Chessick, R. "Socrates—1st Psychotherapist." *American Journal of Psychoanalysis* 42 (1982): 71–83.

Chroust, A. H. *Socrates: Man and Myth; The Two Socratic Apologies of Xenophon*. Notre Dame, IN: University of Notre Dame Press, 1957.

———. "Socrates and Pre-Socratic Philosophy." *Modern Schoolman* 29 (1952): 119–35.

———. "Socrates as a Source Problem." *New Scholasticism* 19 (1945): 55ff.

———. "Socrates in the Light of Aristotle's Testimony." *New Scholasticism* 26 (1952): 327–65.

———. "Xenophon, Polycrates, and the Indictment of Socrates." *Classica et Mediævalia* 16 (1955): 1–77.

Ciholas, P. "Socrates, Maker of New Gods." *Classical Bulletin* 57 (1981): 17–20.

Clark, P. M. "A Cock to Asclepius." *Classical Review* 2 (1952): 146–47.

Clay, D. "Socrates' Mulishness and Heroism." *Phronesis* 17 (1972): 53–60.

Cocke, Z. "In Praise of Xanthippe." *New England Magazine* 37 (1907–1908): 241–46.

Cohen, M. "Confucius and Socrates." *Journal of Chinese Philosophy* 3 (1976):159–68.

Cohen, S. M. "Socrates on the Definition of Piety: *Euthyphro* 10a–11b." In *Socrates: A Collection of Critical Essays*, edited by G. Vlastos. Notre Dame, IN: University of Notre Dame Press, 1980, pp. 158–76.

Cornford, F. M. *Before and After Socrates*. Cambridge: Cambridge University Press, 1964.

———. *Principium Sapientiæ: A Study of the Origins of Greek Philosophical Thought*. New York: Harper Torchbooks, 1965.

Courtney, W. L. "Socrates, Buddha, and Christ." *North American Review* 77 (1885): 63–77.

Croiset, M. *Aristophanes and the Political Parties at Athens*, translated by James Loeb. London: Macmillan, 1909.

Crombie, I. M. *Plato: The Midwife's Apprentice*. London: Routledge & Kegan Paul, 1964.

Cross, R. N. *Socrates: The Man and His Mission*. London: Methuen, 1914.

Daniel, J., and R. M. Polansky. "The Tale of the Delphic Oracle in Plato's *Apology*." *Ancient World* 2 (1979): 83–85.

Dannhauser, W. J. *Nietzsche's View of Socrates*. Ithaca, NY: Cornell University Press, 1974.

Davis, C. "Socrates." *History Today* 20 (1970): 799–805.

Davis, M. "Socrates' Pre-Socratism: Some Remarks on the Structure of Plato's *Phaedo*." *Review of Metaphysics* 33 (1980): 559–77.

Dawson, M. M. *The Ethics of Socrates*. New York: Putnam's Sons, 1924.

Dewey, J. "The Socratic Dialogues of Plato." *Studies in the History of Philosophy* 2 (1935): 3–23.

Dover, K. J. *Aristophanes: Clouds*. Oxford: Oxford University Press, 1968.

———. "Socrates in the *Clouds*." In *The Philosophy of Socrates: A Collection of Critical Essays*, edited by G. Vlastos. Notre Dame, IN: University of Notre Dame Press, 1980, pp. 50–77.

Drengson, A. R. "The Virtue of Socratic Ignorance." *American Philosophical Quarterly* (1981): 237–42.

Dubbs, H. "The Socratic Problem." *Philosophical Review* 36 (1927): 287–306.

Duff, R. A. "Socrates Suicide?" *Proceedings of the Aristotelian Society* 83 (1982–1983): 35–48.

Duncan, P. "Socrates and Plato." *Philosophy* 15 (1940): 339–62.

Durant, W. "The Present Significance of the Socratic Ethic." In *Philosophy and the Social Problem*. New York: Macmillan, 1917, pp. 5–35.

Eastman, M. "Socrates; The Herald of Logic." In *Seven Kinds of Goodness*. New York: Horizon Press, 1967, pp. 67–75.

Edelstein, L. "Platonic Anonymity." *American Journal of Philology* 83 (1962): 1–22.

Edman, I. "Socrates on Trial." *Atlantic Monthly* 191 (1953): 47–52.

Ehnmark, E. "Socrates and the Immortality of the Soul." *Eranos Rudbergianus* 44 (1946): 105–22.

Eisner, R. "Socrates as Hero." *Philosophy and Literature* 6 (1982): 106–18.

Elias, J. A. "'Socratic' vs. 'Platonic' Dialectic." *Journal of the History of Philosophy* 6 (1968): 205–16.

Eliot, A. *Socrates: A Fresh Appraisal of the Most Celebrated Case in History*. New York: Crown, 1967.

Elliott, R. K. "Socrates and Plato's Cave." *Kant-Studien* 58 (1967): 137–57.

Emerson, R. W. *Socrates*. Boston: American Unitarian Association, 1902.

———. *Two Unpublished Essays: The Character of Socrates and the Present State of Ethical Philosophy*. Boston: Lamson and Wolffe, 1896.

Everett, E. "Socrates and Aristophanes." *North American Review* 14 (1822): 273–96.

Feaver, D., and J. Hare. "The *Apology* as an Inverted Parody of Rhetoric." *Arethusa* 14 (1981): 205–16.

Ferejohn, M. T. "The Unity of Virtues and the Objects of Socratic Inquiry." *Journal of the History of Philosophy* 20 (1982): 1–21.

Ferguson, A. S. "On the Date of Socrates' Conversion." *Eranos* (1964): 70–73.

———. "On the Impiety of Socrates." *Classical Journal* 7 (1913): 157–75.

———. *Socrates: A Source Book*. London: Macmillan, 1970.

Fichter, J. H. "A Christian Attitude on Socrates." *Catholic World* 157 (1943): 488–90.

Field, G. C. "Aristotle's Account of the Historical Origin of the Theory of Ideas." *Classical Quarterly* 17 (1923): 113–24.

———. *Plato and His Contemporaries*. London: Methuen, 1930.

———. *Socrates and Plato*. Oxford: Parker, 1913.

———. "Socrates and Plato in the Post-Aristotelian Tradition." *Classical Quarterly* 18 (1924): 127–36.

Fischer, J. L. *The Case of Socrates*. Prague: Academia, 1969.

Flacelière, R. *Greek Oracles*, translated by D. German. New York: Norton, 1965.

Forbes, J. T. *Socrates*. New York: Scribner, 1905.

Foulk, G. J. "Socrates' Argument for Not Escaping in the *Crito*." *Personalist* 55 (1974): 356–59.

Frey, R. G. "Did Socrates Commit Suicide?" *Philosophy* 53 (1978): 106–108.

Friedman, J. A. "The Nature of the Dialogues: Freud and Socrates." *Human Studies* 2 (1979): 229–46.

Fureday, J. J., and C. C. Fureday. "Socratic versus Sophistic Strains in the Teaching of Undergraduate Psychology." *Teaching Psychology* 9 (1982): 14–20.

Gavin, W. "Death: Acceptance or Denial; The Case of Socrates Re-Examined." *Religious Humanism* 11 (1977): 134–39.

———. "A Note on Socrates and 'The Law' in the *Crito*." Aitia 7 (1979): 26–28.

Godley, A. D. *Socrates and the Athenian Society of His Day: A Biographical Sketch*. London: Seeley, 1896.

Gomperz, T. *Greek Thinkers: A History of Ancient Philosophy*, translated by G. C. Berry. 4 volumes. London: John Murray, 1905, 1964.

Gontar, D. "The Problem of the Formal Charges in Plato's *Apology*." *Tulane Studies in Philosophy* 27 (1978): 89–101.

Gooch, P. W. "Socrates; Devious or Divine?" *Greece and Rome* 32 (1985): 32–41.

Gordon, R. M. "Socratic Definitions and Moral Neutrality." *Journal of Philosophy* (1964): 433–50.

Greene, P. "Strepsiades, Socrates, and the Abuse of Intellectualism." *Greek, Roman and Byzantine Studies* 20 (1979): 15–20.

Griggs, E. H. *Socrates, Teacher and Martyr*. Croton-on-the-Hudson, NY: Orchard Press, 1932.

Grote, G. *Life, Teachings, and Death of Socrates*. New York: Sanford & Delisser, 1858.

———. *Plato and the Other Companions of Socrates*. 3 volumes. London: John Murray, 1875.

Guardini, R. *The Death of Socrates; An Interpretation of the Platonic Dialogues Euthyphro, Apology, Crito, and Phaedo*. New York: Sheed and Ward, 1948.

Gulley, N. "Ethical Analysis in Plato's Earlier Dialogues." *Classical Quarterly* 2 (1952): 74–82.

———. *The Philosophy of Socrates*. New York: St. Martin's, 1968.

Guthrie, W. K. C. *Socrates*. London: Cambridge University Press, 1971.

———. *Socrates and Plato*. Brisbane: University of Queensland Press, 1958.

Hackforth, R. *The Authorship of the Platonic Epistles*. Manchester: Manchester University Press, 1913.

———. *The Composition of Plato's Apology*. Cambridge: Cambridge University Press, 1933.

———. "Great Thinkers: Socrates." *Philosophy* 8 (1933): 259–72.

Hadas, M., and M. Smith. "The Image of Socrates." In *Heroes and Gods: Spiritual Biographies in Antiquity*. New York: Harper & Row, 1965, pp. 49–59.

Haden, J. "Socratic Ignorance." In *New Essays on Socrates*, edited by E. Kelly. Lanham, MD: University Press of America, 1984, pp. 17–28.

Harlap, S. "Thrasymachus' Justice." *Political Theory* 7 (1979): 347–70.

Hart, R. "Socrates on Trial." In *New Essays on Socrates*, edited by E. Kelly. Lanham, MD: University Press of America, 1984, pp. 143–50.

Harvey, F. D. "*Nubes* 1493ff. Was Socrates Murdered?" *Greek, Roman and Byzantine Studies* 22 (1981): 339–43.

Havelock, E. A. "The Evidence for the Teaching of Socrates." *Transactions of the American Philological Association*, 1939, pp. 282–95.

———. "The Orality of Socrates and the Literacy of Plato: With Some Reflections on the Historical Origins of Moral Philosophy in Europe." In *New Essays on Socrates*, edited by E. Kelly. Lanham, MD: University Press of America, 1984, pp. 67–93.

———. "The Socratic Problem: Some Second Thoughts." In *Essays in Ancient Greek Philosophy*, edited by J. P. Anton. Vol. 2. Albany: State of New York Press, 1963, pp. 147–73.

———. "The Socratic Self as It Is Parodied in Aristophanes' *Clouds*." In *Yale Classical Studies (22): Studies in Fifth Century Thought and Literature*, edited by A. Parry. Cambridge: Cambridge University Press, 1972, pp. 1–18.

———. "Why Was Socrates Tried?" In *Studies in Honour of Gilbert Norwood*, edited by M. E. White. Toronto: University of Toronto Press, 1952, pp. 95–109.

Hawtrey, R. S. "Plato, Socrates, and the Mysteries." *Antichthon* 10 (1976): 22–24.

———. "Socrates and the Acquisition of Knowledge." *Antichthon* 6 (1972): 1–9.

Hefferman, W. C. "Not Socrates, but Protagoras: The Sophistic Basis of Legal Education." *Buffalo Law Review* 29 (1980): 399–423.

Hegel, G. W. F. *Lectures on the History of Philosophy*, translated by E. S. Haldane. 3 volumes. London: Routledge & Kegan Paul, 1963.

Heidegger, M. *An Introduction to Metaphysics*, translated by R. Manheim. New Haven, CT: Yale University Press, 1959.

Henry, M. "Socratic Piety and the Power of Reason." In *New Essays on Socrates*, edited by E. Kelly. Lanham, MD: University Press of America, 1984, pp. 95–106.

Hess, M. W. "Kierkegaard and Socrates." *Christian Century* 82 (1965): 736–38.

Higgins, W. E. *Xenophon the Athenian: The Problem of the Individual and the Society of the Polis*. Albany: State University of New York Press, 1977.

Hughen, R. E. "Some Thoughts in Support of the Socratic Thesis That There Is No Such Thing as the Weakness of the Will." *Journal of Thought* 17 (1982): 85–93.

Hyland, D. A. "Why Plato Wrote Dialogues." *Philosophy and Rhetoric* 1 (1968): 38–50.

Ikushima, K. "An Analysis of the Dispute between Thrasymachus and Socrates in Book A of Plato's *Republic*." *Journal of Classical Studies* 13 (1965): 87–97.

Jackson, B. D. "The Prayers of Socrates." *Phronesis* 16 (1971): 14–37.

Jackson, D. "Socrates and Christianity." *Classical Folia* 31 (1977): 189–206.

Jackson, H. "The *daimonion* of Socrates." *Journal of Philology* 5 (1874): 232–47.

Jordan, J. N. "Socrates' Wisdom and Kant's Virtue." *Southern Journal of Philosophy* 4 (1973): 7–24.

Kachi, Y. "Gods, Forms, and Socratic Piety." *Ancient Philosophy* 3 (1983): 82–88.

Kahn, C. H. "Did Plato Write Socratic Dialogues?" *Classical Quarterly* 31 (1981): 305–20.

Karavites, P. "Socrates in the *Clouds*." *Classical Bulletin* 50 (1973): 65–69.

Kelly, E., ed. *New Essays on Socrates*. Lanham, MD: University Press of America, 1984.

Kendrick, A. C. "The Life and Philosophy of Socrates." *Christian Review* 10 (1845): 155–81.

Kierkegaard, S. *The Concept of Irony, With Constant Reference to Socrates*, translated by L. M. Capel. New York: Harper & Row, 1965.

———. *Philosophical Fragments or a Fragment of Philosophy*, translated by D. P. Swenson. Princeton, NJ: Princeton University Press, 1944.

Klein, J. P. "Socratic Dialog vs. Behavioral Practice in the Development of Coping Skills." *Alberta Journal of Educational Research* 21 (1975): 255–61.

Kostman, J. "Socrates' Self-Betrayal and the 'Contradiction' between the *Apology* and the *Crito*." In *New Essays on Socrates*, edited by E. Kelly. Lanham, MD: University Press of America, 1984, pp. 107–30.

Kraus, R. *The Private and Public Life of Socrates*, translated by B. Mussey. New York: Doubleday, 1940.

Kraut, R. *Socrates and the State*. Princeton, NJ: Princeton University Press, 1984.

Lacey, A. R. "Our Knowledge of Socrates." In *The Philosophy of Socrates: A Collection of Critical Essays*, edited by G. Vlastos. Notre Dame, IN: University of Notre Dame Press, 1980, pp. 22–49.

Laguna, T. "The Interpretation of the *Apology*." *Philosophical Review* 18 (1909): 23–27.

Landmann, M. "Socrates as a Precursor of Phenomenology." *Philosophy and Phenomenological Research* 2 (1941–1942): 15ff.

Lélut, L. F. *Du démon de Socrate. Specimen d'une application de la science psychologique à celle de l'histoire*. Paris: Trinquart, 1836.

Leonard, W. E. "The Personality and Influence of Socrates." *Open Court* 29 (1915): 313–18.

———. *Socrates, Master of Life*. Chicago: Open Court, 1915.

Lesser, H. "Suicide and Self-Murder." *Philosophy* 55 (1980): 255–57.

Levin, R. L. *The Question of Socrates*. New York: Harcourt Brace and World, 1961.

Levy, A. W. "Socrates in the Nineteenth Century." *Journal of the History of Ideas* 17 (1956): 89–108.

Llamzon, B. S. "Philosophy in the University: Athena or Socrates." *Thomist* 40 (1976): 635–64.

Lofberg, J. O. "The Trial of Socrates." *Classical Journal* 23 (1928): 601–609.

Lukic, M. "Socrates and Indifference Towards Death." *Southern Journal of Philosophy* 9 (1971): 393–98.

MacLaughlin, R. J. "Socrates on Political Disobedience." *Phronesis* 21 (1976): 185–97.

Maguire, J. P. "Thrasymachus—or Plato?" *Phronesis* 16 (1971): 142–63.

Mahood, G. H. "Socrates and Confucius: Moral Agents or Moral Philosophers." *Philosophy East and West* 21 (1971): 177–88.

Manning, H. E. *The Daemon of Socrates*. London: Longmans, Green, 1872.

Martin, R. "Socrates on Disobeying the Law." *Review of Metaphysics* 24 (1970): 21–36.

Mason, C. *Socrates, the Man Who Dared to Ask*. Boston: Beacon, 1953.

Mauthner, F. *Mrs. Socrates*, translated by J. W. Hartman. New York: International Publishers, 1926.

McKeon, R. P. "The Choice of Socrates." In *Great Moral Dilemmas in Literature, Past and Present*, edited by R. M. MacIver. New York: Cooper Square Publishers, 1964, pp. 113–33.

McKirahan, R. D. *Plato and Socrates: A Comprehensive Bibliography*. New York: Garland, 1958.

McNaghten, R. E. "Socrates and the *daimonion*." *Classical Review* 28 (1914): 185–89.

Meyer, M. "Dialectic and Questioning: Socrates and Plato." *American Philosophical Quarterly* 17 (1980): 281–90.

Miller, J. W. "The Socratic 'versus' the Platonic Order of the Dialogues." *Pakistan Congress of Philosophy* 1 (1954): 115–21.

Minadeo, R. "Socrates' Debt to Asclepius." *Classical Journal* 66 (1971): 294–97.

Montgomery, J. D. *The State versus Socrates: A Case Study in Civic Freedom*. Boston: Beacon, 1954.

Mooney, C. P. "The Mystical Dimension of Socratic Piety." In *New Essays on Socrates*, edited by E. Kelly. Lanham, MD: University Press of America, 1984, pp. 161–72.

Moss, A. E. *Socrates, Buddha and Jesus*. London: Watts, 1885.

Mosse, C. "The Trial of Socrates." *Histoire* 29 (1980): 34–42.

Mulhern, J. J. "Aristotle and the Socratic Paradoxes." *Journal of the History of Ideas* 35 (1974): 293–99.

Murphy, J. G. "The Socratic Theory of Legal Fidelity." In *Violence and Aggression in the History of Ideas*, edited by P. P. Wiener and J. Fisher. New Brunswick, NJ: Rutgers University Press, 1974, pp. 15–33.

Murray, G. *Aristophanes: A Study*. Oxford: Clarendon Press, 1965.

———. "The Message of Socrates." In *Classics in Sociology*, edited by D. MacRae. Port Washington, NY: Kennikat Press, 1971, pp. 105–10.

Muzzey, D. S. "Socrates, the Champion of Intellectual Piety." *Spiritual Heroes: A Study of Some of the World's Prophets*. New York: Doubleday, 1902, pp. 65–67.

Myers, I. H. "Socrates Up to Date: A Dialogue Concerning Time." *Atlantic Monthly* 143 (1929): 78–83.

Nadler, S. "Probability and Truth in the *Apology*." *Philosophy and Rhetoric* 9 (1985): 198–202.

Nagley, W. E. "Kierkegaard's Early and Later Views on Socratic Irony." *Thought* 55 (1980): 271–82.

Nakhnikian, G. "Elenchic Definitions." In *The Philosophy of Socrates: A Collection of Critical Essays*, edited by G. Vlastos. Notre Dame, IN: University of Notre Dame Press, 1980, pp. 125–57.

Navia, L. E. *Antisthenes of Athens: Setting the World Aright*. Westport, CT: Greenwood Press, 2001.

———. *Classical Cynicism: A Critical Study*. Westport, CT: Greenwood Press, 1996.

———. *Diogenes the Cynic: The War against the World*. Amherst, NY: Humanity Books, 2005.

———. *The Presocratic Philosophers: An Annotated Bibliography*. New York: Garland, 1993.

———. "A Reappraisal of Xenophon's *Apology*." In *New Essays on*

Socrates, edited by E. Kelly. Lanham, MD: University Press of America, 1984, pp. 47–66.

———. *Socratic Testimonies*. Lanham, MD: University Press of America, 2002.

Navia, Luis E., and E. L. Katz. *Socrates: An Annotated Bibliography*. New York: Garland, 1988.

Nelson, L. *Socratic Method and Critical Philosophy*. New Haven, CT: Yale University Press, 1950.

Neumann, H. "Socrates in Plato and Aristophanes." *American Journal of Philology* 90 (1969): 201–14.

Nichols, M. P. *Socrates and the Political Community: An Ancient Debate*. Albany: State University of New York Press, 1967.

Notopoulos, J. A. "Socrates and the Sun." *Classical Journal* 37 (1942): 260–74.

Nussbaum, G. "Some Problems in Plato's *Apology*." *Orpheus* 8 (1961): 53–64.

Ober, W. B. "Did Socrates Die of Hemlock Poisoning?" *Ancient Philosophy* 2 (1982): 155–21.

O'Brien, M. J. *The Socratic Paradoxes and the Greek Mind*. Chapel Hill: University of North Carolina Press, 1967.

Ojoade, J. O. "Socrates: Was He Really a Sophist?" *Phrontisterion* 5 (1967): 48–61.

Oldfather, W. A. "Socrates in Court." *Classical Weekly* 31 (1938): 203–11.

Organ, T. W. "Crito Apologizes." *Personalist* 38 (1957): 366–71.

Osborne, E. B. *Socrates and His Friends*. London: Hodder & Stoughton, 1930.

Parke, H. W. "Chaerephon's Inquiry about Socrates." *Classical Philology* 56 (1961): 249–50.

Parker, M., ed. *Socrates: The Wisest and Most Just?* New York: Cambridge University Press, 1981.

Patzer, A. *Bibliographia socratica*. Freiburg: Verlag Karl Alber, 1985.

Peterman, J. E. "The Socratic Suicide." In *New Essays on Socrates*, edited by E. Kelly. Lanham, MD: University Press of America, 1984, pp. 3–16.

Petrie, R. "Aristophanes and Socrates." *Mind* 20 (1911): 507–20.

Phillipson, C. *The Trial of Socrates*. London: Stevens & Sons, 1928.

Pick, R. *The Escape of Socrates*. New York: Knopf, 1954.

Plumb, R. K. "Socrates Linked to Find in Athens." *New York Times*, December 25, 1953.

"Portrait of Socrates Found." *New York Times*, October 27, 1963.

Pratt, J. B. "On the Philosophy of Socrates." *Open Court* 21 (1907): 513–22.

Priestly, J. *Socrates and Jesus Compared*. Philadelphia: P. Byrne, 1803.

Quandt, K. "Socratic Consolation: Rhetoric and Philosophy in Plato's Crito." *Philosophy and Rhetoric* 15 (1982): 238–56.

Randall, J. H. "The Historical and the Platonic Socrates." *Plato: Dramatist of the Life of Reason*. New York: Columbia University Press, 1970, pp. 93–102.

Raskin, H. D. *Sophists, Socrates, and Cynics*. London: Croom Helm, 1983.

Reeve, M. D. "Socrates' Reply to Cebes in Plato's *Phaedo*." *Phronesis* 20 (1975): 199–208.

Reilly, R. "Socrates' Moral Paradox." *Southern Journal of Philosophy* 8 (1977): 101–107.

Richmond, W. K. *Socrates and the Western World: An Essay in the Philosophy of Education*. London: A. Redman, 1954.

Richter, G. M. A. "A New Portrait of Socrates." In *Essays in Memory of K. Lehman*, edited by L. F. Sandler. New York: New York Institute of Fine Arts, New York University, 1964, pp. 267–68.

Riley, M. T. "The Epicurean Criticism of Socrates." *Phoenix* 34 (1980): 55–68.

Rist, J. M. "Plotinus and the Daimonion of Socrates." *Phoenix* 17 (1963): 13–24.

Roberts, S. V. "Athens Ruin May Be Jail of Socrates." *New York Times*, March 21, 1976.

Robinson, R. "Elenchus." In *The Philosophy of Socrates: A Collection of Critical Essays*, edited by G. Vlastos. Notre Dame, IN: University of Notre Dame Press, 1980, pp. 78–93.

———. "Elenchus: Direct and Indirect." In *The Philosophy of Socrates: A Collection of Critical Essays*, edited by G. Vlastos. Notre Dame, IN: University of Notre Dame Press, 1980, pp. 94–109.

————. "Socratic Definition." In *The Philosophy of Socrates: A Collection of Critical Essays*, edited by G. Vlastos. Notre Dame, IN: University of Notre Dame Press, 1980, pp. 110–24.

Rogers, A. K. "The Ethics of Socrates." *Philosophical Review* 34 (1925): 117–43.

————. *The Socratic Problem*. London: Oxford University Press, 1933.

Rorty, A. O., ed. "Akrasia and Pleasure: *Nicomachean Ethics* Book 7." In *Essays on Aristotle's Ethics*. Berkeley: University of California Press, 1980.

Rosen, S. "Socrates' Dream." *Theoria* 42 (1976): 161–88.

Ross, W. D. "The Problem of Socrates." *Classical Association Proceedings* (1933): 7–24.

Rothschild, R. *Jefferson, Lenin, Socrates: Three Gods Give an Evening to Politics*. New York: Random House, 1936.

Rowe, C. J. "Plato on the Sophists as Teachers of Virtue." *History of Political Thought* 4 (1983): 409–27.

Santas, G. X. *Socrates: Philosophy in Plato's Early Dialogues*. London: Routledge & Kegan Paul, 1979.

————. "The Socratic Fallacy." *Journal of the History of Philosophy* 10 (1972): 127–41.

"Santayana and Socrates." *New York Times*, August 1, 1926, Sec. 2.

Sarf, H. "Reflections on Kierkegaard's Socrates." *Journal of the History of Ideas* 44 (1983): 255–76.

Sauvage, M. *Socrates and the Human Consciousness*, translated by P. Hepburne. New York: Harper & Row, 1961.

Schleiermacher, F. *Introductions to the Dialogues of Plato*, translated by W. Dobson. New York: Arno Press, 1973.

Schopenhauer, A. "Socrates." In *Fragments of the History of Philosophy*, translated by E. B. Bax. London: George Bell & Sons, 1909, pp. 45–52.

Scolnicov, S. "Reason and Passion in the Platonic Soul." *Dionysius* 2 (1978): 35–49.

Scott, J. A. *Socrates and Christ: A Lecture Given at Northwestern University*. Evanston, IL: Northwestern University Press, 1928.

Scottag, M. J. "Socratic Irony and Self-Deceit." *Ratio* 14 (1972): 1–15.

Seeskin, K. "Is the 'Apology of Socrates' a Parody?" *Philosophy and Literature* 6 (1982): 94–105.

Seiler, C. *The Husband of Xanthippe, and Other Plays*. Boston: Walter H. Baker, 1929.

Senter, N. W. "Socrates, Rhetoric, and Civil Disobedience." *Southwestern Philosophical Studies* 1 (1976): 50–56.

Sharvy, R. "*Euthyphro* 9d–11b: Analysis and Definition in Plato and Others." *Nous* 6 (1972): 119–37.

Sheeks, W. "Isocrates, Plato, and Xenophon against the Sophists." *Personalist* 56 (1975): 250–59.

Shorey, P. "The Question of the Socratic Element in Plato." *Proceedings of the Sixth International Congress of Philosophy*. New York: Longmans, Green, 1927, pp. 316–23.

Sichel, B. A. "Socratic Ignorance and Teaching." *Proceedings of the Philosophy of Education Association* 31 (1975): 75–89.

Sider, D. "Did Plato Write Dialogues before the Death of Socrates?" *Apeiron* 14 (1980): 15–18.

Sigad, R. "Fichte, Sartre, Socrates." *Iyuun* 29 (1980): 37–43.

Sills, T. "Socrates Was Executed for Being Innovative." *English Journal* 70 (1981): 41–42.

Silverberg, R. *Socrates*. New York: Putnam's Sons, 1965.

"Site of Trial of Socrates Is Unearthed." *New York Times*, June 22, 1970.

Skousgaard, S. "Genuine Speech vs. Chatter: A Socratic Problematic." *Kinesis* 6 (1974): 87–94.

Smith, M. "Did Socrates Kill Himself Intentionally?" *Philosophy* 55 (1980): 253–54.

"Socrates' Death Sentence Is Appealed." *New York Times*, April 1, 1927.

Socrates in the Agora. Princeton, NJ: American School of Classical Studies at Athens, 1978.

"Socrates Not so Bald." *New York Times*, January 24, 1926, Sec. 2.

Soupios, M. "Reason and Feeling in Socrates." In *New Essays on Socrates*, edited by E. Kelly. Lanham, MD: University Press of America, 1984, pp. 137–41.

Spiegelberg, H., ed. *The Socratic Enigma*. Indianapolis, IN: Bobbs-Merrill, 1964.

Spitzer, D. C. *Know Thyself: A Leader's Guide to the Study of Socrates*. Boston: Beacon, 1954.

Steinkraus, W. "Socrates, Confucius, and the Rectification of Names." *Philosophy East and West* 30 (1980): 261–64.

Stephens, J. "Socrates on the Rule of Law." *History of Philosophy Quarterly* 2 (1985): 3–10.

Stewart, D. J. "Socrates' Last Bath." *Journal of the History of Philosophy* 10 (1972): 253–60.

Stone, I. F. "I. F. Stone Breaks the Socrates Story." *New York Times*, April 8, 1979, Sec. 6.

———. *The Trial of Socrates*. New York: Little, Brown, 1987.

Strauss, Leo. *Socrates and Aristophanes*. Chicago: University of Chicago Press, 1980.

———. *Xenophon's Socrates*. Ithaca, NY: Cornell University Press, 1972.

———. *Xenophon's Socratic Discourses*. Ithaca, NY: Cornell University Press, 1970.

Strong, L. A. *The Man Who Asked Questions: The Story of Socrates*. London: Thomas Nelson & Sons, 1934.

Sypher, W. "Nietzsche and Socrates in Messina." *Partisan Review* 16 (1949): 702–13.

Tapscott, F. T. "Socratic Anticipation of Christianity." *Bibliotheca Sacra* 92 (1935): 58–76.

Tarrant, D. "The Pseudo-Platonic Socrates." *Classical Quarterly* (1938): 167–73.

———. "The Touch of Socrates." *Classical Quarterly* (1958): 95–98.

Taylor, A. E. "The Impiety of Socrates." In *Varia socratica: First Series*. Oxford: J. Parker, 1911, pp. 1–39.

———. *Plato: The Man and His Work*. London: Methuen, 1926.

———. "Plato's Biography of Socrates." *Proceedings of the British Academy* (1918): 93–132.

———. *Socrates*. Garden City, NY: Doubleday, 1953.

———. "Socrates and the Myths." *Classical Quarterly* 27 (1933): 158–59.

———. *Varia socratica: First Series*. Oxford: J. Parker, 1911.

Tejera, V. "Ideology and Literature: Xenophon's *Defense of Socrates* and Plato's *Apology*." In *New Essays on Socrates*, edited by E. Kelly. Lanham, MD: University Press of America, 1984, pp. 151–60.

Thesleff, H. "The Interpretation and Date of the *Symposia* of Plato and Xenophon." *Bulletin of the Institute of Classical Studies of the University of London* 25 (1978): 157–70.

Thomas, J. E. "On the Duality of Socrates' What-Is-X Question." *Laval Théologique et Philosophique* 30 (1974): 21–27.

Tillich, P. "Socrates (A Speech Delivered by Paulus)." In *From Place to Place: Travels with Paul Tillich*, by H. Tillich. New York: Stein and Day, pp. 86–91.

Tofallis, K. *Socrates: Man and Philosopher*. London: Greek Institute, 1978.

Toynbee, A. J. "The Search for a Prophet: Socrates and Jesus." In *The State versus Socrates: A Case Study in Civic Freedom*, edited by J. D. Montgomery. Boston: Beacon, 1954, pp. 203–21.

Trainor, P. "Immortality, Transcendence, and the Autobiography of Socrates in the *Phaedo*." *Southern Journal of Philosophy* 21 (1983): 595–610.

Turlington, B. *Socrates: The Father of Western Philosophy*. New York: Franklin Watts, 1969.

———. "Socrates' Courtroom Ethics." *American Bar Association Journal* 59 (1973): 505–509.

Vanderpool, E. "The Prison of Socrates." *Illustrated London News* 264, no. 6 (1976): 87–88.

Vermeule, C. C. "Socrates and Aspasia." *Classical Journal* 54 (1958): 49–55.

Versenyi, L. *Socratic Humanism*. Westport, CT: Greenwood Press, 1963.

Versfeld, M. *The Socratic Spirit*. Cape Town: University of Cape Town Press, 1971.

Vlastos, G. "Afterthoughts on the Socratic Elenchus." In *Oxford Studies in Ancient Philosophy*, edited by J. Annas. Vol. 1. Oxford: Clarendon Press, 1983, pp. 71–74.

———. "On the Socrates Story." *Political Theory* 7 (1979): 533–36.

———. "The Paradox of Socrates." In *The Philosophy of Socrates: A Collection of Critical Essays*. Notre Dame, IN: University of Notre Dame Press, 1980, pp. 1–21.

———, ed. *The Philosophy of Socrates: A Collection of Critical Essays*. Notre Dame, IN: University of Notre Dame Press, 1980.

————. *Socrates: Ironist and Moral Philosopher*. Ithaca, NY: Cornell University Press, 1991.

————. "Socrates on Akrasia." *Phoenix* 23 (1969): 71–88.

————. "Socratic Knowledge and Platonic 'Pessimism.'" *Philosophical Review* 66 (1957): 226–38.

————. "Was Polus Refuted?" *American Journal of Philology* 88 (1967): 454–60.

Vogel, C. J. "The Present State of the Socratic Problem." *Phronesis* (1955): 26–35.

————. "Who Was Socrates?" *Journal of the History of Philosophy* 1 (1963): 513–22.

Wade, F. C. "In Defense of Socrates." *Review of Metaphysics* 25 (1971): 311–25.

Walsh, J. J. "The Socratic Denial of Akrasia." In *The Philosophy of Socrates: A Collection of Critical Essays*, edited by G. Vlastos. Notre Dame, IN: University of Notre Dame Press, 1980, pp. 235–63.

Walton, C. "Xenophon and the Socratic Paradoxes." *Southern Journal of Philosophy* 16 (1978): 687–700.

Watson, W. "The Voices of God." In *New Essays on Socrates*, ed. E. Kelly. Lanham, MD: University Press of America, 1984, pp. 173–79.

Weiss, R. L. "Kierkegaard's 'Return' to Socrates." *New Scholasticism* 45 (1971): 573–83.

Wellman, R. R. "Socratic Method in Xenophon." *Journal of the History of Ideas* 37 (1976): 307–18.

Wenley, R. *Socrates and Christ: A Study in the Philosophy of Religion*. Edinburgh: Blackwood, 1809.

West, E. J. "Plato and Socrates: The Men and Their Methods." In *New Essays on Socrates*, edited by E. Kelly. Lanham, MD: University Press of America, 1984, pp. 131–36.

Whelan, F. G. "Socrates and the 'Meddlesomeness' of the Athenians." *History of Political Thought* 4 (1983): 1–29.

"Who Killed Socrates?" *New York Times*, March 17, 1940, Sec. 4.

Wiggers, G. F. *A Life of Socrates*. London: Taylor & Walton, 1840.

Wilson, Pearl C. *The Living Socrates*. Owings Mills, MD: Stemmer House, 1975.

Winspear, A. D., and T. Silverberg. *Who Was Socrates?* New York: Cornon, 1939.

Wolz, H. G. "The Paradox of Plenty in Plato's *Euthyphro* in the Light of Heidegger's Conception of Authenticity." *Southern Journal of Philosophy* 12 (1974): 493–511.

Wood, N. "Socrates as Political Partisan." *Canadian Journal of Political Science* 7 (1974): 3–31.

Woodbury, L. "Socrates and Archelaus." *Phoenix* 25 (1971): 299–309.

———. "Socrates and the Daughter of Aristides." *Phoenix* 27 (1973): 7–25.

Woodhead, W. D. "The *Daimonion* of Socrates." *Classical Philology* 35 (1940): 425–26.

Woodruff, P. "Socrates and Ontology: The Evidence of the *Hippias Major.*" *Phronesis* 23 (1978): 101–17.

———. "Socrates' Approach to Semantic Incompleteness." *Philosophy and Phenomenological Research* 38 (1978): 453–68.

Woozley, A. D. *Law and Obedience: The Arguments of Plato's Crito.* Chapel Hill: University of North Carolina Press, 1979.

———. "Socrates on Disobeying the Law." In *The Philosophy of Socrates: A Collection of Critical Essays,* edited by G. Vlastos. Notre Dame, IN: University of Notre Dame Press, 1980, pp. 299–318.

Young, G. "Socrates and Obedience." *Phronesis* 19 (1974): 1–29.

Younger, I. "Socrates and Us." *Commentary* 70 (1980): 46–49.

Zeller, E. *Socrates and the Socratic Schools,* translated by O. J. Reichel. New York: Russell and Russell, 1962.

Zimmerman, M. E. "Socratic Ignorance and Authenticity." *Tulane Studies in Philosophy* 29 (1980): 133–50.

Zubirí, X. "Socrates and Greek Wisdom." *Thomist* 7 (1944): 1–64.

Index of Names